RECORDS OF CIVILIZ ... UDIES

EDITED
OF THE DEPARTMENT

TY

GENERAL EDITOR

W. T. H. Jackson
Professor of German and History

PAST EDITORS

1915-1926
James T. Shotwell
*Bryce Professor Emeritus of the History
of International Relations*

1926-1953
Austin P. Evans
Late Professor of History

1953-1962
Jacques Barzun
Seth Low Professor of History

RECORDS OF CIVILIZATION
IN NORTON PAPERBACK EDITIONS

ODO *of* DEUIL

De profectione Ludovici VII in orientem
The Journey of Louis VII to the East

Edited, with an English Translation
by VIRGINIA GINGERICK BERRY

W · W · NORTON & COMPANY · INC · *New York*

TO MY MOTHER AND MY FATHER

Published simultaneously in Canada by
Penguin Books Canada Ltd,
2801 John Street, Markham, Ontario L3R 1B4.

W. W. Norton & Company, Inc., 500 Fifth Avenue, New York, N.Y. 10110
W. W. Norton & Company Ltd., 37 Great Russell Street, London WC1B 3NU

ISBN 0-393-09662-9

Printed in the United States of America

6 7 8 9 0

Contents

Acknowledgments

I TAKE great pleasure in expressing my thanks to those who have in various ways assisted me in the preparation of this volume. The University of Chicago libraries obtained for me photostatic copies of the manuscript on which this study is based. Professors Blanche B. Boyer, James Lea Cate, and Einar Joranson gave much valuable assistance when the work was originally written as a doctoral dissertation under the Committee on the History of Culture at the University of Chicago. Since then Professor Austin P. Evans, in his capacity as editor of this series, has given me much useful help. Professor Boyer of Chicago, Professor K. M. Setton, and my husband, Professor E. G. Berry, of the University of Manitoba have read the draft and aided with numerous suggestions. Miss Rosalie Green, the Reverend Eric Smith, S.J., and Mr. Austin Faricy have contributed generously of their time and ability during the several revisions. For any errors, however, I alone am responsible. Finally, I wish to acknowledge the assistance toward publication given me by the Canadian Humanities Research Council.

Winnipeg, Manitoba.   V. G. B.

September, 1947

Introduction

I

EVEN A SUMMARY OUTLINE of the Second Crusade[1] reveals its tragic character and emphasizes the woeful contrast between the sanguine hopes with which it was begun and the undeniable failure in which it ended. The leadership of such powerful princes as Louis VII of France and Conrad III of Germany, the inspired exhortations of St. Bernard, the enrollment of vast though motley armies, and the extensive preparations, caused western Europeans to expect that the expedition would be even more successful than the First Crusade. Yet after the laborious journey overland, there followed a series of reverses due to strained relations with the Greeks, lack of discipline and unity of plan in the armies,[2] and ruinous disregard for the conditions obtaining among the Turks and the Eastern Christians. While marching through Asia Minor the crusaders suffered great losses from famine, thirst, pestilence, and numerous Turkish raids. Consequently, the large armies broke up. Although many of the Germans went home, some of them spent the winter in Constantinople; the French nobles, after abandoning the rest of the army at Adalia, sailed to Antioch. In the spring of 1148, after Raymond of Antioch had been unable to enlist the French in an expedition against Aleppo and Caesarea, the remnants of the two armies joined the Syrian Christians in besieging Damascus. With the failure of this siege because of treachery

[1] For a detailed account of the Second Crusade see the following works: Wilken, *Geschichte der Kreuzzüge*, Vol. III; Sybel, "Über den zweiten Kreuzzug," *Zeitschrift für Geschichtswissenschaften*, IV (1845), 197–228; Jaffé, *Geschichte des deutschen Reiches unter Conrad dem Dritten;* Kugler, *Studien zur Geschichte des zweiten Kreuzzugs;* Giesebrecht, *Geschichte der deutschen Kaiserzeit*, Vol. IV; Kugler, *Analekten zur Geschichte des zweiten Kreuzzugs;* Neumann, *Bernhard von Clairvaux und die Anfänge des zweiten Kreuzzugs;* Bernhardi, *Konrad III;* Kugler, *Neue Analekten;* Hüffer, "Die Anfänge des zweiten Kreuzzugs," *Historisches Jahrbuch*, VIII (1887), 391 ff.; Vacandard, *Vie de Saint Bernard;* Chalandon, *Jean II Comnène et Manuel I Comnène.*

[2] This point has been especially well expressed by Giesebrecht, *op. cit.*, p. 270: "If the crusaders had believed that they would take up the fight against the infidels supported by all of Christendom, they were badly mistaken. The dissenting and opposing interests within Christendom were becoming apparent at the very moment when the call to arms came. The religious fervor with which the cross had been taken dissipated more and more; on the other hand, difficulties appeared which they neither saw nor wanted to see during the high tide of enthusiasm."

and the abandonment of an undertaking against Ascalon, the futile military activity of the crusade ceased, and the crusaders straggled back to their homes.

Such patent lack of success discouraged men from writing histories of the expedition. Contemporaries felt that the events did not deserve a record more complete than that afforded by the entries in local chronicles and annals. The *Chronicon Mauriniacense*[3] tersely describes the stay of Louis in Syria as follows: "he was not able to do anything useful, anything worthy of mention, or, actually, anything worthy of France"; and this sentiment is often repeated by accounts like the *Continuatio* of the *Gesta abbatum sancti Bertini*.[4] Even the great Otto of Freising, who had written with gloomy majesty of so many cataclysms in his *Chronicon*, refused later to record his experiences on the Second Crusade, saying, "But since everyone knows the outcome of the aforesaid expedition, an outcome exacted because of our sins, we have left it to be recorded by other writers, or on another occasion, for we have resolved to write a cheerful account this time, and not a tragedy."[5]

The one exception to this prevailing tendency on the part of Western historians[6] is Odo of Deuil, who in his *De profectione Ludovici VII in orientem* describes the journey of the French army as far as Antioch.[7] Because of his unique position questions arise as to who Odo was and why he recorded a large part of the crusade. Unfortunately nothing is known about Odo's early life except that he was a monk of the monastery of St. Denis and evidently came from Deuil, in the valley of Montmorency.[8] Only in 1147, when

[3] RHGF, XII, 88.

[4] "They [the crusaders] accomplished little or nothing." MGSS, XIII, 664.

[5] *Gesta Friderici*, ed. by G. Waitz (3d ed.), I, xlvii.

[6] Eastern writers on this subject are the Greek historians, Nicetas and Cinnamus, and William of Tyre. The last named recently appeared in translation as *A History of Deeds Done Beyond the Sea*, translated by Babcock and Krey in "The Columbia University Records of Civilization." For an excellent discussion of these Eastern historians see Kugler, *Studien zur Geschichte des zweiten Kreuzzugs*, pp. 1–43. This work will be referred to hereafter as *Studien*.

[7] Since Louis VII remained in the East for another year, the *De profectione* does not describe the entire crusade. One should remember, however, that the strength of his army and Conrad's was largely spent by the time he reached Antioch. Thus, the fiascos at Damascus and Ascalon stem in large measure from the conditions which obtained during the early part of the crusade, and Odo's account proves less fragmentary than the chronology might indicate.

[8] See the salutation of Odo's letter on p. 3, below. All following references to Odo's work are paged according to my edition and translation.

he left France as Louis VII's chaplain for the Second Crusade,[9] does he emerge as an individual. Yet the very fact that he was royal chaplain suggests that Odo had attained a position of importance and trust at St. Denis. Perhaps he was already regarded as a possible successor to the abbot, Suger, and therefore had taken a growing part in the business of the monastery, just as Suger had done during the lifetime of Abbot Adam.[10] However that may be, Odo accompanied Louis during the entire crusade and, late in 1149, returned to France with him. There he did not remain attached to the court, but entered upon a career of monastic administration which again points to the possibility of his having been trained to succeed Suger. In a few months he was chosen to carry out the difficult task of ejecting a corrupt order of canons from Compiègne and of functioning there as the first abbot for a group of monks from St. Denis. After a vigorous struggle he accomplished this task,[11] but he did not remain in Compiègne long. When Suger died, in 1152, Odo became the abbot of St. Denis.[12] As at Compiègne, he entered upon this office amid turbulent conditions; some of the monks soon charged him with alienation of the abbey property, of mistreatment of Suger's relatives, and even of murder.[13] Conspicuous in his defense, however, was St. Bernard, who advocated a thorough investigation of the charges in order to clear the abbot.[14] Evidently he was vindicated or the charges were

[9] Page 5, below.

[10] See M. Combes, *L'Abbé Suger* (Paris, 1853), p. 122, for reference to Suger's activity during the life of Adam.

[11] For details about this reform see the letters of Eugenius III to Suger (RHGF, XV, 458–59); Baldwin of Noyon to Eugenius (*ibid.*, p. 459); Suger to Baldwin of Noyon, Eugenius, and Peter of Cluny (in Suger, *Œuvres complètes de Suger*, ed. by A. Lecoy de la Marche [Paris, 1867], pp. 270–74).

[12] See the *Breve chronicon ecclesiae sancti Dionysii*, RHGF, XII, 216; *Historia pontificalis*, MGSS, XX, 544.

[13] "But, with no regard for Suger's acts of kindness, Odo tried to destroy all of his kindred, and he weakened the church and harmed it among the common people." *Historia pontificalis, ibid.*

"If he has been burdened with debts (although there are hardly any) the manifest reason lay in the time itself. As to the charge of alienating land, it is proved manifestly untrue. Yet I do not think that even his enemies themselves could have suspected him of the death of G., since, with much difficulty, he rescued this same G. and all his men when they had been hemmed in by enemies and were at the very point of death." Letter of St. Bernard to the bishop of Ostia, PL, CLXXXII, 492–93.

[14] "But let an inquiry be instituted, for an examination will cause a more definite belief in these facts than an oath will; and if conditions are found identical with the villainous charges, the abbot will not be acquitted, no matter how they came about. If they are not,

dropped, for the disturbance soon died down. Thenceforth Odo's administration was apparently uneventful, since no details have come to us except records of Odo as the witness to or the beneficiary of charters and the recipient or the subject of a few routine letters which have been preserved.[15] His death, in 1162,[16] brought to a close a career which would have been worthy of little note had it not included the writing of the best contemporary account of the Second Crusade.

It is natural to wonder why Odo described so large a part of a crusade which was so universally unappealing to other writers. In the letter to Suger which accompanies his history Odo presents himself as a mere transmitter of facts, a man who is furnishing raw material for Suger to use in a history of Louis VII which will be similar to the *Vita Ludovici Grossi*, which he had written recently.[17] At some length Odo contrasts Suger's eminent fitness for performing such a task with his own unfitness to record the material.[18] And yet, as Kugler has pointed out,[19] this modesty is peculiar to the letter. That does not mean that Odo wrote the history first and then added the letter as a polite afterthought; the tone of the whole work is not unsuited to a personal dispatch, and even in the history Odo at times addresses Suger personally.[20] But the technique and the plan do not harmonize with the idea of Odo as a mere gatherer of facts. In the course of the history one discovers that Odo is an accomplished craftsman in his own right and that he was certainly not unconscious of his artistry. He presents the material with much thought and care, not as a series of rough

the accusers will not lose anything by their falsehood." Letter of St. Bernard to Eugenius, *ibid.*, p. 492.

[15] For the charters see Luchaire, *Études sur les actes de Louis VII*, pp. 188–89, 197, 233; M. Félibien, *Histoire de l'abbaye royale de Saint Denys* (Paris, 1706), pp. cix–cx; GC, VII, 378. For the letters see RHGF, XV, 656, 666–67.

[16] His death is dated by the fact that for the first time his name does not appear on the charter granted in 1162 to St. Denis by Louis VII in memory of his wife Constance. See Félibien, *op. cit.*, pp. cx–cxi.

[17] This *Vita* has been ed. and trans. by H. Waquet.

[18] All further references to Odo's work, unless otherwise indicated, refer to this edition and translation.

[19] *Studien*, p. 11.

[20] For example, he apologizes for being prolix (p. 21); calls Suger's special attention to Louis' attempt to regain Estusin and Esslingen for St. Denis (p. 103); advises him to be comforted because Louis is safe (p. 143).

notes.[21] Then, too, in the entire first book he recounts events that happened in France before the crusaders set out. Suger knew these well; he had a part in every phase of the development from the time when he voiced disapproval of the crusade at Bourges[22] until he said farewell to Louis at St. Denis.[23] One is led to think, therefore, that Odo announced his real motive for writing in the phrase, "Then, too, since I have enjoyed the renowned King Louis' generous favors and have been closely associated with him during the crusade, I am eager to thank him,"[24] and that the conclusion, "yet my powers are meager," reveals a modesty which is not wholly sincere, perhaps because it was a conscious literary device[25] or because the writer was deferring to Suger.

Louis certainly does dominate the history; his actions, ideas, and virtues constantly appear in a most favorable light. In addition to eulogizing his sovereign, however, Odo has a second and equally compelling purpose. He wishes to record information which will be useful for the French when they again undertake the journey East. Thus, he tells about the disadvantages which ensued because the pilgrims brought heavy carts;[26] he describes virtuous deeds so that they may serve as an example to those who may follow the same road later;[27] he gives the names of towns in order to indicate the route traveled;[28] he depicts the condition of the different localities, so that people will know where to observe caution with regard to provisioning.[29] This care is partially explained by the statement,

For never will there fail to be pilgrims to the Holy Sepulchre; and they will, I hope, be the more cautious because of our experiences.[30]

It is emphasized and clarified when he says,

[21] See pp. xxiv ff.
[22] "Vita Sugerii," in Lecoy de la Marche, *op. cit.*, p. 393.
[23] Page 19.
[24] Page 3.
[25] It is interesting to note in this connection that the *De expugnatione Lyxbonensi* also takes the form of a letter. *De expugnatione Lyxbonensi*, ed. and trans. by C. W. David.
[26] Page 25.
[27] Page 29.
[28] *Ibid.*
[29] *Ibid.*
[30] *Ibid.*

And both nations will always have something to bewail if the sons of these men do not avenge their parents' death. To us who suffered the Greeks' evil deeds, however, divine justice, and the fact that our people are not accustomed to endure shameful injuries for long, give hope of vengeance. Thus we comfort our sad hearts, and we shall follow the course of our misfortunes so that posterity may know about the Greeks' treacherous actions. [31]

We may say, then, that Odo wrote his history because he wished to show gratitude and admiration for his sovereign and because he wanted to disclose to his countrymen the nature of the misfortunes which the French suffered in the East. As I have pointed out, this reaction to the Second Crusade was unique. Yet the value of Odo's narrative does not arise merely from the fact that the other accounts are few and meager. Even if there were many other histories of the crusade, Odo's would be an outstanding source of information, because it contains a wealth of authoritative detail, the breadth and variety of which is really amazing. Kugler has expressed the range aptly:

He presents the parleys and views of the contesting factions very lucidly; amid the confusion of bloody battles he stresses clearly geographically and strategically decisive facts; he maintains an ever lively interest in new and strange phenomena, in Greek customs, and in the Turkish mode of combat. [32]

The De profectione *as a source of information about the Second Crusade.*—Odo was well situated for the performance of his task. In the first place, he had excellent opportunities for gaining firsthand information, because he either witnessed or took part in most of the events about which he wrote. If by the year 1145 he was considered as a possible abbot of St. Denis, he probably accompanied Suger to the councils in which the business concerning the crusade was transacted, [33] and some time before the expedition set out he evidently joined the royal retinue. [34] On the journey

[31] Page 99.
[32] *Studien*, pp. 12–13.
[33] See above, p. xv.
[34] He describes Louis' visit to the leper colony: "There I myself saw him enter"; p. 17.

his position as chaplain brought him into close relationship with Louis.[35] Thus, in addition to the ordinary crusader's opportunity for seeing new lands, cities, and peoples and for participating in the marches, battles, and respites of the journey, Odo had access to information which could be gained only by an intimate associate of the king. He usually attended important councils where the negotiations and decisions vital to the progress of the crusade took place;[36] he observed the words and actions of the foreign legates and of the foremost crusaders; he accompanied the king to such places as Constantinople, which was closed to the great majority of the army. Inasmuch as he was chaplain and an educated man, he probably had access to the diplomatic documents which came to the royal camp. Since many of these were read aloud before the king and supplemented by oral messages,[37] the value of this privilege is less apparent in the case of Odo than in that of a historian who has to base the bulk of his narrative on archival material, but it probably aided him to verify impressions after the audiences.

From the foregoing description it is obvious that Odo's knowledge centered about the French crusading army, especially with regard to official and royal matters. This type of information was usually adequate, because Odo had chosen Louis as the principal theme of his history, but at times he had to refer to the policy of the Greeks and Hungarians or to the progress of the Germans in order to explain conditions which the French encountered.[38] For these purposes Odo got material from the accounts of witnesses and from the results of his own observation and deduction. For instance, he learned much from reports that were made to Louis. Some of these reports came from French officials, as was the case when the embassy which had been sent ahead to Constantinople met Louis,[39] or when Arnulf and Bartholomew told of their visit

[35] See below, pp. 3–5.
[36] The most apparent exception to Odo's attendance at such meetings is his absence when Louis and the French barons met Manuel in Asia Minor in order to do him homage. See pp. 81 ff.
[37] See, for example, the embassy of the Greeks to Louis at Ratisbon, pp. 25 ff.
[38] Odo recognizes this fact when he explains why he describes the German army: "the king and the emperor both came to mind when I was writing about Ratisbon; for, although the king is my main subject, their mutual experiences force me to include a few words about the emperor" (p. 33).
[39] Page 59.

to Manuel after the robbing of the money-changers,[40] or when the Count of Flanders and Archibald of Bourbon described the plight of the pilgrims left behind at Adalia.[41] News of other events, such as the German defeat near Dorylaeum (and probably the flood at Choerobacchi and the division of the German armies at Nicaea) he obtained from the German embassy which met the French at Nicaea[42] and from Conrad.[43] An emir who was captured on the Maeander evidently supplied information about the preparations the Turks made for their skirmish against the crusaders.[44] Many times, however, the facts came through less formal channels. It seems likely that the Greeks in Thrace told stories about the march of the Germans.[45] At Constantinople the Greeks certainly circulated false rumors of German successes against the Turks.[46]

Odo also depended on his own powers of observation. In Germany, for example, he observed the fine new bridges which Conrad had built for the army;[47] at Branitz, the large fleet which the Germans had been forced to abandon.[48] Both indicated the splendor with which the emperor had set out. Corpses of dead Germans in Greece attested the disorder which had marked their passage through the otherwise peaceful land;[49] and the manner in which the inhabitants fled before the French and, later, lowered provisions in baskets from the towns seemed to confirm this.[50] Blood on the mountains near Laodicea indicated the place where Otto of Freising's army had been defeated.[51]

In the second place, Odo's standard of veracity was high. This becomes apparent when one reads other references to the expedition; for, although his work is the only history wholly devoted to the subject and is the most important single source of information for the Second Crusade, portions of it can be checked and

[40] Page 77.
[41] Page 139.
[42] Page 91.
[43] Pages 105 ff.
[44] Page 111.
[45] For example, the flood which they suffered at the Drave River (p. 47); the damage which they did to Philippopolis (p. 43 ff.); the great numbers that crossed the Arm (p. 51).
[46] Page 73.
[47] Page 33.
[48] Page 41.
[49] Page 47.
[50] Page 41.
[51] Page 115.

supplemented by other contemporary records.[52] Almost invariably these records confirm the reliability of Odo's work.[53]

It is only natural, however, that the trustworthiness generally characteristic of our author is sometimes impaired. We have seen already that one of his aims in writing the history was to show the French how the crusaders had suffered at the hands of the Greeks. Such a didactic aim inevitably colored the historian's interpretation of facts.[54] Furthermore, he sometimes had to make use of secondary information derived from prejudiced persons. These conditions promoted a tendency to oversimplify the immediate relation of cause and effect without taking into account the many elements which influenced the events.[55] Yet these defects need not entirely invalidate the material in question. Usually the facts can be separated from the interpretation by making allow-

[52] Chief among these are the Greek historians Nicetas (CSHB, Vol. XXII) and Cinnamus (CSHB, Vol. XXV), who describe the crusade as an episode in the reign of Manuel Comnenus and are most valuable for information concerning the journey through Thrace and the stay around Constantinople; and Otto of Freising, who has treated the preliminaries to the second crusade in his *Chronicon* (trans., under the title *The Two Cities*, by C. Mierow) and the episodes of the departure of Conrad's army and the flood at Choerobacchi in *Gesta Friderici* (ed. by G. Waitz [3d ed., Leipzig, 1912]). William of Tyre's *A History of Deeds Done Beyond the Sea*, Vol. II, translated by Babcock and Krey, New York, 1943, the *Historia Pontificalis* (MGSS, XX, 521 ff.), the *Annales Palidenses* (MGSS, XVI, 82–83), *Annales Magdeburgenses* (*ibid.*, pp. 188–90), *Annales Herbipolenses* (*ibid.*, pp. 3–8), *Chronicon Mauriniacense* (RHGF, XII, 88), Helmold's *Cronica Slavorum* (MGSS, XXI, 56–58), translated by Francis Tschan as *The Chronicle of the Slavs, by Helmold, Priest of Bosau* in the "Columbia University Records of Civilization," New York, 1935, *Gesta Eugenii III Papae* (RHGF, XV, 423–25), *Gesta Ludovici VII* (RHGF, XII, 199–201), and *Vita et res gestae Sancti Bernardi*, III (RHGF, XIV, 370 ff.) contribute additional information. Since the authenticity of some of this material is doubtful, it is well for the nonspecialist to read the section, "Zur Kritik der Quellen," in Kugler's *Studien*, pp. 1–43, in order to get his bearings. Although some of the individual points made by Kugler in this section have since been disproved, in general his judgment has been held valid. Letters which enlarge our knowledge of the expedition are those of Bernard to the clergy and people of eastern France (RHGF, XV, 606), of Bernard to Manuel (RHGF, XV, 607–8), of Bernard to the people of England (PL, Vol. CLXXXII, No. 365), of Conrad to Wibald (RHGF, XV, 533–34), of Eugenius to Louis (RHGF, XV, 429–30), of Louis to Suger (RHGF, XV, 487, 488, 496), of Manuel to Eugenius (RHGF, XV, 440–41), of Manuel to Louis (RHGF, XVI, 9), and of Nicholas the monk to the count and barons of Brittany (RHGF, XV, 607).

[53] For some cases in which Odo's account varies from that of other sources, see below, p. 10, *n.* 22, p. 12, *n.* 29, p. 15, *n.* 36, p. 47, *n.* 18, p. 59, *n.* 54, p. 88, *n.* 3, p. 92, *n.* 8, p. 92, *n.* 9.

[54] Odo anticipated this criticism unsuccessfully when he said: "Let no one think that I am taking vengeance on a race of men hateful to me and that, because of my hatred, I am inventing a Greek whom I have not seen" (p. 57).

[55] In theory Odo deplored this practice. "The man who partially knows a case makes a partial judgment, but the man who does not know the entire case cannot make a just judgment" (p. 73).

ance for the historian's viewpoint[56] and by supplementing his information in the case of incidents at which he was not present.[57]

Fortunately, these cases of prejudice and faulty information form the exception rather than the rule. Odo usually presents both sides of a question. Often he does so by reporting the speeches of rival factions in the French army.[58] At other times he invents an imaginary reader who objects to the course of events and must be refuted.[59] Much more revealing in this connection, however, are the casual statements of fact which Odo never stresses, such as the lack of baronial subservience to the royal commands,[60] the disorderly conduct of the Franks in Greek territory,[61] and the necessity of having the Templars reorganize the army in Asia Minor.[62]

In the third place, he was extremely close to his material. He wrote during the crusade, as he indicates in the letter to Suger, when he describes himself as "still engaged in the hardships of the journey,"[63] and as the following passage of his history shows.

But please allow me this failing, father. I was engrossed in happy affairs, and, while writing the words connected with my native land and while remembering its affairs, unweariedly I recalled for too long a time what I had seen when a happy man.[64]

[56] Thus in the portrait of Manuel, who is the archvillain of the story, one finds an instructive example of Odo's method of adverse interpretation. He has created a strong impression of the treachery and dissimulation of the emperor by assigning base motives to apparently innocent actions on the part of Manuel (see pp. 69, 77-83), by making Manuel personally responsible for hostile acts on the part of his subjects (see pp. 53, 113), and by interpreting all of Manuel's inimical deeds as motivated solely by a cunning desire to trap the Franks (see pp. 55, 137).

[57] Odo usually marks such passages by "as we have heard" or a similar phrase. Sometimes he rationalizes about the value of the story as in the case of the white knight at the ford on the Maeander: "As to this, I should not wish to deceive anyone nor to be deceived; but I do know that in such straits such an easy and brilliant victory would not have occurred except by the power of God, nor would the rain of iron from the opposing army have fallen without causing death or wounds" (p. 113). That some episodes can be corrected by comparison with other sources is shown by the additional information about the German defeat at Laodicea gained from Conrad's letter to Wibald (cf. below, p. 92, n. 2, p. 108, n. 10). All such supplementary evidence which I have noted is given in the footnotes to the translation, where it can readily be compared with Odo's account.

[58] See pp. 69 ff.; 79 ff.; 131 ff.

[59] See pp. 57, 107, 135.

[60] See pp. 21, 79.

[61] See pp. 41, 45, 57, 67, 97.

[62] See pp. 125 ff.

[63] Page 3.

[64] Page 21.

These passages, when linked with the fact that the narrative stops at Antioch, suggest the spring or summer of 1148 as the time of composition. Confirmatory evidence is furnished by the fact that Odo's viewpoint before the army reached Antioch is consistently that of a man who looks back over events and interprets them in the light of what has happened later, while only one statement points forward.[65] Moreover, this statement, "the flowers of France withered before they could bear fruit in Damascus,"[66] is a singularly colorless reference which is far from Odo's usual vein in dealing with such ignominious events as the siege of Damascus. It therefore seems likely that Odo is referring to the plan to go against Damascus, which was doubtless in the air before the crusaders left Antioch in June; the actual expedition has no part in his narration.[67]

We have seen that Odo had excellent opportunities for gaining first-hand information, was highly dependable in his account and recorded events before they had time to become confused in outline or had faded entirely from his mind. The chief defect of his work as a source of information for the Second Crusade lies in its limited sphere. Even though the outcome of the entire crusade had largely been determined by the events and conditions described before the French arrived in Antioch, Odo has not recorded the latter part of the expedition. Whether the work was never finished or whether the rest of it was lost has never been solved. In its present form,

[65] This tendency seems too inherent to be the result of revision. For example, he interprets the actions of the Greeks at Constantinople in the light of the disillusionment which grew during the crusaders' experiences in Asia Minor; he points out, while reporting Conrad's advice about taking the long road from Lupar, that this advice caused the French to undergo the same misfortunes which the Germans suffered; he considers that the respite at Adalia was more costly than all the hardships of the journey.

[66] See p. 119.

[67] It has been asked whether the *De profectione* was subsequently revised by Odo or someone else. The small part which Eleanor of Aquitaine plays in the narrative (bare references on pp. 17, 57, 77, 79) may point to a revision which took place after Eleanor's divorce from Louis and marriage to Henry II. As Kenneth Setton has suggested, the difficult passage "Occasionally the empress wrote to the queen, and then the Greeks degenerated entirely into women" (p. 57) gains in meaning if one posits a lacuna after "queen," because of a revision which removed all outstanding accounts of Eleanor from the history. Less convincingly, Wilken (*Geschichte der Kreuzzüge*, III, 137) interprets the puzzling sentence as meaning that the letters were not actually written by the empress. Such a change as Setton suggests would be a process of cutting out rather than a careful reworking of the material and would reinforce the idea that the actual writing took place during the crusade rather than after a lapse of time.

however, it gives us valuable information about the inception and early stages of the crusade, emphasizing the important role therein which Odo assigned to the Greeks.

The De profectione *as a piece of historical writing.*—The *De profectione* is outstanding not only as a source of valuable information but also as a history which presents the facts ably and artistically. It is a good piece of historical writing even for the twelfth century, which can boast such works as Suger's *Vita Ludovici Grossi*, Otto of Freising's *Chronicon* and *Gesta Friderici*, and William of Tyre's *Historia*. The narrative owes much of its effectiveness to Odo's careful organization of the material which he had at hand. At no time do we have the impression that he was jotting down events in a haphazard or merely chronological manner. On the contrary, he divides his history into seven books, each of which develops a theme that contributes to the forward movement of the entire account. Thus, they might be given separate titles, such as "Preparations for the Crusade," "The March from France to the Borders of Greece," "The Journey through Greece to Constantinople," "Constantinople," "Misfortunes of the Germans in Asia Minor," "The Defeat of the Franks at Laodicea," and "Efforts to Recover after Laodicea"; yet through them runs the unifying thread of his double aim, to eulogize the king and to instruct the French by revealing the disasters which befell the crusaders.

Equally indicative of his careful organization of the subject matter is the way Odo confides to the reader his technique of writing. He desires to be brief in order to adhere to the theme and to avoid wearying the reader.[68] Evidently he had the common experience of discovering that the complexity of the material makes it difficult for even a systematic person to follow a well-planned outline. In order to clarify his procedure, therefore, he sometimes sketched it beforehand, as when he says:

---

[68] Odo's desire to be brief is shown when he refrains from describing the miracles at Vézelay, lest describing too many should cause him to abandon his theme (p. 9); when he decides not to record the laws enacted by Louis at Metz because they were not well obeyed (p. 21); when he says that he cannot repeat the honors shown Louis by all the different communities along the way to Constantinople (p. 25); when he does not record the names of the men who came via Apulia because he saw their untimely death and because it might be tedious for the reader who looks for an example of usefulness and worth in the material which he reads (p. 81).

Now, however, at this new beginning I gird myself for difficult tasks, intending to enter strange countries in my description just as we did in fact, and accordingly I shall bring to a swifter conclusion the hardships which ensued.[69]

Now, after this brief interruption, I want to write of how the Germans were led to Constantinople, nay, even across the sea; for a story ought to be recounted in the order in which it has happened.[70]

He realized the difficulty of his task to the full when he explained:

It is necessary to go back and forth, to progress and to turn back in my story; for although many things present themselves for description, the account should not be confused by the wealth of subjects. Many events happen at the same time, but in discourse one must observe a sequence. For instance, the king and the emperor both came to mind when I was writing about Ratisbon; for, although the king is my main subject, their mutual experiences force me to include a few words about the emperor.[71]

Despite these troubles, however, he achieves a lucid narrative, the parts of which are carefully tied together.[72]

It has already been suggested that Odo's definite outline led him to oversimplify the relation of cause and effect, especially with regard to the immediate explanation of events in which the purposes of Manuel and the Greeks figure.[73] It would probably be more correct to say that the characteristic of Odo's mind which enabled him to formulate such a definite plan of writing was also responsible for his reduction of cause and effect to a system. For a like simplification occurs whenever Odo pictures God as an ulti-

[69] Page 21.

[70] Page 47.

[71] It is interesting to compare with this statement of the confused way in which events often happen the following observation in regard to the German defeat: "The Germans were asked about the order, method, and cause of such a great misfortune; but perhaps all of those inquiries were made improperly, since confusion actually has no order, aberration no method, and the unreasonable no cause" (p. 91).

[72] For example, "we shall refer to their lamentable and swift misfortunes at the proper time and place; but in the meantime, let us return to our own men" (p. 51); "the messengers sent ahead by him encountered the king at the Lake of Nicaea, as has been said already, and they told him the events we have described" (p. 97).

[73] See above, p. xxi.

mate cause. In such cases the Deity, far from being an abstraction, appears as an active protagonist. He was interested in the crusade because it was an expedition in His service.[74] Through various agents—the forces of nature,[75] men,[76] and a supernatural being[77]— He aided His chosen people. With no less vigor He avenged injuries.[78]

At other times, however, Odo explains events as the result of human actions. Then the divine and human causes appear in his narrative more as contradictory than as complementary factors. Thus, although God apparently favors the crusaders, the Greeks work against them with marked success. The resolution of this dilemma probably lies in the customary explanation that the ways of God are inscrutable[79] and that He is a trier of men.[80] It is significant, however, that Odo is inconsistent in advancing such a theory to account for the disasters of the Franks on the journey. In his version the human cause usually seems the more vivid, the divine cause the more conventional and colorless; a passive interpretation centering about God as the chastiser of the French was not germane to a man who so keenly hoped for revenge on the part of the Franks that he wrote in order to incite it.

Odo's manner of expression reveals the same cultivation and careful thought as does his organization of subject matter; yet he writes with a skill which only occasionally becomes mannered because of over-nicety.[81] Probably the best feature of his art is a knack for using words well. He has command of a large vocabulary, which enables him to write with an admirable combination of flexibility in subject matter and precision in expression. For this he employs a great number of poetic words,[82] which lend special effectiveness to descriptive passages.[83] His enjoyment of words

[74] See pp. 81, 93, 101, 105. Cf. Erdmann, *Die Entstehung des Kreuzzugsgedankens*, pp. 166–325.
[75] See pp. 45, 107, 109, 117, 119, 133, 143.
[76] See pp. 23, 99.
[77] See p. 113.
[78] See pp. 71, 91, 101, 141.
[79] See pp. 13, 137.
[80] See p. 133.
[81] A sample of his most affected style is found on pp. 83–85, where he describes the eclipse and the reasons advanced for it.
[82] In this connection note his constant use of syncopated forms, such as *intrasse, deportarunt*.
[83] See the admirable description of Constantinople, pp. 63–67; the picture of the storm in the valley of Ephesus, p. 109.

and their use is also shown by the manner in which he adopts new ones; for when he introduces a comparatively rare word[84] or one borrowed from the Greek,[85] he carefully indicates its shades of meaning. Unlike many medieval and renaissance authors of similar tastes, however, Odo does not stud his pages with long quotations from other writers.[86] As his use of Biblical expressions indicates,[87] he is more likely to adapt and to paraphrase than to quote directly, a process which probably points to the use of material which he has assimilated, not to new borrowings from phrase books.

Throughout the history Odo's style is highly rhetorical. The figures are comparatively few in number, but he employs them with an assiduity and resourcefulness which give a certain variety to the frequently repeated motifs. Most prominent of all is his use of different forms of anaphora. By reiterating the same word,[88] different forms of the same word,[89] and words which derive from the same root[90] he achieved vivid effects marked by strong emphasis. This interest in repetition sometimes tempted him to indulge in plays on words, involving the same word with two different meanings[91] or two words of similar sound, but different meanings.[92] It also lent itself to the extensive use of parallel constructions.[93] Odo spiced the narrative with contrasts which he

[84] For example, *garritus*, p. 44.

[85] For example, *polychronias*, p. 56.

[86] Further study of Odo's vocabulary and his quotation from classical and medieval writers would be of value as an index to Odo's personal learning and, thence, to the educational climate of St. Denis in the mid-twelfth century.

[87] See, for example, the quotation from Romans on p. 3, and the one from Psalms on p. 77.

[88] "sanctae curae . . . sancto operi . . . sancto abbati" (p. 8); "tam robustum exercitum tam subito . . . tam leviter" (p. 90); "altare contra altare" (p. 70); "de crastino in crastinum" (p. 90); "pariter eligerunt quod pariter tolerarent" (p. 12).

[89] "pratum est nemorosum vel nemus pabulosum" (p. 32); "nostri cum stupore dolent et cum dolore stupent" (p. 90); "non enim cito credit sibi noceri qui nocendi non habet animum" (p. 66).

[90] "percutientes et repercussi" (p. 44); "duci, immo etiam et transduci" (p. 46); "saepiebant . . . persaepe" (p. 24).

[91] "dux cum turba suorum ut sedarent turbam" (p. 42); "sic secunda dies terminata est non secunda" (p. 14); "ad sinistram partem sinistro auspicio" (p. 88).

[92] "sicut divitiis . . . sic etiam vitiis" (p. 64); "spatiosus et speciosus" (p. 48); "prece et precio" (p. 36); "post Alemannos properare et prosperari" (p. 90); "caedendum est et cadendum" (p. 70).

[93] "iam cibus deficiebat hominibus, qui . . . iam fames vexabat equos, qui . . ." (p. 124); "turres habebant et muros duplices ad tutelam et in mari naves ad fugam" (p. 106); "diligens pro persona, praeferens pro aetate, venerans pro fortuna" (p. 102); "si gestus corporis, si alacritas faciei, si verba cordis" (p. 60).

obtained from juxtaposition of words which were diametrically opposed in meaning,[94] from formal contrasts turning upon the word *quam*,[95] and from the device of making a statement and then contradicting it.[96] To a somewhat lesser extent he employed the more ornate figures of metaphor,[97] simile,[98] and personification.[99]

The style, then, is relatively simple, depending for richness on the color of individual words, repetition, contrast, and comparison. As such it is admirably suited to a historical work, since such a work gains value if it narrates attested facts in an intelligible and coherent fashion. We have already seen that Odo was in possession of many reliable facts,[100] that he followed a definite outline which enabled him to present the material clearly,[101] and that he hoped to be brief.[102] His most successful attempts to combine these qualities reveal him, at the height of his powers, a competent historian with a narrative style which is crisp, vivid, and telling in every detail.[103] Only when he falls short are his sentences mannered and stiff.

[94] "in rerum abundantia penuriam non ferentes" (p. 40); "regiam maiestatem humilitate condire" (p. 48); "sapientes, stultorum genibus provoluti, humilitate et ratione insaniam sedaverunt" (p. 44).

[95] "audacter amplius quam prudenter" (p. 36); "magis praevalerent dolis quam viribus" (p. 72); "certe melius est in opulentia diu honeste vivere quam cito turpiter in egestate perire" (p. 104).

[96] "tamen a duce (immo a truce suo)" (p. 90); "cum transirem regionem istam aspera mihi montibus videbatur; nunc autem planam iudico respectu Romaniae" (p. 30).

[97] "mortem volantem" (p. 94); "ferrea pluvia" (p. 112); "marcescunt flores Franciae antequam fructum faciant in Damasco" (p. 118); "ut pluvia eos potius raperet quam aspergeret" (p. 48).

[98] "hostesque nos sicut fera quae sanguine gustato fit trucior" (p. 124); "loricati pedites inter densos hostes submerguntur velut in pelago" (p. 118); "Constantinopolis . . . ad formam veli navalis in trigonum ducitur" (p. 62); "aer obscurior, quasi vellet ante nostrum iter divina providentia desecari" (p. 108).

[99] "sic uterque nostrorum impetus cito et facile de cadaveribus partis utriusque campos usque ad latibula montium seminavit" (p. 110); the passage involving "virtus ieiuna" (p. 92); the personification of Constantinople (p. 86).

[100] See above, p. xviii.

[101] See above, p. xxiv.

[102] See above, p. xxiv.

[103] See the impression of insistence he gives when he tells of Louis's request for Esslingen and Estusin from Conrad: "On hearing this the king himself, and then his men, besought both Conrad and Frederick, first privately and then in public; importuning the emperor's friends and renewing his insistence about the matter, he asked it as a favor for himself, he urged it as a means of pleasing God and the glorious martyr" (p. 103). Especially effective is the sharp, incisive way in which he describes the army on the mountain near Laodicea: "The mountain was steep and rocky, and we had to climb along a ridge so lofty that its summit seemed to touch heaven and the stream in the hollow valley below to descend into hell. Here the throng became congested while ascending, pushed forward, then crowded

The De profectione *as part of a historical tradition.*—Odo's technique of organizing and writing history causes me to believe that he was following a developed tradition of historiography. One has not far to seek for an example of history writing which must have exerted a strong influence on him. The Abbot Suger made a redaction of his *Vita Ludovici Grossi* in 1144,[104] only a little more than a year before the opening events of Odo's work occurred. Odo showed his familiarity with and respect for Suger's account when he suggested that the abbot use the material in the *De profectione* as the basis for a similar life of Louis VII.[105] More than that, he seems to have followed Suger's lead in the matter of composition. A recent editor of the *Vita Ludovici Grossi* has summarized the method and the art of Suger as follows: he knew how to write history so that it was agreeable as well as instructive, and he disliked boring the reader with monotonous details; because he wanted to awaken the curiosity of his readers and to arouse their surprise and emotion he often passed over dull incidents in order to hasten to others which were more interesting; he wrote in an animated and colorful way which revealed his sympathy with nature, his psychological treatment of people, his patriotism; because his chief aim was to entertain and his chief ability was to write a warm, vivid account, his work succeeds more as a piece of literature than as a history.[106] Superficially, this might be a characterization of the *De profectione.* Odo, too, made great efforts to interest the reader, emphasizing the picturesque incidents at the expense of less striking ones.[107]   He depicted the forces of nature,[108] analyzed men psychologically,[109] introduced his patri-

closely together, stopped, and taking no thought for the cavalry, clung there instead of going ahead. Sumpter horses slipped from the steep cliffs, hurling those whom they struck into the depths of the chasm. Dislodged rocks also caused destruction. Thus, when the men had scattered far and wide in order to seek out paths, all feared that they would misstep or that others would strike them violently" (p. 117).

[104] Waquet, ed. and trans., *Suger: Vita Ludovici Grossi*, Paris, 1929, p. xi.

[105] See above, p. xvi.

[106] Waquet, *op. cit.*, pp. xiv–xvii.

[107] See the episode of the snake charmer at Philippopolis (p. 43); the visit of Louis to the leper colony outside Paris (p. 17).

[108] For example, the flood at Choerobacchi (pp. 47–9); the storm in the valley of Ephesus (p. 109).

[109] See the scattered passages on the Greeks as a people, on Manuel, and on the generosity of Louis. Odo also revealed character by means of the speeches which he inserted in the narrative; such are the argument of Godfrey of Langres and his opponents at Constantinople (pp. 69 ff.) and that of Louis and the barons at Adalia (pp. 131 ff.).

otic reactions into the narrative.[110] But by and large he surpasses his master in soberness of narrative, breadth of view, and spaciousness of design. His view of the historian's task is deeper and more mature than that of Suger; he aims more to instruct and to admonish than to amuse.

Odo must, therefore, have absorbed principles which were due not merely to Suger; he must have had access to another source of inspiration. To this source, also, Suger may be our chief guide, since the historical tradition from which he derived his technique of writing was probably the same which Odo used, even though the emphasis of the two men was slightly different. We do not know the external facts about Odo's education, but presumably he acquired it at St. Denis and other monasteries, as was the custom at the time.[111] St. Denis harbored an urbane learning, marked with a strong historical tinge. Suger's biographer records the abbot's frequent quotations from the Scriptures and from Horace,[112] his interest in and readiness to recount incidents from Frankish history,[113] his custom of reading and commenting upon the works of the church fathers and the ecclesiastical historians.[114] From Waquet's researches concerning the *Vita Ludovici* we learn additional information about Suger's use of classical authors. In that work he quoted from Horace,[115] Juvenal,[116] Lucan,[117] Ovid,[118]

---

[110] See pp. 57, 73, 119, 135.

[111] See the life of Suger in Cartellieri, *Abt Suger von Saint-Denis*.

[112] "For he was so steeped in the knowledge of Holy Scripture that he had ready an apt and succinct reply on any point about which he had been asked. On account of his tenacious memory, however, he could not forget the heathen poets, with the result that he often recited to us from memory pertinent Horatian verses, to the number of twenty or thirty." Lecoy de la Marche, ed., *Œuvres complètes de Suger*, p. 381.

[113] "He had such a very great knowledge of history that, no matter what king or prince of the Franks one mentioned, he immediately and without hesitation would hasten to recount his deeds." *Ibid.*, p. 382.

[114] "After dinner in any season, either summer or winter, since he was satisfied with very little sleep, he was accustomed either to read or to hear someone read for a long time or to instruct those around him by telling famous stories. Also there was reading from the authentic books of the church fathers, and sometimes a selection from the ecclesiastical historians was read." *Ibid.*, p. 389.

[115] *Ars poetica* (p. 7 in the Waquet edition of the *Vita Ludovici*. The references in the following six notes refer to the same work); *Epistles* (p. 40); *Odes* (p. 5).

[116] *Satires* (p. 189).

[117] *Pharsalia* (pp. 7, 33, 61, 71, 93, 110, 113, 116, 149, 163, 170, 183, 184, 231, 232, 258, 287).

[118] *De arte amandi* (p. 101); *Heroides* (p. 180); *Metamorphoses* (p. 96).

Sallust,[119] Terence,[120] and Vergil,[121] authors of great popularity in twelfth-century curricula.[122] At St. Denis, therefore, Odo could have come in contact with the works of classical and ecclesiastical historians and of poets who were masters of style. From them he could have derived his interest in didactic and eulogistic history, his delight in elegant expression.[123] We may be justified in saying that the historical interests of Suger and the monastery's well-stocked library[124] united to make St. Denis a center for history writing and that Odo's *De profectione* stems from this union, just as Suger's writings and the *Grandes chroniques de France* did.

The value of the De profectione *for further research.*—This study of the *De profectione* has aimed to be more suggestive than exhaustive. If it has called attention to the rich potentialities of the text, it has been successful. First of all we have seen the unique role which the history plays among the sources of the Second Crusade and the fidelity with which it records facts concerning this little-known expedition. On its information the historian of that movement must always be dependent to a great extent. In addition we have observed the skill with which the *De profectione* was written and have speculated about the historiographical tradition into which it fits. It is in the sphere of such investigations, which make use of the ideas and customs of the mid-twelfth century, that its importance has not been fully appreciated. The German historians, best exemplified by Kugler, have long valued Odo's account of the events of the Second Crusade;

[119] *Catilina* (p. 167).
[120] *Andria* (p. 127).
[121] *Aeneid* (p. 110).
[122] Cf. M. Manitius, *Geschichte der lateinischen Literatur des Mittelalters*, Vol. III (Munich, 1931), *passim*. It is interesting to note in this connection that the library of St. Denis contained a sixth-century Vergil and a ninth-century Terence.
[123] For example, the *Ars poetica* indicates how an author should take a subject equal to his strength, narrate it in clear order, and distinguish between important and unimportant facts (ll. 38–45); how he should wish either to amuse or to instruct, or to combine these two functions in his writing (ll. 333–37); how he should hasten to the issue, hurrying the hearer into the midst of the story as if it were already known (ll. 148–49). Lucan celebrates the power of the historian, which rises from his ability to give immortality to men and their deeds (Bk. vii, ll. 205–13; Bk. ix, ll. 980–86). Sallust says how valuable history is in inciting men to great deeds (*Jugurtha* IV). Eusebius, Orosius, and Augustine constantly remind one of the importance of careful organization and interpretation of historical facts.
[124] See note 122, above, and p. xxxiii, below.

but the topics relating to cultural subjects have never been fully exploited. The history affords information on a variety of thought-provoking subjects of this type. For example, Odo's narrative is an essential document in the history of the anti-Greek sentiment among the French which culminated in the Fourth Crusade; it gives a vivid picture of the personal reactions to the sophistication of the late Byzantine Empire of such different people as the king, a vehement bishop like Godfrey of Langres, the conciliatory party in the camp, and Odo himself. Another mine of information centers around the person of the king. Odo has described the personal character and conduct of Louis in affectionate detail. He has also portrayed the function of the sovereign in a large military expedition, in the exchange of diplomatic matters, and in council with his barons. These are only a few of the questions on which the *De profectione* sheds light. Thus, it stands as a comparatively new field for the investigator, particularly for one who is interested in expanding the cultural history of the mid-twelfth century.

II

The history of the manuscript.—The only known manuscript of Odo's *De profectione Ludovici VII in Orientem* occupies folios 15v–41 in MS No. 39, in the College of Medicine at Montpellier. In addition to Odo's letter and history, this late twelfth- or early thirteenth-century codex contains a collection of historical items, such as the *Descriptio cujusdam de locis sanctis* attributed to Fretellus, the various components of the *Liber sancti Jacobi*, and the *Vita Amicii et Amelii karissimorum*.[1] All were composed in the twelfth century,[2] and, with the exception of the *De profectione*, all were often copied.[3]

Information concerning the history of the manuscript is scant. Not until 1660 did it elicit particular notice. Then Chifflet, who edited Odo's history, designated it simply as "codex MS Clare-

---

[1] For a more detailed description see below, pp. xxxv–xxxvii.

[2] Fretellus, *ca.* 1130; Odo, *ca.* 1148; *Liber sancti Jacobi, ca.* 1150; *Vita Amicii et Amelii,* first half of the twelfth century.

[3] It is interesting to note that selections from the *Liber sancti Jacobi* and the *Vita Amicii et Amelii* were included in Montpellier No. 78 (Bouhier), No. 139 (Pithou), No. 235 (Bouhier), and that they, together with the work of Fretellus, appear in Montpellier No. 142 (Pithou). Thus, in Montpellier No. 39 Odo's work is the one unusual item which has been admitted to a conventional combination.

vallensis.''[4] Evidently the volume remained in the possession of
the monastery of Clairvaux until the time of the French Revolution, when the library was declared national property and taken
first to Bar-sur-Aube and then to Troyes. In 1804 Chardon de la
Rochette, who had been commissioned by the government to bring
rare books and manuscripts from the libraries of the *départements*
to the Bibliothèque Nationale, came to Troyes, especially attracted
by the famous Bouhier collection which had been purchased in
1781 by the library of Clairvaux. With him was Prunelle, a professor of medicine at Montpellier. De la Rochette selected 147
manuscript volumes, and Prunelle, 328. Instead of reaching the
Bibliothèque Nationale, however, the group chosen by Prunelle
went to the College of Medicine in Montpellier, where they have
remained until the present time.[5] Among them was the volume
now catalogued as No. 39.

From the meager evidence afforded by this later history of the
manuscript and from its contents it is tempting to try to recon-
struct the early history. Two monasteries immediately proclaim
their part in such a history: Clairvaux because, as we have already
seen, the monastery owned the manuscript in 1660; St. Denis because of the contents of the volume and the fame which that
monastic library enjoyed during the Middle Ages. Since Odo evidently sent his letter and history to Suger, the holograph, which
has now disappeared, presumably belonged to St. Denis. Likewise
the text of Turpin, which occurs in the *Liber sancti Jacobi*, is connected with the same monastery; for Chapter xxx, in describing
the council which Charlemagne held at St. Denis after his return
from Spain, narrates that he granted to St. Denis the same sort of
supremacy over France as he had granted to St. James of Compostella in regard to Spain.[6] This passage, which has sometimes
been considered an interpolation,[7] made the Chronicle of Turpin

---

[4] Preface to the *Bernardi Clarevallensis illustre genus assertum* (Dijon, 1660).

[5] For the story of the dissolution of the library of Clairvaux see Delisle, *Le Cabinet des manuscrits*, II, 16, 278–79, and *Analecta Bollandiana*, XXXIV (1915), 228.

[6] See the various forms of this passage in the editions of F. Castets (Paris, 1880), W. Thoron (Boston, 1934), C. Meredith-Jones (Paris, 1936), and H. M. Smyser (Cambridge, Mass., 1937).

[7] This theory was advanced by Gaston Paris in *De Pseudo-Turpino* (Paris, 1865). Although it has been followed to some extent, Bédier rejects it in *Les Légendes épiques* (Paris, 1912), III, 50.

of immense value to the monastery. Even more definite evidence that the monastery possessed a copy is furnished by the fact that Renaud, count of Boulogne, had the St. Denis text used for the basis of the French translation made for him in 1206.[8] Thus one might conclude that Montpellier No. 39[9] was written at and belonged to the monastery of St. Denis. But this need not have been the case. For example, no marks such as bookplates, inscriptions, or names have been found in the manuscript.[10] This is suggestive for two reasons. In the first place, the monks of St. Denis were prone to mark their manuscripts carefully. Secondly, the absence of any such distinctive mark prompts the hypothesis that the manuscript remained from the beginning in the same library where it was in 1660, thus running much less risk of being marked than would a manuscript which was constantly changing hands.

Such evidence, tenuous though it is, suggests that the manuscript was copied at Clairvaux from material belonging to St. Denis.[11] As is indicated by the incident of the Count of Boulogne and the often-repeated claim of the trouvères that they found the material for their writings in the library of St. Denis,[12] the monastery was justly famous for its collection of manuscripts. It would be very natural, therefore, for the monks of Clairvaux to borrow books for copying from St. Denis; and they may have been attracted to the work of Odo, which is the least generally popular item of the collection, because of the role which St. Bernard plays in the first section of the narrative. Be that as it may, when D was written, at the end of the twelfth or the beginning of the

---

[8] Delisle, *Le Cabinet des manuscrits*, I, 205.

[9] For the sake of convenience we shall hereafter call the manuscript D, because of its ultimate provenance from St. Denis. Use of C for Clairvaux or M for Montpellier would be confusing, since Odo's work has been printed by Chifflet and Migne, who are referred to in the critical notes as C and M.

[10] Since I have not seen the manuscript itself and have seen photostatic copies of folios 15–42 only, I cannot speak from autopsy. The fact that such marks are not mentioned by Waitz in *Archiv der Gesellschaft für ältere deutsche Geschichtskunde*, VII (1839), 196, or *Catalogue des manuscrits* (Paris, 1849), I, 301, or *Analecta Bollandiana*, XXXIV, 247–49, indicates that presumably they do not exist.

[11] The lack of inscription rules out the possibility that D was a gift book made at St. Denis for Clairvaux.

[12]   Ce n'est mie menchoigne, mais fines vérités
         A Saint Denis en France fu li raules trouvés;
         Plus de cent cinquante ans a yl esté celez

is an example of these claims, quoted by Delisle, *op. cit.*, I, 205. See Bédier, *op. cit.*, for further evidence.

thirteenth century, Clairvaux was finishing her first energetic century of development. At that time the monastery contained a
library, a small library for books in actual use, and a little cloister
with eight cells for scribes—ample accommodations for the copying and preservation of manuscripts.[13] From the first, historical
works formed a part of the library. By 1472, according to the
earliest catalogue of the library, there were sixty-six volumes con-
taining collections of such historical items as Josephus, the *Tri-
partite History*, Eusebius, Solinus, Suetonius, Caesar, Gregory of
Tours, Valerius Maximus, Orosius, many chronicles (especially
those concerning the kingdom of Jerusalem), *The Golden Legend*,
and different lives of the saints.[14] Of these, many dated from the
twelfth and thirteenth centuries. Then, too, the general appearance of the manuscript—large pages written in two columns and
adorned only by colored initials—corresponds to the description
of manuscripts written at Clairvaux during this period. From such
evidence we may say that the manuscript was probably copied at
Clairvaux from material loaned by the monastery of St. Denis and
that it remained at Clairvaux until the French Revolution, when
it was removed to Bar-sur-Aube, Troyes, and ultimately to Montpellier.

The description of the manuscript.—D is an in-folio written on vellum that is consistently fine[15] and usually thin enough to permit
wrinkles to appear and letters to show through faintly from the
opposite side of the leaf. It is composed of 111 folios, divided as
follows:[16] "Descriptio cujusdam de locis sanctis," 1–15v; "Epistle"
and "De profectione" of Odo, 15v–41; blank page on which the
creed has been filled in by a much later hand, 41v; "Liber miracu-
lorum S. Iacobi," 42–43; "Prologus Calixti super translationem
S. Iacobi," 43–43v; "Translatio S. Iacobi apud fratris Iohannis
evangelistae," 43v–47; "Calixtus papa de tribus sollemnitatibus
S. Iacobi," 47–49v; "Argumentum b. Calixti papae de miraculis
S. Iacobi," 49v–66; "Proemium domni Calixti papae in Passione
b. Eutropii," 66–70; "Historia famosissima Karoli Magni," 70–

---

[13] Viollet le Duc, *Dictionnaire de l'architecture française* (Paris, 1875), I, 267–69.

[14] H. d'Arbois de Jubainville, *L'Etat intérieur des abbayes cisterciennes* (Paris, 1858), p. 79.

[15] Rough places occur infrequently, and there are only two holes and one carefully mended tear in ff. 15–42.

[16] *Analecta Bollandiana, loc. cit.*, pp. 247–49.

SAMPLE PAGE OF MANUSCRIPT: BEGINNING OF BOOK ONE

97v; "De corporibus sanctorum qui in itinere S. Iacobi requiescunt," 97v–101; "Aimericus Pivaudi de Partiniaco," 101–101v; "Versus Calixti papae," 101v; "Versus beati Fortunati Pictavensis," 101v–102; "Epistola domni papae Innocentii confirmativa,"

102–102v; "Epistola Chromatii et Elidori de ortu B. Mariae," 102v–103; "Vita Amicii et Amelii," 103–111v.

The pages measure 33 x 23.5 centimeters. They are always laid out in two columns of thirty-one lines, each of which affords a space of 27 x 9 centimeters for writing. The lines appear to have been drawn directly onto the page, not impressed from one sheet to another by the use of a pointed instrument. Pin pricks are often visible at the edges, but they do not correspond to the ruling of the lines. No title or marginal index occurs. Likewise, there is no numbering system or mark which would indicate the gatherings. This last omission is especially unfortunate, since the photostats used for this study do not permit one to observe how the gatherings were arranged.

Although D contains no illuminations or elaborate decorative devices, the well-planned pages, neat script, capitals, and frequent punctuation contribute to a pleasing appearance which is enhanced by the incipit and explicit rubrics and by the eight initial letters. These initials are from 2¼ to 4½ centimeters in height and about 2¼ centimeters broad, varying according to the form of the letter represented and the extent to which it is permitted to extend into the margin. With the exception of the first initial, they appear to have been red, as were the incipits and explicits. The first, however, may have been gold or blue. It is further distinguished from the others by penwork in the shape of flowers and foliage, which fills the initial and makes a stiff little border in the margin beside it.

One scribe evidently wrote the entire text. The variation in size and general appearance of the letters from page to page is comparatively slight and may be attributed to the natural variations found in any one hand. Sometimes, however, it appears that the scribe did leave spaces, which were later filled by a corrector.[17] The script is an example of the early Gothic which developed in the late twelfth and early thirteenth century in France.[18] The firm strokes and flowing quality of the whole give the impression that it was written with complete mastery of the form and hence with ease and speed. Although there is a certain amount of lateral

[17] For further discussion of this point see below, p. xxxix.
[18] On p. xxxvi is a reproduction of a page from the manuscript.

compression and linking of letters, these features have not been carried to the extremes which mark the fully developed Gothic style. Hair strokes and forked letters are also few, but the letters *b*, *d*, *l*, *h*, *i*, *m*, *n*, *p*, *q*, and *u* are somewhat clubbed. The angular tendency crops out especially in letters such as *c*, *e*, *o*, and *p*. Some letters (such as *a*, *d*, and *g*) occur in several forms. Although the letters are not usually confusing because of similarity with one another, *b* sometimes resembles *h*, upright *d* resembles *cl*, and small *l* resembles *i*. Ligatures occur with moderate frequency. *Ct*, *et*, and *st* are the most common; *fi*, *fl*, *li*, *ti*, *tr*, and *tu* are usual; examples of *ns*, *nt*, and *ut* are rare. M-strokes are almost ubiquitous.

The orthography of D is typical of the time in which it was written. Although free from the more distorted forms used during the earlier periods and in less-well-informed localities during the Middle Ages, it departs somewhat frequently from classical usage. Those departures are not always consistent. Sometimes the same word appears in classical form in one place and in nonclassical form in another, as is the case of *martyres* and *martire*, *abundantior* and *habundantiori*, *turres* and *turibus*. It has seemed advisable, therefore, always to print the classical version in the text in order to facilitate the reading.[19]

Although the folios do not give the impression of being loaded with abbreviations, the scribe employed a large number and a wide variety, which occur unevenly throughout the manuscript as the exigencies of space demand; i.e., after several columns in which the number is small and the writing flowing, the number increases materially and the writing becomes more cramped. As a whole, the abbreviations are clear and easy to expand.[20]

The scribe has punctuated the text rather generously. In most cases this punctuation is an aid to the reader, but sometimes it separates clauses or words in a way which makes them difficult to understand. The scribe indicated full stops by using a semicolon (very rarely) or a dot which rests above the base line. Dots or

---

[19] Anyone interested in a list of the departures from the classical usage can find it in my unpublished dissertation, "Odo of Deuil's *De profectione Ludovici VII in Orientem*," deposited in the University of Chicago library, pp. xxxii–xxxv.

[20] A list of the abbreviations and the number of times they appear may be found in the unpublished version of my thesis, *loc. cit.*, pp. xxxv–xxxviii.

dots with strokes over them (⸫) denote partial stops. Although
he used dots for both full and partial stops, the scribe did not
utilize the device of placing them at different heights from the
base line in order to distinguish between the two types. These
dots sometimes stand alone, but more often they are connected by
a hair line with the letters which precede. Question marks are
rare. Usually when a word is divided at the end of a line the
division is indicated by a hair line which resembles the modern
hyphen. With the possible exception of the initial letters at the
beginning of every book, there is no indication of paragraphing.
Capital letters occur only after full stops, and not always then.
Proper names in the present sense are not capitalized.

Although the scribe usually copied his exemplar accurately, he
did, of course, make some mistakes. Of these he corrected many
immediately, either by erasing and rewriting or by remaking the
offending letter or letters.[21] A corrector, whose hand is discern-
ible in insertions made throughout the manuscript, emended others.
The corrector's script belongs to the same period and type as that
of the scribe and is, therefore, often difficult to identify. It is usually characterized, however, by the abundant occurrence of abbreviations, the use of slightly different abbreviation marks from
those used by the scribe, the presence of the figure seven *et*, the
use of suprascript *a* and *s* within the line rather than only at the
end, and the more compressed and pointed appearance of the letters. Since the majority of entries made by this hand are in spaces
which the scribe left to be filled in later, one can say that the two
men worked at the same time, using the same exemplar, and that
the corrector was evidently expert in deciphering the abbreviations
and symbols which puzzled the scribe. In addition to filling such
difficult passages, he made corrections, the most common of which
were of unintentional omissions of m-strokes, letters, and words.

In addition to these two comparatively well-defined groups are
other corrections (e.g., by erasure or expunction) which defy classi-
fication and identification with the corrections of the scribe (henceforth to be known as D1) or those of the corrector (henceforth to

[21] His corrections have to do with letter confusions, omissions, dittography and a few
other errors of judgment which he noted on the spot. All corrections have been noted in
the critical apparatus of the text, pp. 1–142, below. A detailed analysis of them may be
found in my thesis, *loc. cit.*, pp. xxxix–xliv.

be known as D2). Examination of the manuscript would undoubt-edly give much aid in the solution of this problem because of the information furnished by the various tints and consistencies of the inks used, the imprint remaining on the vellum of letters which are now erased, etc. In this study, which has been based upon the examination of photostats, it has been necessary to combine all such puzzling corrections into an amorphous group (designated as Dx) without drawing any finer distinctions. These were probably the work of several correctors, as the variety in types of correc-tion, which far surpasses that of D1 and D2, suggests. By making over letters, crossing out, erasing, and expuncting Dx corrected letter and word confusions; he supplied omitted m-strokes, abbre-viation marks, and letters and corrected cases of dittography. Dx is also responsible for the detection and changing of several in-correct forms which had come into the text, for deleting appar-ently superfluous words, for indicating a change in word order, and for emending some abbreviations which the scribe misinter-preted. To this list should be added the few marginal notes which can be deciphered: *potius*, p. 48; *licet*, p. 50; *ego*, p. 50; and *apanis*, p. 114. Of these, the first three were undoubtedly guideposts for the corrector, as probably were the marginal comments which are now erased; the last is cryptic.

Despite the care taken by the scribe and the correctors, D still contains some few errors of the types which we have already seen corrected in many instances. These consist of confusions of let-ters, abbreviations, and words; omission of letters, m-strokes, and abbreviation marks; and the insertion of letters. As in the case of the errors already corrected, however, very few have to do with grammatical inaccuracy.

Previous editions of the manuscript.—We owe the first edition of the *De profectione* to the learned Jesuit, Peter Francis Chifflet, who included in his *Sancti Bernardi genus illustre assertum*, published at Dijon in 1660, "the works of Odo of Deuil, John the Hermit, Herbert of Tours . . . and other writers, which have to do with the history of the twelfth century A.D."[22] His choice of Odo's history as the first item of this collection is explained by the statement that Odo narrated the events of the first year of the

[22] Title-page.

Second Crusade more accurately than any other writer;[23] and, in addition to this opinion on his own part, he indicated that other scholars had recognized the importance of the history and had hoped that it would be made accessible.[24] To fulfill this hope Chifflet printed the entire text of D in a clear and readable form, substituting spelling according to classical usage for the medieval forms, supplying contemporary capitalization and punctuation, and making emendations wherever he considered necessary. Since the conventions of the science of paleography as we now know it had not then been established and his interest lay in presenting the subject matter to the reader rather than disclosing the processes by which he arrived at that presentation, he did not point out his emendations, or the original reading of the manuscript in such places, or other details, such as the changes made in the manuscript by the scribe and the correctors. He allotted no discussion to the subjects of abbreviation and orthography; and his textual notes consist of the three suggestions that *Sisto* should perhaps be read as *Xysto* and *nongentes* as *nonaginta* and that a verb should be supplied in one sentence. Chifflet's work is extremely accurate, however, and the majority of his emendations show both sagacity and technical knowledge. Only a few misprints, errors in transcription and spelling, changes in word order, and unnecessary emendations occur.[25]

As one would expect from the man whose aims have just been outlined, Chifflet took pains to place the history in the proper setting. First he wrote a short introduction, in which he identified Odo, summarized the inception of the crusade and the march as far as Antioch, and suggested that Suger used Odo's material in the *Gesta Ludovici*.[26] Then he printed an itinerary which he had drawn up for the period between the Christmas court at Bourges in 1145 and the arrival of the crusaders in Antioch in 1148.[27] In this list he translated into terms of the days of the months the

---

[23] Page 1.

[24] "The very same information which the king imparted to Suger in barely a single page Odo explained to him in seven books, and these books, which have been very much sought after and desired for this long time, we publish now at last from a manuscript at Clairvaux."

[25] These points can be verified in the critical notes, pp. 2–142.

[26] Pages 1–3.

[27] Pages 3–5.

dates which Odo mentioned in relation to church feasts, included
some information which he had gained from other sources, and
identified some of the geographical names. And finally Chifflet
flanked Odo's history with two twelfth-century documents, the
letter which Louis VII wrote to Suger from Antioch,[28] and an
account of the eclipse of 1147, written at the Cathedral Church of
St. Stephen of Catalonia.[29]

Many scholars of the nineteenth century used Chifflet's excellent
edition. Wilken translated and paraphrased much of it in his famous *Geschichte der Kreuzzüge*.[30] His example was followed by
Michaud in *Bibliothèque des Croisades*[31] and by Paris in the *Histoire
littéraire de la France*.[32] Guizot also used Chifflet's text when he
translated Odo's entire history for the *Collection des mémoires relatifs
à l'histoire de France*.[33] In addition to being used as a tool for translation and historical narration, the text itself was incorporated in
two collections of documents. In 1877 Delisle reprinted the parts
which dealt immediately with France; i.e., most of the letter, all
of Book I, and the beginning of Book II.[34] Two years later Migne
reprinted the whole of Chifflet's work, including his introduction,
itinerary, Louis VII's letter, and the account of the eclipse of
1147.[35] Since neither of these men re-examined the manuscript,
their editions did not make any advance in critical technique over
the edition of 1660. In some cases, of course, they corrected obvious errors, such as mistakes in printing and spelling; and Migne
made several clever emendations of the printed text.[36] Those im-
provements are counterbalanced, however, by a repetition of many
of Chifflet's errors and by an increase in mistakes, caused by misprints, haste in copying, or unnecessary emendation. The Bouquet
edition follows the general policy of the collection in which it is

[28] Pages 6–8.
[29] Pages 77–79, with an explanatory note on p. 80.
[30] Leipzig, 1817.
[31] Paris, 1829.
[32] Paris, 1869.
[33] Paris, 1825; Vol. XXIV.
[34] The excerpts printed are: *Ecclesiae B. Dionysii . . . suo dilexit et*, p. 2; *ad tempus illud
. . . vobis commisit*, p. 2; *Vos patris eius . . . Ego vero*, pp. 2–4; *rerum quae . . . et cubanti*,
p. 4; *Summatim vobis . . . eloquentia venustandam*, p. 4; *Anno Verbi . . . omnium prosecutus*,
pp. 6–18; *Post discessum . . . nec ego retinui*, p. 20. RHGF, XII (Paris, 1877), 91–93.
[35] PL, CLXXXV (Paris, 1879), 1202–46.
[36] These have been included in the critical notes, pp. 2–142, below.

included as to the brief identification of names, dates, and other supplementary information whenever possible. Migne determined the source of one classical and several Biblical quotations.

Very soon, however, an independent edition appeared in the *Monumenta Germaniae historica.*[37] Because Waitz, like Chifflet, valued Odo's history greatly, classifying it as "among the principal records of this age," he was tempted to print the whole;[38] but the nature of the *Monumenta* undertaking forced him to restrict himself to excerpts which dealt with the Germans.[39] The Waitz[40] edition illustrates the increase of interest in medieval studies and in paleographical method during the two hundred years after Chifflet's edition. The spelling of the manuscript, far from being changed to conform with classical usage, was retained wherever the medieval forms occurred and, for the sake of consistency, was sometimes changed from the classical to medieval forms. Emendations of the text were much fewer, and the editor indicated their presence by printing the manuscript reading in the critical notes. An extraordinarily high standard of accuracy prevailed throughout. Waitz continued the work of the previous editors in identifying the Biblical quotations used by Odo, in locating the places mentioned by him and modernizing their geographical names, and in giving information concerning the men who played a part in the crusade. His notes, which include valuable references to other twelfth-century sources and to modern treatises, indicate what a wealth of material is now available for augmenting Odo's account.

[37] MGSS, XXVI (Hanover, 1882), pp. 59–73.

[38] *Ibid.*, p. 60.

[39] Waitz interpreted this restriction broadly: "I have kept the passages which can illumine, even to a small extent, the fate of the Germans and the ones in which the Count of Flanders participated." The following list includes the passages selected for his edition: *Ecclesiae beati . . . meruit omnium,* pp. 2–4; *Anno Verbi . . . eum sequi,* p. 6; *Rex quasi . . . socium promittebant,* p. 10; *Alemannorum et . . . societate scribebant,* p. 10; *Omnes igitur . . . Stampas vocat,* p. 12; *predictus etiam . . . Christi adiunxerat,* p. 12; *inter haec . . . principi congregandis,* p. 14; *Mettis ergo . . . vocati veniunt,* pp. 20–24; *In his quae . . . Hungaria educit,* pp. 28–38; *Hucusque lusimus . . . annorum firmasse,* pp. 40–54; *Ceterum multo studio . . . voces eorum,* p. 58; *Constantinopolis Graecorum gloria . . . pignoribus venerandae,* pp. 62–66; *Forum tamen . . . defendendo possideat,* p. 72; *Ecce pertransivimus . . . exercitus violari,* pp. 72–4; *Dum haec aguntur . . . colloquium respuit,* p. 80; *Illo die . . . est hiemare,* pp. 82–108; *Nunc venit . . . spolia diviserunt,* p. 112; *Erant ibi . . . occiderant inimici,* p. 114; *Parcat Deus . . . divinam gratiam conquirebant,* pp. 136–142.

[40] Although Waitz had seen the manuscript at Montpellier in 1837 (*Archiv der Gesellschaft für ältere deutsche Geschichtskunde,* VII [1839], p. 196) and in 1840 (MGSS, XXVI, p. 60), the transcription was made for him by V. Cl. Baist.

The present edition.—*Speculum* for 1935 printed a note mentioning the need for a modern edition of Odo's *De profectione*.[41] In view of the fact that the two most recent editions are the version in Migne (which, as we have seen, is only a repetition of Chifflet's work) and the selections in the MGSS and that the document in question is the principal source of information for the Second Crusade, the need seems obvious. And so the present text, established after a detailed examination of D and a collation of the other editions, has been prepared. It has been the policy of the editor to use the resources of modern scholarship, while trying to retain Chifflet's aim of printing a text that is readily intelligible to the general reader. In the introduction I have furnished a setting for and evaluation of the work and have treated such technical subjects as the description of the manuscript, the orthography and abbreviations, and the methods employed by the scribe and correctors.[42] The text itself has been set up with present-day punctuation, capitalization, and paragraphing; with the classical type of spelling, which remains more familiar than the medieval usage; and with a brief critical apparatus which includes notes on peculiarities in the manuscript, manuscript readings in cases where emendation seemed advisable,[43] and readings from the other editors.

In order to increase the usefulness of this edition I have also prepared the first complete English translation of Odo's history. The only other complete translation in any language is that which Guizot based on Chifflet's text and published in 1825. In the main, the two translations agree; but some differences of interpretation, arising in large part from variation between the two texts, do appear. Further tools for interpreting the account are furnished by the rather full supplementary notes which accompany the text and translation.

[41] Page 229.

[42] See pp. xxxv–xl.

[43] Whenever it has been at all possible, the original reading of the manuscript has been retained. The few emendations made are usually simple grammatical corrections of gender, case, tense, or number.

De profectione
Ludovici VII in orientem

The Journey
of Louis VII to the East

Epistola Odonis
ad Venerandum Abbatem Suum Sugerium[a]

Ecclesiae beati Dionysii venerando abbati Sugerio monachorum eius minimus, Odo de Deogilo, salutem.

Velle[b] adiacet mihi, perficere autem non invenio, ut de via sancti Sepulcri vobis aliqua idonee denotem[c] quae mandetis stilo vestro memoriae sempiternae, nam detentus adhuc in agone itineris, et imperitia praepedior et labore. Est tamen temptandum aliquando id etiam quod nequimus ut nostro [16r] conatu viros strenuos[d] ad hoc quod volumus et non possumus incitemus. Ego igitur, cum in via sancti Sepulcri gloriosi regis Ludovici beneficia ubertim senserim et secretius familiaritati adhaeserim, referendarum gratiarum affectum quidem habeo; sed non ministrant vires effectum. Sit hoc beati Dionysii, cuius amore haec[e] fecit, et vestrum,[f] quia monachum vestrum loco vestro suscepit. Vos tamen multum pro vobis debetis, quem specialiter in regno suo dilexit et[g] zelo ductus fidei propagandae[h] ad tempus illud dimittens vobis commisit. Ibi tamen vigilavit sibi sua credens expertae fidei et[i] sapientiae singulari.

Vos patris eius gesta scripsistis, sed criminis erit fraudare[j] posteros notitia filii cuius omnis aetas est forma virtutis; nam cum regnare coeperit paene puer non fuit illi gloria saeculi materia voluptatis, sed dedit augmentum virtutibus eius et lucem. Unde si quis gesta eius ab itinere Ierosolymitano describere coeperit, futuris regi-

---

[a] In these notes the following abbreviations obtain: D for the work of the scribe of Montpellier 39, D1 for the corrections made by the scribe, D2 for the corrections made by the corrector, and Dx for the corrections whose source has not been determined. See above, pp. xxxvii ff. The editions referred to as C, B, M, and W are those of Chifflet, Bouquet, Migne, and Waitz, all of which have been discussed above on pp. xl ff.

[b] Vellet > Velle Dx.

[c] denoiem > denotem D1.

[d] strenuo > strenuos D2.

[e] hoc CBM.

[f] vestri B.

[g] ei M.

[h] propanande > propagande D1.

[i] *om.* CM.

[j] laudare M.

---

[1] For a discussion of Suger's connection with the history, see above, pp. xvi, xxix ff.; for the life of Odo, pp. xiv–xvi.

[2] Romans 7:18. In the translation, quotations from the Bible follow the King James version, though the wording is not always identical.

Odo's Letter
to His Venerable Abbot, Suger

To Suger,[1] the venerable abbot of the Church of St. Denis, the least of his monks, Odo of Deuil, sends greeting.

I wish to point out to you capably, with a view to your perpetuating them in writing, some facts about the crusade, yet I cannot,[2] for, as I am still engaged in the hardships of the journey,[3] I am hampered both by fatigue and lack of skill. Nevertheless, we must sometimes essay even the impossible, in order that our effort may incite able men to the task which we wish to perform, but cannot. Then, too, since I have enjoyed the renowned King Louis'[4] generous favors and have been closely associated with him during the crusade, I am eager to thank him; yet my powers are meager. Let this be the task of St. Denis, out of love for whom the king did these favors, and your own, because he accepted your monk as yourself. You, moreover, owe him much on your own behalf, for he has particularly favored you in his realm and on leaving it for a time, influenced by zeal for extending the faith, he has entrusted that very realm to you.[5] Nonetheless, he was thereby protecting his own interests by confiding them to a man of proven loyalty and unique wisdom.[6]

You have recorded his father's deeds,[7] and it will be a crime to cheat posterity of knowing the son, whose entire life is a model of virtue; for when as a mere boy he began to reign, worldly glory did not cause him sensual delight, but brought increase and luster to his virtues. Wherefore, if anyone begins to depict his life only from the time of the journey to Jerusalem, he will cut off the

---

[3] The letter and history were probably written in the winter of 1148. See above, p. xxiii.
[4] Louis VII is the central figure of the following history. This fact and the relation of Odo to his sovereign are discussed above, p. xvii. The most complete treatment of Louis VII is Hirsch, *Studien zur Geschichte König Ludwigs VII.*
[5] Suger was the principal regent of France during the crusade. See below, pp. 15 ff., 21.
[6] Suger's activity in the interest of Louis VI and Louis VII is best told by Cartellieri, *Abt Suger von Saint-Denis.*
[7] In the *Vita Ludovici Grossi*, ed. and trans. by Waquet.

bus exempli propositi a Deo maximam partem truncabit; nos enim magis miramur in puero Nicolao quartam et sextam feriam papillarum et reliquam indolem quam[k] praesulatus eius admirabilem sanctitatem.[1] Vos igitur, cui iure debetur reverentia scribendi de filio, qui prius patrem stilo[m] traxistis in lucem et qui iure debetis obsequium, abundantiori gratia functus amborum, incipite a pueritia ubi coepit virtus[n] oriri, quod vos melius scitis[o] quia sicut nutricius secretius didicistis. Ego vero, etsi impeditus sermone (sed non scientia rerum quae in via sancti Sepulcri gestae[p] sunt, quippe qui sicut capellanus illi surgenti saepius aderam et cubanti), ut ita dixerim quasi balbutiendo, summatim vobis offeram veritatem litterali eloquentia venustandam. Nec ideo vos pigeat exsequi quod debetis si hoc auditis a pluribus usurpari; immo gratum habetote si laudes habet multorum qui meruit omnium.

Explicit Epistola

---

[k] quo > quam D1.
[l] sci- > sancti- D2.
[m] *om.* B.

[n] virtus coepit B.
[o] nostris B.
[p] gesta D.

greatest part of the example set forth by God for future kings; for we marvel more at Nicholas' fourth- and sixth-day abstinence and other traits when an infant than at his wonderful sanctity as bishop.[8] Do you, therefore, to whom is justly due the honor of writing about the son, since you formerly made the father illustrious in literature, and since you owe them deference, having enjoyed the abundant favor of both, start with his boyhood, when his virtue began to flourish, as you very well know, for you learned it when you were his private tutor. Now, although I am lacking in style (but not in knowledge of the events which occurred on the crusade, since, as his chaplain, I was often present when he arose and when he retired) so that I stutter, as it were, I shall furnish you in brief the facts to be embellished by your literary eloquence. And do you not be reluctant to perform your duty, even if you hear that this task has been assumed by many; rather be grateful if he who has merited the praise of all enjoys the praise of many.[9]

End of the Letter

[8] K. Fissen, *Das Leben des heiligen Nikolaus* (Göttingen, 1921), p. 18, quotes the ninth-century Latin version of the life of St. Nicholas, written by John the Deacon: "While he was still being fed by his mother's milk he began to partake only twice on the fourth day of the week and once on the sixth day."

[9] Suger was not able to realize this hope of Odo's. Cf. Guillelmus, *Vita Sugerii Abbatis*, ed. by A. Lecoy de la Marche, in Suger, *Œuvres complètes*, p. 382: "Also he described the deeds of King Louis in a brilliant piece of writing and likewise began to write about his son Louis; but because he was prevented by death, he did not bring this work to a close."

Incipit Libellus[a] Primus

Anno Verbi incarnati millesimo centesimo quadragesimo sexto[b] gloriosus rex Francorum et dux Aquitanorum, Ludovicus, regis filius Ludovici, cum esset viginti quinque annorum, ut dignus esset Christo, Vezeliaco in Pascha baiulando crucem suam agressus est eum sequi.[1] In natali Domini praecedenti cum[c] idem pius rex Bituricas curiam celebrasset, episcopis et optimatibus regni ad coronam suam generalius solito de industria convocatis secretum[d] cordis sui primitus revelavit.[2] Tunc religiosus vir episcopus Lingonensis [16v] de Rohes,[e] quae antiquo nomine vocatur Edessa, depopulatione et oppressione Christianorum et insolentia paganorum satis episcopaliter peroravit; et de flebili materia fletum plurimum excitavit monens omnes ut cum rege suo ad subveniendum[f] Christianis Regi omnium militarent. Ardebat et lucebat in rege zelus fidei, contemptus voluptatis et gloriae[g] temporalis—exemplum omni sermone praestantius; tamen quod serebat[h] verbo episcopus, rex exemplo non ilico messuit.[i][3] Statutus est ergo dies alius, Vezeliaco in Pascha, quo in passione Domini omnes unanimiter[j] convenirent et

[a] lider B.
[b] VĪIDW.
[e] eum > cum Dx.
[d] secretis > secretum D1.
[e] clerohes D.

[f] c > d Dx.
[g] gl[orie] *over erasure of* exe- D1.
[h] serebant > serebat Dx; serebant M.
[i] messu[it] *over erasure of* -erunt D2; messuerunt CBM.
[j] ununimiter > unanimiter D1.

[1] Cf. Luke 14:27; John 19:17.

[2] See below, p. 9. Odo goes back to events before the meeting at Vézelay in order to show how it came about.

[3] This passage and Otto of Freising's *Gesta Friderici*, ed. by G. Waitz, 3d ed., I, xxxv, 54 (34), indicate that Louis planned to go to the East before he was urged to do so by the pope, a point which has caused much debate. Most valuable on this subject are the views advanced by Sybel in *Zeitschrift für Geschichtswissenschaften*, IV, 197; Kugler, *Studien zur Geschichte des zweiten Kreuzzugs;* Giesebrecht, *Geschichte der deutschen Kaiserzeit*, Vol. IV; Kugler, *Analekten zur Geschichte des zweiten Kreuzzugs;* Neumann, *Bernhard von Clairvaux und die Anfänge des zweiten Kreuzzugs;* W. Bernhardi, *Konrad III* (Leipzig, 1883), "Jahrbücher der deutschen Geschichte," Vol. XIV; Kugler, *Neue Analekten;* Hüffer, "Die Anfänge des zweiten Kreuzzugs," in *Historisches Jahrbuch*, VIII (1887), 391 ff.; Vacandard, *Vie de Saint Bernard.* Among the various motives ascribed to Louis are his desire to do penance (for his burning of Vitry in 1143 and for his breaking the oath that Pierre de la Chatre should not enter the city of Bourges as archbishop) and his wish to fulfill his dead brother Philip's (d. 1131) vow of going to Jerusalem.

[4] According to GC, IV, 575 ff., and W. Williams, *Saint Bernard of Clairvaux* (Manchester, 1935), Godfrey de la Roche, one of the original monks of Clairvaux and one of St. Bernard's

Beginning of Book One

In the year of the Incarnation of the Word 1146, the illustrious king of the Franks and duke of the Aquitanians, Louis, son of King Louis, in order to be worthy of Christ, undertook to follow Him by bearing His cross[1] on Easter in Vézelay,[2] at the age of twenty-five. On the preceding Christmas, when the same devout king had held court at Bourges, he had revealed for the first time to the bishops and magnates of the realm, whom he had purposely summoned in greater numbers than usual for his coronation, the secret in his heart.[3] On that occasion the pious bishop of Langres[4] spoke in his episcopal capacity concerning the devastation of Rohes, whose ancient name is Edessa, and the oppression of the Christians and the arrogance of the heathen;[5] and by this doleful theme he aroused great lamentation, while at the same time he admonished all that, together with their king, they should fight for the King of all in order to succor the Christians. There burned and shone in the king the zeal of faith, the scorn of pleasure and of earthly glory—an example finer than any discourse; but what the bishop sowed by word the king did not harvest immediately through his example.[6] Therefore another time was appointed, Eastertide at Vézelay, where all were to assemble on the Sunday

most zealous followers, was the first abbot of Fontenay 1119-30, the prior of Clairvaux 1130-38, the bishop of Langres 1138-62/3. On the crusade he vied with Arnulf of Lisieux (see below, p. 23), for the honor of being the most important churchman of the expedition, basing his claim on the fact that St. Bernard had entrusted Louis VII to his care. The *Historia pontificalis*, MGSS, XX, 534-35, which tells the story of the bitter rivalry, pictures Godfrey as more wise and generous than Arnulf, but also more violent. A. Ruville, *Die Kreuzzüge* (Leipzig, 1920), p. 131, indicates that Godfrey had just returned from the East when he appeared at Bourges. Although I have found no evidence to confirm it thus far, that fact, if true, would explain Godfrey's anti-Greek tendencies to some extent.

[5] For a description of conditions in the East which led to the fall of Edessa see the works of Kugler, Bernhardi, Giesebrecht, and Vacandard cited above and Wilken, *Geschichte der Kreuzzüge*, Vol. II. The contemporary Western accounts of the capture of Edessa seem in the main to stem from the letter of Eugenius III to King Louis, RHGF, XV, 429-30. See, for example, *Chronicon Richardi Pictaviensis*, RHGF, XII, 415-16; *Gesta Ludovici*, RHGF, XII, 199.

[6] Suger opposed the expedition openly (*Vita Sugerii, loc. cit.*, pp. 393 ff.). According to Otto of Freising, *Gesta*, I, xxxv, 54 (34), the magnates wished to consult St. Bernard before making a decision.

in resurrectione quibus foret caelitus[k] inspiratum crucis gloriam exaltarent.

Rex interim, pervigil in incoepto, Romam Eugenio papae super hac re nuntios mittit. Qui laetanter suscepti sunt laetantesque remissi, referentes omni favo litteras dulciores, regi oboedientiam,[1] armis modum et vestibus imponentes, iugum Christi suave suscipientibus peccatorum omnium remissionem parvulisque eorum et uxoribus patrocinium promittentes, et quaedam alia quae summi pontificis sanctae curae et prudenti visa sunt utilia continentes.[m] Optabat ipse tam sancto operi manum primam praesens imponere, sed tyrannide Romanorum praepeditus non potuit, sancto vero Clarevallensi abbati Bernardo curam istam delegavit.

Tandem dies adfuit regi optatus; abbas etiam, apostolica auctoritate et propria sanctitate munitus, et convocatorum maxima multitudo loco et termino pariter adfuerunt. Suscepit ergo rex a summo pontifice[n] sibi missum crucis insigne, et proceres multi cum eo. Et quoniam locus in castro[o] non erat qui tantam multitudinem capere posset, extra in campo fixa est abbati lignea machina, ut de eminenti circumstantibus loqueretur. Hanc ascendit cum rege cruce ornato; cumque caeleste organum more suo divini verbi rorem fudisset, coeperunt undique conclamando cruces[p] expetere. Et cum earum fascem[q] praeparatum seminasset potius quam dedisset, coactus est vestes suas in cruces scindere et seminare. In hoc laboravit

---

[k] one quibus foret celitus in D2.
[l] obedientie > obedientiam D1.
[m] continente > continentes Dx.
[n] pentifice > pontifice D1.

[o] in castro locus CBM.
[p] cruces cruces CBM.
[q] falcem > fascem Dx.

---

[7] The Pisan Bernard de Paganelli, a monk of Clairvaux, in 1140 became the first abbot of San Anastasio alle Tre Fontane, near Rome, and in 1145 was elected Pope Eugenius III. The controversy as to whether he provided the impetus for the Second Crusade has been referred to on p. 6 above, n. 3. For information about his life see H. Mann, *The Lives of the Popes in the Middle Ages* (London, 1914), IX, 127–221; J. Haller, *Das Papsttum* (Stuttgart, 1939), II, 63 ff.

[8] Cf. Psalms 19:10.

[9] Hüffer, *loc. cit.*, p. 406, n. 1, interprets this phrase as meaning the obedience of the king to the pope during the crusade, a view which seems unlikely in this context.

[10] Cf. Matthew 11:30.

[11] Cf. the letter of Eugenius to Louis, RHGF, XV, 430.

[12] See Otto of Freising, *The Two Cities;* trans. C. Mierow, VII, 31, for a description of the disorders in Rome at the time when Eugenius became pope; and VII, 34, for an account of the pope's brief reconciliation with the Romans from Christmas, 1145 to March, 1146.

[13] On the subject of this delegation of power to Bernard see *Vita sancti Bernardi*, III, RHGF,

before Palm Sunday, and where those who should be divinely inspired were to take up the glorious cross on Easter Sunday.

Meanwhile the king, who was ever active in the undertaking, sent messengers concerning it to Pope Eugenius at Rome.[7] They were received gladly and sent home glad, bearing letters sweeter than any honeycomb,[8] which enjoined obedience to the king[9] and moderation in arms and clothing, which promised those taking the easy yoke of Christ[10] the remission of all sins and the protection of their wives and children, and which contained certain other provisions that seemed advisable to the pope's holy wisdom and solicitude.[11] He wished personally to give the initial blessing to such a holy undertaking, but, since he could not, hindered as he was by the tyranny of the Romans,[12] he delegated that charge to Bernard, the holy abbot of Clairvaux.[13]

At last the day long desired by the king was at hand. So, too, the abbot, endowed with the papal authorization and his own holiness, and the huge multitude of those who had been summoned were at hand at the appointed time and place. Then the king, and many nobles with him, received the sign of the cross which had been sent by the pope. And since there was no place within the town which could accommodate such a large crowd, a wooden platform was erected outside in a field, so that the abbot could speak from an elevation to the people standing round about. He mounted the platform accompanied by the king, who was wearing the cross;[14] and when heaven's instrument poured forth the dew of the divine word, as he was wont, with loud outcry people on every side began to demand crosses.[15] And when he had sowed, rather than distributed, the parcel of crosses which had been prepared beforehand, he was forced to tear his own garments into crosses and to sow them abroad. He engaged in this as long as he remained in the vicinity of the town. I refrain from describ-

XIV, 370–71; Otto of Freising, *Gesta Friderici*, I, xxxvii, 58 (36); *Continuatio Sanblasiana*, MGSS, XX, 304–5. An excellent life of St. Bernard is Vacandard, *op. cit.*

[14] The *Chronicon Senonense sanctae Columbae*, RHGF, XII, 288, states that the platform, with the exception of the portion where Louis stood, fell, but that no one was injured. This may be one of the miracles which Odo mentions.

[15] The eloquence of St. Bernard's appeals can be gauged by reading his *Epistola ad clerum et populum orientalis Franciae*, RHGF, XV, 605–7. At this time the letter of the pope was read (cf. *Epistola Nicolai monachi ad comitem et barones Britanniae*, RHGF, XV, 607) and Louis evidently made a speech of exhortation too (*Chronicon Mauriniacense*, RHGF, XII, 88).

quamdiu fuit in villa. Supersedeo scribere miracula quae tunc ibidem acciderunt, quibus visum est id placuisse Domino,[r] ne, si pauca scripsero,[s] non credantur plura fuisse vel, si multa, materiam videar omisisse. Tandem edicto quod post annum progrederentur, omnes ad sua cum gaudio repedarunt.

Abbas vero, sub tenui corpore et paene praemortuo [17r] robustum tegens spiritum, ubique circumvolat praedicando, et multiplicati sunt super numerum in parvo tempore crucem portantes. Rex, quasi iam nactus gaudium suum fidei propagandae, de spe futuri exercitus copiosi Apuliam regi Rogerio nuntios mittit. Qui de omnibus rescripsit ad libitum; insuper viros remisit nobiles qui regnum suùm in victualibus et navigio et omni necessitate et se vel suum filium itineris[t] socium promittebant. Misit etiam alios Constantinopolitano imperatori, cuius nomen ignoro quia non est scriptum in libro vitae.[u] Hic in longo rotulo prolixam adulationem depinxit et, regem nostrum nominando "sanctum amicum et fratrem," promisit plurima quae opere non implevit. Sed haec alias! Alemannorum et Hungarorum[v] etiam reges de foro et transitu requisivit, quorum nuntios et litteras ad suam voluntatem recepit. Harum quoque regionum[w] duces multi et comites, eius exemplo provocati, de itineris illi societate scribebant. Sic ad nutum omnia procedebant. Interea fama volat; Angliam transfretat et aliarum

[r] Domino placuisse CBM.	[u] Viiae C.
[s] scrro- > scrip[sero] D1.	[v] Hug > Hung[arorum] D1.
[t] iteneris > itineris Dx.	[w] regiorum C.

[16] This plan was changed at Étampes. See below, p. 15.

[17] Cf. *Bernardi epistola ad Eugenium*, RHGF, XV, 603: "As for the rest, you have commanded and I have obeyed, and the authority of him who gives orders has made the obedience fruitful: whenever I have announced and spoken of the crusade, the crusaders have been multiplied beyond number. Cities and castles are emptied, and seven women now can hardly find one man whom they may apprehend, and so women everywhere remain behind in a widowed state while their husbands are still alive."

[18] Probably Roger, duke of Apulia (*ca.* 1118–48).

[19] For the relation of Roger to the Second Crusade see below, pp. 15, 59, 83; E. Caspar, *Roger II* (Innsbruck, 1904), pp. 370 ff.; F. Chalandon, *Histoire de la domination normande en Italie et en Sicile* (Paris, 1907), II, 131 ff.; E. Curtis, *Roger of Sicily* (New York, 1912), pp. 212–42.

[20] These negotiations have been recorded also by Helmold in his *Chronicle of the Slavs*, trans. by Tschan, New York, 1935, pp. 172–3, and by Nicetas in his *Historia*, CSHB, XXII, 80.

[21] This expression, meaning "register of the elect," is found in *Revelation*, particularly in 20:15. For information about Manuel Comnenus see Chalandon, *Jean II Comnène et Manuel Comnène.* Odo's concept of him is discussed above, p. xxii, n. 56.

[22] *Epistola Manuelis ad Ludovicum*, RHGF, XVI, 9. It is interesting to note that Odo passes

ing the miracles which occurred there at that time, by reason of
which it appeared that the undertaking had pleased the Lord, for
fear, if I write of only a few, it will not be believed that there were
more, and lest, if I write of many, I seem to have abandoned my
theme. Finally, after the proclamation that they should set out
at the end of a year, all returned home joyfully.[16]

The abbot, however, who bore a hardy spirit in his frail and
almost lifeless body, hastened about, preaching everywhere, and
soon the number of those bearing the cross had been increased
immeasurably.[17] As if already realizing his joy in extending the
faith, the king sent messages to King Roger in Apulia, to com-
municate his plan for the large army which was being raised.
Roger replied very willingly on all counts; moreover, he sent nobles
who pledged his realm as to food supplies and transportation by
water and every other need and promised that he or his son[18]
would go along on the journey.[19] Also King Louis sent other
messengers to the Emperor of Constantinople,[20] whose name I ig-
nore because it is not recorded in "the book of life."[21] On a long
scroll the emperor inscribed extravagant flattery and, calling our
king his "holy friend and brother," made a great many promises
which he did not fulfill.[22] But of these things at another time!
Louis also asked the kings of the Germans[23] and the Hungarians[24]
for the rights of marketing in and passing through their lands,
and from them he received messengers and letters granting his requests. Then, too, many dukes and counts of these countries,
stimulated by his example with regard to the crusade, enrolled in
it. Thus everything progressed favorably. Meanwhile the news
flew; it crossed to England and penetrated the remote parts of

over the fact that Manuel, after granting Louis' wish, refers to the gravity and weightiness
of the matter. Similar in content is the *Epistola Manuelis ad Eugenium*, RHGF, XV, 440–41,
which contains a more explicit reference to demands on the part of Manuel: "But it is my
imperial will that they honor me just as the Franks who formerly came honored my famous
grandfather." The question of homage is apparently already in his mind.

As Claude Cahen in *La Syrie du Nord a l'époque des croisades*, Paris, 1940, pp. 380–81, points
out, the presence of king and emperor as leaders of this crusade weakened Manuel's demand
for homage from the crusaders. For the crusaders' realization of this, see pp. 79–81 below.

[23] For the role of Conrad III in the Second Crusade see the works of Giesebrecht, Kugler,
and Bernhardi, already cited, and of Jaffé, *Geschichte des deutschen Reiches unter Conrad dem
Dritten*.

[24] Geisa II, king of Hungary 1141–61, was still a minor at the time of the crusade. Cf.
Otto of Freising, *Gesta Friderici*, I, xxxiii, 51 (32) and Chalandon, *Jean II Comnène*, p. 74.

recessus penetrat insularum. Parant naves maritimi cum rege navigio processuri.

Ceterum dum rex lustrans omnia statum regni ordinat, dum subditis in posterum[x] pacem firmat, omnes undique nuntii Parisius[y] convenerunt. Revertenti omnes pariter adfuerunt. Imperatorum sacras et ducum chartas offerunt, verboque et litteris quicquid poposcerat pollicentur.

Habet rex optionem cui fidem habeat, in quo compendium credat; sed illi mos erat ut socii essent consilii qui forent et laboris. Omnes igitur ad Circumdederunt[z] Me Stampas vocat, ut pariter eligerent quod pariter tolerarent. Qui sicut fuerunt in veniendo[a] alacres[b] sic utinam essent in electione prudentes! Congregata enim loco et termino episcoporum et nobilium multitudine, tam gloriosa quam magna, praedictus etiam abbas, et praedicandus, praesentiam suam obtulit et rumorem attulit; et utroque laetabundam[c] reddidit contionem. Nam de Alemannia veniebat,[d] regemque et regni proceres militiae crucis Christi adiunxerat. Deinde diversarum regionum leguntur litterae, nuntii audiuntur; et haec usque ad vesperum[e] protenduntur. In his duxerunt laetam diem, et quod superfuit in crastinum distulerunt. Venit dies laeta magis[f] quam prospera. Interfuere [17v] congregatis[g] qui Graecos dicerent[h] sicut lectione et[i] experientia noverant fraudulentos. Rex autem et sui qui merito nullarum gentium vires timebant fraudes utinam timuissent! Sed

---

[x] imposterum CB.	[d] v *over erasure of* d, D2 *correcting himself.*
[y] Parisiis M.	[e] ver > v Dx.
[z] dederunt *over erasure* D1.	[f] magis laeta CBM.
[a] inveniendo M.	[g] *expunction mark under* s *erased* Dx.
[b] -s *over erasure* D1.	[h] dicerent dicerent > dicerent Dx.
[c] -da . . . inter D2.	[i] lectione et *over erasure* D1.

---

[25] St. Bernard sent a letter to England, No. 365 in the *Epistolae Bernardi*, PL, Vol. CLXXXII. The effect of the news is recounted in *Gesta Stephani*, ed. by R. Howlett in *Chronicles of the Reigns of Stephen, Henry II and Richard I* ("Rolls Series," No. 82; London, 1886), Pt. III, p. 122; ed. and trans. by T. Forester, *Chronicle of Henry of Huntingdon*, "Bohn's Antiquarian Library," p. 418.

[26] A possible reference to the Lisbon expedition. The most complete account of this enterprise is *De expugnatione Lyxbonensi*, ed. and trans. by C. W. David ("Columbia University Records of Civilization," Vol. XXIV). I have found no evidence that the French crusaders were accompanied by a fleet as were the Germans.

[27] For a partial record of the activities of Louis during this period see Luchaire, *Études sur les actes de Louis VII*, pp. 152 ff.

[28] This is merely a recapitulation of the negotiations described immediately above, and it occurred during the summer of 1146.

[29] February 16, 1147. Odo has summarized the time between the meetings at Vézelay and

other islands.[25] The people living along the coast, who were to advance with the king by ship, prepared their vessels.[26]

Now while the king set the condition of his realm in order by examining everything, while he ensured future peace for his subjects,[27] all the messengers from the different countries assembled at Paris. All were there together when he returned. They presented the emperors' letters and the dukes' charters, and in word and writing they promised to grant his requests.[28]

The king had the liberty of choosing someone in whom he might confide, to whom he would entrust his revenue; but it was his custom to associate in counsel with himself those who would also be associated with him in action. Therefore he summoned everyone to Étampes on Circumdederunt Me Sunday[29] to choose together what they would endure together. Would that they had been as wise in choosing as they were swift in coming! When the multitude of bishops and nobles (which was as illustrious as it was large) had gathered at the appointed time and place, the abbot, mentioned before and eminently worthy of mention,[30] presented himself and brought news; he made the assembly glad on both counts, for he was returning from Germany, and he had won the king and the magnates of that realm to the soldiery of the cross of Christ.[31] Next the letters from the different countries were read, the messengers heard; and these transactions were prolonged until evening. In these pursuits they spent a pleasant day, and they put off the rest of the business until the morrow. That day came, more pleasant than fortunate. There were men in the assembly who said that the Greeks, as they had learned either by reading or by experience, were deceitful. Would that the king and his men, who were right in fearing the strength of no nation, had entertained some fear of deceitful wiles! But because mortal wisdom and pru-

---

Étampes very briefly, omitting the meeting at Châlons of Louis, St. Bernard, legates of Conrad III, and Duke Welf. Cf. *Vita Sancti Bernardi*, III, RHGF, XIV, 378.

[30] Despite my lack of success in attempting to English the Latin plays on words, I have retained some attempts as closer to the spirit of the original than a literal translation would be.

[31] *Vita Sancti Bernardi*, III, *loc. cit.*, XIV, 378, narrates the story of Conrad's enrollment in the crusade. The circumstances of Bernard's preaching of the crusade in Germany are little known from contemporary records and, hence, have furnished much opportunity for controversy. Cf. the works of Kugler, Giesebrecht, Neumann, Bernhardi, Hüffer, Vacandard, and Williams, cited above, p. 6, nn. 3, 4.

quia non est consilium nec prudentia contra Deum, elegerunt viam
per Graeciam morituri. Sic secunda[j] dies terminata est non secunda. Tunc viri nobiles, regis Rogeri nuntii, confusi abeunt, do-
lentium habitu, domini sui satis expresse monstrantes affectum, de
dolis Graecorum praedicentes nobis quod postea sumus experti.
Nec mirum si Rogerius, rex potens et sapiens, regem optabat, si
Francos diligit nostrarum partium oriundus.

Postremo revolvit diem tertiam gratia Trinitatis, et congregati,
gratia prius sancti Spiritus invocata (quam pridie utinam similiter
invocassent!), deinde a sancto abbate sermone habito spiritali, de
regni custodia prosequuntur. Rex autem, more suo[k] sub timore
Dei reprimens potestatem, praelatis ecclesiae et regni optimatibus
eligendi indidit libertatem. Eunt igitur ad consilium; et post ali-
quantulam[l] moram, cum quod erat melius elegissent, sanctus abbas
praecedens revertentes, sic ait "Ecce gladii duo hic. Satis est," te,
pater Sugeri, et Nivernensem comitem monstrans. Quod valde
placuit omnibus si soli[m] comiti placuisset. Sed se ille Carthusiae
devoverat, quod cito post effectui mancipavit[n] nec regis nec omnium diutinis precibus potuit revocari. Imponitur tandem tibi soli
onus amborum, quod inconcussa pace tulisti, et hoc esse onus
Christi ex levitate sensisti. Inter haec indicitur dies in Pentecosten
profecturis et in Octavis[o] undecumque Mettis[p] glorioso[q] et humili
principi congregandis.

Post haec, ne aliquid deesset benedictionis aut gratiae, Romanus
pontifex Eugenius venit et pascha Domini in ecclesia beati Dionysii
honore quo decuit celebravit. Affluunt multi multarum partium

[j] sco > scd- D1.
[k] au more suo D2, *who wrote* an > a̅u̅.
[l] aliquantam B.
[m] solo D.

[n] et *inserted* CBM.
[o] optatis CBM.
[p] Mettis *over erasure of* Metesis D1.
[q] gl[oso] et *over erasure* D1.

[32] Proverbs 21:30.

[33] It is commonly supposed that this choice was caused by the desire of the Franks to
follow the route of the First Crusade (on this point, see below, pp. 59, 131) and to the enmity
between the Sicilian Normans and the Germans. Kugler, *Studien*, p. 103, considers that this
step, a change from Louis' original plan, was made necessary by the participation of the
Germans in the crusade.

[34] Luke 22:38.

[35] William II, count of Nevers 1089–1147, had long been a devoted supporter of the French
monarchy. For a summary of his life see *L'Art de vérifier les dates*, 2d part, "*Depuis la naissance
de Jésus-Christ*" (4th ed.; Paris, 1818), XI, 211–15. He died very soon after becoming a
Carthusian (*Origo et historia brevis Nivernensium comitum*, RHGF, XII, 316; *Historia Vizeliacensis
monasterii, ibid.*, pp. 318–19).

dence do not exist against God,[32] they who were destined to die
chose the route through Greece.[33] Thus, the second day ended
without seconding the business. Then the noblemen, King Roger's
messengers, went away confounded, like men in grief, showing
clearly enough their love for their master and foretelling to us the
Greek trickery which we later experienced. And it is not strange
that Roger, a wise and powerful king, favored our king's undertaking, or that one who came originally from our part of the world
cherished the Franks.

At last, by the grace of the Trinity, the third day rolled around,
and after the grace of the Holy Ghost had first been invoked (would
they had invoked it in the same manner on the previous day) and
then a sermon had been delivered by the holy abbot, the assembly
continued with the problem of the custody of the realm. Now the
king, limiting his power out of fear of God, as was his wont, gave
the prelates of the church and the nobles of the realm the privilege
of election. They went to take counsel, and after they had chosen
the better course of action after some little delay, as they were
returning, led by the holy abbot, the latter said, "Behold, here
are two swords; it is enough,"[34] pointing out you, Father Suger,
and the count of Nevers. This would have pleased everyone a
great deal if only it had pleased the count, but he had vowed himself to Chartreuse, and he accomplished his vow shortly afterward
and could not be recalled from it by the prolonged prayers of the
king or of all the others.[35] Then on you alone was placed the burden assigned to both, and you bore it in unruffled peace and felt
that it was the easy burden of Christ.[36] In the meantime a day in
Pentecost was appointed for the departure and one in the Octave[37]
for meeting the humble and illustrious prince at Metz.

Afterwards, so that no blessing or favor should be lacking, Eugenius, the Roman Pontiff, came and celebrated Easter in the Church
of St. Denis with proper ceremony.[38] Many people from many

---

[36] Cf. the words of Christ in Matthew 11:30, "My yoke is easy, and my burden is light."
Odo passes over the fact that Suger did not wish to accept the regency, "because he con-
sidered it a burden rather than an honor," and that he did so only in obedience to the pope.
Cf. *Vita Sugerii, loc. cit.*, pp. 393–94; *Breve chronicon sancti Dionysii*, RHGF, XII, 215–16.

[37] June 15, 1147.

[38] The visit of Eugenius to Paris and St. Denis is attested by *Breve chronicon sancti Dionysii,
loc. cit.*, pp. 215–16; *Gesta Eugenii III Papae*, RHGF, XV, 423–25; *Appendix ad Sigebertum*,
RHGF, XIII, 291; *Anonymi chronicon Cassinensis*, RHGF, XIII, 736.

utrique miraculo, videlicet regi et apostolico peregrinis. Papa vero
bene ordinata confirmat, enormia multa componit dum regis pro-
motionem expectat. Illo anno in quarta feria Pentecostes edictum
accidit; sic regi celebria cuncta succedunt. Dum igitur a beato
Dionysio vexillum et abeundi licentiam petiit, qui mos semper
victoriosis regibus fuit, visus ab omnibus planctum maximum excitavit et intimi affectus omnium benedictionem [18r] accepit.

Dum vero pergeret rem fecit laudabilem, paucis[r] imitabilem et
forsitan suae celsitudinis nulli; nam cum prius religiosos quosque
Parisius[s] visitasset, tandem foras progrediens leprosorum adiit offi-
cinas. Ibi certe vidi eum cum solis duobus arbitris intrasse[t] et per
longam moram ceteram suorum multitudinem exclusisse. Interim
mater eius et uxor et innumeri alii ad beatum Dionysium praecur-
runt. Quo[u] ipse postmodum veniens, papam et abbatem et ecclesiae
monachos invenit congregatos. Tunc ipse humillime humi pro-
sternitur;[v] patronum suum adorat. Papa vero et abbas auream[w]
portulam reserant et argenteam thecam paululum extrahunt, ut
osculato rex et viso quem diligit anima sua alacrior redderetur.
Deinde sumpto vexillo[x] desuper altari et pera[y] et benedictione a
summo pontifice, in dormitorium monachorum multitudini se sub-

---

[r] tamen *inserted* CBM.	[v] prostratus CBM.
[s] Parisiis M.	[w] *om.* B.
[t] interesse CBM.	[x] velulo > vexillo Dx.
[u] Et CBM.	[y] petra > pera Dx.

---

[39] The word *edictum* is often used for *indictum* to mean "fair." Cf. C. du Cange, *Glossarium
mediae et infimae Latinitatis* (Paris, 1840). Scheduled for the second Wednesday of June, the
Lendit Fair fell on June 11 in 1147.

[40] Odo exaggerates the antiquity of the custom in relation to the king. The oriflamme, a
vermilion banner mounted on a golden lance, was housed in the church of St. Denis and was
given by the abbot to his patron, the count of the Vexin, as a holy banner (a symbol of the
saint going forth into battle) whenever it was necessary for the count to go to war. At the
time of Louis VI the Vexin became one of the royal holdings, and the king gained the right
to carry the oriflamme. Cf. Du Cange, *Glossarium*, "auriflamma"; C. Erdmann, "Kaiser-
fahne und Blutfahne," *Sitzungsberichte der preussischen Akademie der Wissenschaften* (Berlin,
1932), pp. 889 ff.; S. M. Crosby, *The Abbey of St. Denis*, New Haven, 1942, pp. 50-52.

[41] Before going to St. Denis; Odo has again summarized an event and then proceeded to
narrate it in detail, without indicating the process clearly to the reader.

[42] Odo's presence in the retinue of the king before the visit to St. Denis indicates that he
had been in Louis' personal service before the crusade was actually begun.

[43] Adelaide, the daughter of Humbert II of Maurienne and the sister of Pope Calixtus II,
had married Matthew of Montmorency in 1138, one year after the death of Louis VI.

[44] The famous Eleanor of Aquitaine, who in 1147 had been queen of France for ten years,
has very little part in Odo's narrative. Although she was present, and often active, at
nearly all the events which he describes and she must have been well known to him, she is

places thronged together because of the double marvel, that is, the king and the apostolic father as pilgrims. The pope, moreover, confirmed the arrangements which were satisfactory and corrected many irregularities while waiting for the king to arrive. In that year the Lendit Fair of St. Denis fell on the Wednesday after Pentecost;[39] therefore all the great crowds who went to the fair drew near the king. While thus in the sight of everyone he requested from St. Denis the oriflamme and the permission to depart (a ceremony which was always the custom of our victorious kings),[40] he aroused great lamentation and received the blessing of everyone's deepest affection.

Upon setting out,[41] he did a praiseworthy thing, which few, perhaps no one of his lofty rank, could imitate; for, first having visited some monks in Paris, he went outside the gates to the leper colony. There I myself saw him enter, with only two companions, and shut out the rest of his great retinue for a long time.[42] Meanwhile his mother[43] and his wife[44] and countless others went ahead to St. Denis. When the king arrived there presently, he found the pope and the abbot and the monks of the church gathered together. Then he prostrated himself most humbly on the ground; he venerated his patron saint. Indeed, the pope and the abbot opened the small golden door and drew out the silver reliquary a little way, so that the king might be rendered the more eager for his task by seeing and kissing the relic of him whom his soul venerated.[45] Then, when the banner had been taken from above the altar,[46] after he had received the pilgrim's wallet and a blessing from the pope, he withdrew from the crowd to the monks' dormi-

---

mentioned only briefly on pp. 57, 77, 79, below. A possible explanation of this fact can be found on p. xxii. For an account of her life see A. Richard, *Histoire des comtes de Poitou* (Paris, 1903), Vol. II, and Sister Angèle Gleason, "The Political Influence of Eleanor of Aquitaine" (unpublished Master's thesis, Dept. of History, University of Chicago, 1929). Less satisfactory are F. Magne, *La Reine Aliénor* (Paris, 1931); M. Rosenberg, *Eleanor of Aquitaine* (Boston, 1937); Vital-Mareille, *La Vie ardente d'Eléonore d'Aquitaine* (Paris, 1931).

[45] The restoration of St. Denis had been finished by Suger in 1144, and at that time the body of St. Denis and his companion martyrs had been placed in silver reliquaries in the high altar, which was covered with golden plates. Suger has told the story of the restoration most vividly in *De rebus in administratione sua gestis*, ed. by A. Lecoy de la Marche, *op. cit.*, pp. 185–209, and in *De consecratione ecclesiae sancti Dionysii, ibid.*, pp. 213–38. These have been edited and translated by Panofsky, *Abbot Suger*, Princeton University Press, 1946.

[46] Presumably by Suger, since the count of the Vexin was accustomed to receive the banner from the abbot of St. Denis.

ducit. Non enim patiebantur moras oppressio populorum et mater
et uxor, quae inter lacrimas et calorem paene spiritum exhalabant;
sed luctum et planctum qui ibi[z] inerat velle describere tam stultum
est quam impossibile. Illo die retentis paucis suorum in refectorio
comedit cum fratribus et osculatis postmodum omnibus recessit
orationibus et lacrimis omnium prosecutus.

Explicit Primus

---

[z] inibi B.

tory. The crowds and the king's wife and his mother, who nearly perished because of their tears and the heat, could not endure the delay; but to wish to depict the grief and wailing which occurred then is as foolish as it is impossible. On that day the king and a few of his retinue dined in the refectory with the brothers, and, after receiving the kiss of peace from all, he departed, accompanied by the tears and prayers of all[47].

End of Book One

[47] Odo ignores the unrest in France caused by the heavy taxes for the crusade. Cf. *De tributo Floriacensibus imposito*, RHGF, XII, 94–95; *Epistola Johannis abbatis Ferrariensis ad Sugerium*, RHGF, XV, 497.

Incipit Secundus

Taediosa est semper longa loquacitas pluribus occupato; unde vereor ne nostra oratio nimis prolixe sine respiratione cucurrerit. Sed date quaeso mihi, pater, hanc noxam. Intereram laetis rebus, et patriae meae nomina scribens et rerum reminiscens quod laetus videram sine taedio diutius recolebam; non enim cito afferunt iocunda laborem. Modo vero novo principio succingor ad aspera, intraturus exteras regiones, sicut actu fecimus sic sermone, et laboriosa deinceps citius terminabo.

Post discessum gloriosi regis ab ecclesia beati Dionysii nihil in regno eius actum est memorandum, nisi forte vultis scribi[a] quod in regni cura vobis dedit socium Remensem archiepiscopum.[1] Nescio tamen si comes Rodulfus (quia tunc excommunicatus erat) debeat a communione nostri sermonis excludi; qui, ne vobis duobus deesset saecularis gladius,[b] tertius additus est, ut triplex funiculus difficile[c] rumperetur [18v].

Mettis ergo quia ibi convenimus stilum vertamus. Ubi rex cum iure dominii nihil suum invenerit, omnes tamen invenit ex gratia, sicut Verduno iam fecerat,[d] quasi servos. Fixis ergo tentoriis extra urbem, paucis diebus venientem exercitum expectavit;[e] statuitque leges paci ceterisque utilitatibus in via[f] necessarias, quas principes sacramentis et fide firmaverunt. Sed quia ipsi non bene tenuerunt eas, nec ego retinui.

[a] scibi > scribi D1; scire B.
[b] gladius sacularis CBM.
[c] diffu- > diffic- D1.

[d] fererat > fecerat D1.
[e] exercitum exercitum > exercitum expectavit D1.
[f] viam CBM.

---

[1] Samson, archbishop of Rheims since 1140, did little in the regency, according to the evidence of A. Luchaire, *op. cit.*, pp. 170–76. Cartellieri, *op. cit.*, p. 48, considers his inclusion in the regency to have been a matter of form, motivated by the desire to keep the bishops and the archbishops of the realm from resisting the power of Suger.

[2] Raoul I, count of Vermandois and Valois 1117–52, was a strong supporter of Louis VI and became his seneschal. After a short term as seneschal under Louis VII he retired because of disagreements with Suger, but he returned to office in 1138 and held it until 1152. During the regency he was very active, but to a lesser degree than Suger. The excommunication to which Odo refers resulted in 1142 because Raoul put away his wife (the sister of Theobald of Champagne) in order to marry Adelaide, Eleanor of Aquitaine's sister. For information about Raoul see Luchaire, *op. cit.*, pp. 44–46; Cartellieri, *op. cit.*, pp. 35–36, 48–49; *L'Art de vérifier les dates*, Paris, 1818–44, Part 2, Vol. XII, pp. 195–97.

Beginning of Book Two

Extreme garrulousness is always wearisome to a very busy man; and so I fear that my account has run on too long without affording a breathing space. But please allow me this failing, father. I was engrossed in happy affairs, and, while writing the words connected with my native land and while remembering its affairs, unweariedly I recalled for too long a time what I had seen when a happy man; for pleasant events do not soon cause fatigue. Now, however, at this new beginning I gird myself for difficult tasks, intending to enter strange countries in my description, just as we did in fact, and accordingly I shall bring to a swifter conclusion the hardships which ensued.

After the illustrious king's departure from the Church of St. Denis nothing memorable was done in his realm, unless, perhaps, you wish to have recorded the fact that he made the archbishop of Rheims your associate in the administration of the realm.[1] Then, I do not know whether I ought to leave Count Raoul out of the communion of our account (because he was at that time excommunicate);[2] he was added as the third administrator, lest you two should lack a temporal sword,[3] so that "a threefold cord should not be quickly broken."[4]

To Metz, then, let us direct our account, since we assembled there. Although the king found nothing there which belonged to him by right of domain, he nevertheless found all subject to him voluntarily, as had already been true at Verdun. And so, after camp had been pitched outside the city, he waited a few days for the army to arrive; and he enacted laws necessary for securing peace and other requirements on the journey, which the leaders confirmed by solemn oath. But because they did not observe them well, I have not preserved them either.

---

[3] Odo has used the familiar figure of the two swords to indicate spiritual and temporal power in the regency on p. 15, above.

[4] Ecclesiastes 4:12.

Inde praemittit Wormatiam prudentes et religiosos viros, Alvi-sum[g] Atrebatensem episcopum et sancti Bertini abbatem[h] Leonem, ut in Rheno, qui ibi praeterfluit, navigium subsequenti exercitui praepararent; quod optime compleverunt congregata undique tanta multitudine navium ut ponte non egerent.

Huius clerus et populus civitatis in sollemnitate apostolorum Petri et Pauli regem valde sollemniter susceperunt. Hic primam nostri populi stultam superbiam sensimus. Transmearunt enim milites, inventaque pratorum satis ampla latitudine, venerabilem[i] episcopum Luxoviensem Arnulfum cum suis Normannis et Anglis domino regi placuit expectare.[j] Affluebant nobis per fluvium ab urbe victualia, et erat nostrorum et indigenarum assiduus commea-tus. Oboritur tandem rixa; peregrini autem nautas in fluvium proiecerunt. Quo viso cives currunt ad arma et vulneratis aliquibus unum ilico peremerunt. Turbantur hoc scelere peregrini; clamant[k] ignem pauperes, tam civibus exitiabilem quam etiam quibusdam nostris (divitibus mercatoribus scilicet et cambitoribus). Sed utros-que stultos Deo volente represserunt utrarumque partium sapien-tes. Cives tamen adhuc timent; et subductis utrique ripae navibus auferunt commeatum.[l] Sed religiosus vir Atrebatensis episcopus, navi quadam cum labore reperta, cum quibusdam baronibus trans-meat, turbam sedat et securitatem civibus pollicetur. Postea re-ductis navibus commeant more solito nobisque necessaria mini-strantur. Hucusque[m] de populo malum praesagium habebatur; hic

[g] alvinum D.   [k] clamare M.
[h] abbatem *over erasure* D1.   [l] cummeaatum D.
[i] venenerabilem > venerabilem Dx.   [m] quod *inserted* CM.
[j] [Trans]mearunt . . . expecta[re] D2.

[5] Alvisus of Arras was successively a monk of St. Bertin, prior of St. Vedast of Arras, abbot of the Benedictine monastery of Anchin, bishop of Arras 1131-47. Cf. GC, III, 324 ff. Various attempts to prove that he was Suger's brother have been unsuccessful. Odo attests to his gifts as diplomat and peacemaker, pp. 29, 45.

[6] Leo, abbot of St. Bertin 1138-63, was a friend of Alvisus and traveled with him in the retinue of the count of Flanders; "as priest and in council he presided over a large part of the count of Flanders' army and, commended for his holy conversation, he gave great pleas-ure to the king, the count, and the princes" is the description of him on crusade given by John of Ypres in the *Chronicon Sithiense S. Bertini*, RHGF, XIII, 471. For further information about his life see GC, III, 498.

[7] June 29, 1147.

[8] Arnulf, erstwhile cleric and archdeacon of Séez, was bishop of Lisieux 1142-82. A stu-dent of canon law, the author of Latin poems of very pure form and worldly content, he shone on the crusade because of his eloquence and indefatigability in diplomacy. In opposition to Godfrey of Langres he headed a pro-Greek and strongly Flemish faction in the army. Cf.

From Metz he sent ahead to Worms the prudent and pious men, Alvisus, bishop of Arras,[5] and Leo, abbot of St. Bertin,[6] to prepare for the army that followed a means of crossing the Rhine, which flowed past there; and they performed their task excellently, assembling from all sides a fleet so great that the army had no need for a bridge.

The people and the clergy of Worms received the king with the greatest festivity on the feast day of the Apostles Peter and Paul.[7] Here we first perceived the foolish arrogance of our people. For the army crossed the Rhine, and, when they had found a broad expanse of meadow, the lord king decided to await the venerable Arnulf, bishop of Lisieux,[8] and his Normans and English. From the city a great abundance of victuals came to us by river, and there was constant commerce between the natives and our people. Finally a quarrel arose; the pilgrims even threw the sailors into the river. Seeing this, the citizens of Worms rushed to arms, wounded several of our men, and killed one on the spot. The pilgrims were thrown into confusion by this crime; the poor clamored for fire, which was deadly both to certain of our men (rich merchants, that is, and money-changers)[9] and to the citizens. By the will of God, however, wise men on both sides restrained the fools on both sides. Yet the citizens were still afraid; and, since they had removed the boats from both sides of the river, they halted the commerce. But that pious man, the bishop of Arras, after finding a boat with some difficulty, crossed the river with certain of the barons, calmed the crowd, and promised the citizens safety. Afterwards, when the boats had been brought back again, they engaged in commerce as before and furnished us with necessities. Hitherto, a foreboding about the people was entertained; here it was realized for the first time. Since everything was expensive

---

below, pp. 70–71, 75–79; *Historia Pontificalis*, MGSS, XX, 534–35; GC, XI, 774; M. Manitius, *Geschichte der lateinischen Literatur des Mittelalters*, III, 59.

[9] Among the large number of noncombatants in the army were evidently merchants and money-changers. Cf. Bernard's "If you are a clever merchant, if you are one who searches for the things of this world, I point out certain great markets to you; see that they do not perish. Take the sign of the cross and if, as the others do, you have made confession with a contrite heart, you will obtain indulgence. The selling price of the material for this emblem is small: if the emblem is worn on the shoulder of a pious man, without any doubt its value is equal to the kingdom of God." *Epistola Bernardi ad clerum et populum orientalis Franciae*, p. 606.

primo expertum est. Exinde multi de turba se per Alpes a nobis separaverunt, quia omnia prae multitudine carius[n] emebantur.

Rex quoque castra movet, praemisso Ratisbonae venerando Atrebatensi cum cancellario et abbate sancti Bertini [19r] causa nuntiorum[o] imperatoris Constantinopolitani, qui ante multos dies regem ibi praestolabantur. Ad hanc urbem omnes Danubium ponte optimo transierunt inveneruntque navium multitudinem copiosam quae sarcinas nostras multumque populum usque Bulgariam deportarunt. Bigas etiam et quadrigas nonnulli navibus imponebant, ut damnum praeteritum[p] in desertis Bulgariae compensarent; sed prius et postea magis fuere spei quam utilitati. Ad cautelam haec omnia dicimus posterorum; nam cum esset quadrigarum maxima multitudo, si offendebat una, mora omnibus erat aequalis. Si vero plures vias inveniebant, omnes pariter aliquando saepiebant, et summarii vitantes earum impedimentum persaepe gravius incurrebant. Ex hoc erat mors frequens equorum et de parvis dietis[q] querelae multorum.

Huius populi civitatis regem valde regaliter susceperunt. Sed quoniam id totiens replicari non potest quotiens illi gentes[r] devotionem sui animi demonstrarunt,[s] dicendum semel est omnes villas, castella et civitates usque Constantinopolim honorem illi regium magis et minus, omnes tamen pro viribus exhibuisse. Sed cum esset omnium par voluntas, "magis et minus" dico, quia non erat omnibus[t] idem posse.

Fixis ergo tentoriis et rege hospitato, imperatoris legatarii vocati veniunt. Quo salutato sacrisque redditis responsionem stantes expectant, non enim sederent nisi iussi; post praeceptum vero, positis subselliis quae secum attulerant, subsederunt. Vidimus ibi quem

[n] carois > carius Dx.	[r] gratis CM.
[o] nuncior > nunciorum D2.	[s] demonstraint D.
[p] pretitum D.	[t] omnium CM.
[q] dictis M.	

---

[10] Wilken, *op. cit.*, III, 100, seems justified in identifying these pilgrims as the armies of the counts of Maurienne and Auvergne and the marquis of Montferrat. Odo mentions that they came via Apulia, p.79, below.

[11] Little is known about Bartholomew the chancellor. Luchaire, *op. cit.*, pp. 54–55, asserts that he was chancellor only from mid-June, 1147, to the end of October, 1149; i.e., while he was with the king on the crusade. In 1149 Louis sent Bartholomew back to France to give Suger full information about the crusade. During the journey east he acted on several important embassies, going ahead of the French army to Constantinople, interceding for the Franks who were attacked by the Patzinaks and Cumans there, and treating with Manuel after the theft from the Greek money-changers. Cf. below, pp. 29, 55, 75.

[12] That is, consumption of food supplies. Cf. Wilken, *op. cit.*, III, 101.

because of the throng of people, many of the rank and file left us here and went through the Alps.[10]

The king broke camp after he had sent the venerable bishop of Arras and the chancellor[11] and the abbot of St. Bertin ahead to Ratisbon to meet the emperor of Constantinople's messengers, who had been awaiting the king there for many days. At this city all crossed the Danube on a very fine bridge and found an ample fleet, which conveyed our baggage and many of the people as far as Bulgaria. Some even placed two- and four-horse carts on shipboard in order to compensate in the wastelands of Bulgaria for the losses which they had already endured,[12] but both previously and afterward the carts afforded more hope than usefulness. We say all these things to caution subsequent pilgrims; for, since there was a very great number of four-horse carts, if one was damaged, all were delayed to the same extent; but, if they found many roads, all thronged them at the same time, and the packhorses, in avoiding the obstruction they presented, very frequently ran into more serious hindrances. For this reason the death of horses was a common occurrence, and so were the complaints about the short distance traveled each day.

The inhabitants of Ratisbon received the king in kingly style. But since I cannot repeat that phrase as often as the people showed him the devotion of their hearts, it should be said once and for all that all the towns, strongholds, and cities all the way to Constantinople showed him kingly honor, to a degree greater or less, yet all to the best of their ability.[13] Now, although all were equally desirous of giving him a fine reception, I say "to a greater or less degree" because they did not all have the same resources.

Then, after camp had been pitched and the king provided with quarters, the emperor's messengers[14] were summoned and came. When they had greeted the king and delivered their letters they stood to await his reply, for they would not sit unless commanded to do so; on command they arranged the chairs that they had brought with them and sat down. We saw there what we afterward

---

[13] Cf. the letter written by Louis to Suger from the borders of Hungary, RHGF, XV, 487: "while the Lord is aiding us at every turn the princes of the lands meet us with rejoicing and receive us with pleasure and gladly take care of our wants and devoutly show us honor."

[14] Demetrius and Maurus (whom Chalandon, *Jean II Comnène*, p. 289, n. 1, identifies as John Ducas). Cf. below, p. 29.

postea didicimus morem Graecorum, sedentibus dominis omnem
pariter astare clientelam. Videas[u] iuvenes fixo gressu, reclino ca-
pite, in propriis dominis erectis aspectibus cum silentio, solo nutu
ipsis parere paratos. Non habent amictus; sed vestibus sericis cur-
tisque et clausis[v] undique divites induuntur strictisque manicis
expediti more pugilum[w] semper incedunt. Pauperes etiam excepto
pretio similiter se coaptant.

Chartas autem plenarie[x] interpretari partim non decet, partim
non possum; nam prima pars earum et maxima tam inepte humiliter
captabat benevolentiam ut verba nimis affectuosa, quia non erant
ex affectu,[y] non solum imperatorem sed etiam mimum,[z] dicerem
dedecere.[a] Et ideo pudor [19v] est tendentem ad alia talibus occu-
pari. Non possum[b] autem quia Franci adulatores, etiam si velint,
non possunt Graecos aequare. Rex vero cuncta, licet cum rubore,
prius exponi tolerabat; sed ex quo fonte procederent nesciebat.
Tandem vero, cum eum in Graecia nuntii frequentarent et semper
ab huiusmodi prooemio incoharent, vix ferebat; religiosus autem
et animosus vir Lingonensis[c] episcopus Godefridus, quadam vice
regi compatiens narrantisque et interpretis moras non ferens, ait,
"Fratres, nolite 'gloriam,' 'maiestatem,' 'sapientiam,' et 'religio-
nem' eius tam frequenter iterare.[d] Se ipse novit, et nos bene novimus eum. Sed quod vultis celerius et liberius intimate." Semper
tamen etiam inter quosdam laicos istud proverbium notum fuit,
"timeo Danaos et dona ferentes."

Pars autem ultima chartarum quae ad rem pertinebat continebat
haec duo: scilicet[e] ut rex imperatori de suo regno nullam civitatem
aut castrum auferret;[f] immo restituerit ei si ab aliquo quod sui
iuris esset Turcos excluderet; et hoc sacramentis nobilium firmare-

[u] Videns CW.	[a] dedecem > dedecere Dx.
[v] cu- > cla- D1.	[b] possunt M.
[w] pugillum > pugilum Dx.	[c] linguonensus > linguonensis D1.
[x] plenariae D.	[d] frequenterare > frequenter iterare D1.
[y] effectu M.	[e] Si licet D.
[z] nunium > mimum Dx.	[f] auferet > auferret Dx; offerret M.

[15] The garments here described correspond to the *scaramangion*, a sort of jacket-tunic with
tight sleeves. Cf. N. P. Kondakov, "Les Costumes orientaux à la cour Byzantine," *Byzantion*,
I (1924), 7–49.
   [16] An idea of the fulsome titles and attributes used by the Greek ambassadors can be gained
from Constantine Porphyrogenitus, *De cerimoniis aulae Byzantinae*, II, 46, ed. by J. J. Reiske,

learned is the Greek custom, namely, that the entire retinue remains standing while the lords are seated. One could see young
men standing immobile, with heads bent and gaze directed in-
tently and silently on their own lords, ready to obey their mere
nod. They do not have cloaks, but the wealthy are clad in silken
garments which are short, tight-sleeved, and sewn up on all sides,
so that they always move about unimpeded, as do athletes.[15] The
poor outfit themselves in garments of like cut, but cheaper sort.

To interpret the documents fully is in part inappropriate, in part
impossible, for me; for the first and greatest portion of them sought
with such inept humility to secure our good will that I should say
the words, too affectionate because they were not sprung from
affection, were such as to disgrace not only an emperor, but even
a buffoon. And therefore it is a shame for one to occupy himself
with such matters when hurrying on to others. It is impossible
for me, moreover, because French flatterers, even if they wish,
cannot equal the Greeks. Now, although he blushed at it, the
king at first allowed everything to be set forth; he did not know,
however, from what source these compliments came. But finally,
when messengers visited him repeatedly in Greece and always began with an introduction of this kind, he could scarcely endure it;
and one time that pious and spirited man, Godfrey, bishop of
Langres, taking pity on the king and not able to endure the delays
caused by the speaker and interpreter, said, "Brothers, do not repeat 'glory,' 'majesty,' 'wisdom,' and 'piety' so often in reference
to the king.[16] He knows himself, and we know him well. Just
indicate your wishes more briefly and freely." Nevertheless, the
proverb "I fear the Greeks, even when they bear gifts"[17] has always
been well-known, even among certain laymen.

The last part of the letters, however, which was to the point,
contained these two provisions: namely, that the king should not
take any city or stronghold in the emperor's realm; that, on the
contrary, if he drove the Turks from any place belonging to the
emperor's domain, he should restore that place to the emperor;
and this agreement was to be confirmed by oath on the part of the

CSHB, VIII, 679 (cf. Reiske's commentary, IX, 798–99), where are listed the titles by which
the emperor should address foreign princes and dignitaries.
[17] Vergil *Aeneid*, ii, 49.

tur. Primum satis competens nostris sapientibus videbatur; pro altero vero diu est quaestio de iure ventilata. Quidam dicebant, "Quod sui iuris est[g] habet[h] vel pretio vel ratione vel viribus a Turcis expetere; a nobis autem cur non debet, si nos hoc viderit occasione aliqua[i] possidere?" Alii vero dicebant illud debere nominari, ne de propositione indefinita lites possent[j] in posterum excitari. Inter haec dies plures pertranseunt, et Graeci moras causantur verentes, ut dicebant, ne imperator cavens sibi comburat pabula, destruat immunita. "Hoc enim facturum se praedixerat si nos," inquiunt, "moraremur, quasi sciens ex hoc quod vos pacifici non venitis. Quod si fecerit, postea nec ipso volente in via plenarie necessaria invenietis." Tandem vero quidam ex parte regis de securitate[k] sui regni iuraverunt, et ipsi forum idoneum, concambium competens, et alia quae nostris utilia visa sunt pro suo imperatore sacramento simili firmaverunt. Aliud autem, quod inter ipsos definiri non potuit, mutuae[l] regum praesentiae reservarunt. Post haec unus eorum Demetrius nomine cum festinatione recedit; alius, qui Maurus dictus est, nobiscum remansit. Eliguntur deinde qui cum eodem [20r] Mauro Constantinopolim praemittantur (hoc enim inter alia littèrae requirebant)—Alvisus Atrebatensis, Bartholomeus cancellarius, Archembaldus Burbonensis et quidam alii. Procedunt igitur expeditius legatione suscepta, subsequente rege morosius, sicut ferre poterat constipatio populosa.

In his quae scribimus pro exemplo est descriptio probitatum, pro directione itineris[m] nomina civitatum, pro cautela viatici qualitas regionum. Nunquam enim deerunt sancti Sepulcri viatores; erunt-

[g] esse M.	[k] seiuritate sui > securitate sui D1.
[h] potest CM.	[l] mutae M.
[i] aliqua occasione CM.	[m] iteneris > itineris Dx.
[j] posset D; possint M.	

---

[18] These provisions had evidently been in Manuel's mind when he wrote to Louis VII and Eugenius III in 1146. See above, p. 10, n. 22. For an account of similar demands on the part of Alexius in 1096 see F. Chalandon, *Histoire de la première croisade* (Paris, 1925), pp. 121 ff.

[19] This statement indicates the trepidation with which Manuel awaited the approach of the crusading armies. From the Greek point of view it has been expressed in highly colored form by Nicetas, in CSHB, XXII, 81–82.

[20] The final negotiation between the two sovereigns is depicted on p. 81, below.

[21] Archibald VII, count of Bourbon from an unknown date until 1171, was allied to the French crown by his marriage to Agnes of Savoy, aunt of Louis VII. For a brief account of his life see *L'Art de vérifier les dates,* Part 2, Vol. X, pp. 327–28.

nobles.[18] The first seemed very reasonable to our council; but in regard to the second the question about the emperor's domain was aired at length. Some said, "From the Turks he must try to acquire his domain either by purchase or negotiation or force; why should he not try to acquire it from us, too, if he should see us gain possession of it somehow?" Yet others said that his domain should be defined, so that a future quarrel could not be excited by the indefinite statement. Meanwhile, several days passed, and the Greeks protested against the delays, fearing, so they said, that the emperor would burn the food and destroy the fortifications by way of precaution. "For he warned us that he would do so if we delayed," they said, "on the ground of knowing from your delay that you were not coming peacefully.[19] If he should do this, you would not thereafter find adequate supplies along your route, even though the emperor himself were willing that you should." At last, however, certain men swore to the security of the Greek realm on behalf of the king, and by a similar oath on behalf of their emperor the Greeks confirmed the promise of a sufficient market, suitable exchange, and other privileges which seemed necessary to us. The second provision, about which they could not come to a decision, they reserved, however, for a time when both sovereigns should be present.[20] After these negotiations one of the Greeks, Demetrius by name, departed hastily; the other, who was called Maurus, stayed with us. Later the men were chosen who were to be sent ahead to Constantinople with this Maurus, whom I have mentioned (for the letters made this request among others)— Alvisus of Arras, Bartholomew the chancellor, Archibald of Bourbon,[21] and certain others.[22] Thus, when they had undertaken the embassy, they advanced swiftly, while the king followed slowly at the pace which the dense crowd would permit.

In this account the description of virtuous deeds furnishes the reader a good example, the names of towns indicate the route of the journey,[23] the nature of the localities depicted suggests the caution which should be observed in provisioning. For never will there fail to be pilgrims to the Holy Sepulcher; and they will, I

---

[22] Among these were Manasses of Bulles, Evrard of Breteuil, Anselm the seneschal of Flanders, Evrard of Barres. See below, p. 55.

[23] For the route followed, see the map on p. 87.

que, si placet, de nostris eventibus cautiores. Igitur—Mettis, Wormatia, Wirceburgis, Ratisbona, Batavia, civitates opulentissimae,[n] tribus diebus[o] a se invicem distant. A postremo nominata quinque dietae sunt usque ad Novam-urbem; ab hac, una usque ad portas Hungariae. Quae interiacent nemorosa sunt et, nisi deferantur de civitatibus, non sufficiunt exercitui victualia ministrare. Rivis tamen abundant et fontibus et pratis. Cum transirem regionem istam aspera mihi montibus videbatur; nunc autem planam iudico respectu Romaniae. Hungaria ex hac parte aqua lutosa cingitur; ex alia[p] vero a Bulgaria amne lucido separatur. In medio sui fluvium habet Droam, qui scamni[q] more, unam ripam proclivem habet et alteram arduam. Unde[r] modica pluvia effluit, et adiutus vicinis paludibus etiam aliquanto remota submergit. Audivimus eum multos Alemannorum qui nos praecesserant subito inundasse; nos autem ubi castra eorum fuerant vix potuimus transvadare.[s] In hoc parvas naves habuimus et[t] paucas, et ideo fuit opus equos natare. Qui facilem ingressum et egressum difficilem habentes, cum labore quidem, sed tamen, Deo volente, sine damno transibant. Cetera omnis aqua terrae huius lacus sunt et[u] paludes et fontes (si tamen fontes sunt quos paululum fossa humo, etiam[v] in aestate, faciunt transeuntes), excepto Danubio, qui hanc satis in directum praeterfluit et multarum regionum divitias nobili civitati Estrigim navigio convehit.[w] Terra haec in tantum pabulosa est ut dicantur in ea pabula Iulii Caesaris extitisse. In hac pro voto nobis fuerunt et forum et concambium.

Haec dietas quindecim habet. Deinde Bulgaria in ingressu castrum attollit quod Belgrada [20v] dicitur Bulgarensis, respectu cuiusdam quae in Hungaria est eiusdem nominis civitatis; inde ad unam dietam, interposito quodam fluvio, Brundusium civitatem

[n] opulintissime > opulentissime D1.	[s] transvadere CM.
[o] dietis CM.	[t] *om.* CM.
[p] olia > alia D1.	[u] *om.* M.
[q] stanni DCMW.	[v] etiam *over erasure* D1.
[r] Un- *over erasure* D1.	[w] invehit CM.

[24] Odo's purpose in writing is discussed on pp. xvi ff.

[25] Kugler, *Studien*, p. 135, has pointed out that Odo's account of the number of days marched is too small even for a modern army and is, therefore, very much too small for Louis' army, which was impeded in various ways. He thinks that Odo computed the distance as for an army going at top speed in order to reach a destination; i.e., the crusading army of the future, to which he looked forward eagerly.

[26] Because of the nature of the rest of the route followed by the army, it seems probable that Odo's "Nova Urbs" stands for Klosterneuburg rather than for Neustadt. The only

hope, be the more cautious because of our experiences.[24] Well then—Metz, Worms, Würzburg, Ratisbon, and Passau, very wealthy towns, are each separated from the other by a three-day journey.[25] From the last-named it is a five-day journey to Klosterneuburg;[26] from there, one day's journey to the Hungarian border. The regions which lie between the towns are wooded, and if provisions should not be brought from the cities they cannot furnish an army with supplies. Nevertheless, they contain a wealth of streams, springs, and meadows. When I was crossing that territory I thought it rugged with mountains, but now, in comparison with Romania, I consider it level. On this side Hungary is bounded by muddy water; but on the other it is separated from Bulgaria by a clear stream. In its center flows the river Drave, of which one bank is sloping and the other steep, like a balk, with the result that the river overflows if a light rain falls and, when augmented by neighboring swamps, floods places which are even considerably distant. We heard that it had suddenly deluged many of the Germans who had preceded us, and we could hardly ford the place where their camp had been. For this crossing we had few ships and small, and so the horses had to swim. Since they entered the stream at an easy place and left it at a difficult one, they crossed with hardship indeed, but, by the aid of God, without loss. All the rest of the water in this land takes the form of lakes, swamps, and springs (if those are springs which travelers create, even in summer, by lightly digging the surface of the ground), with the exception of the Danube, which flows by in a fairly straight course and ships the wealth of many districts to the noted town of Gran. This land produces so much food that Julius Caesar's commissaries are said to have been located in it.[27] Here we had such marketing privileges as we wished.

We took fifteen days to cross Hungary. Then, at the border, Bulgaria presented a fortified town called the Bulgarian Belgrad, to distinguish it from a Hungarian town of the same name, and thereafter, one day away and across a certain river, a poor little town, Brandiz. The rest of the country is wooded meadow or

Neustadt which lies near the route is Wiener Neustadt, which was not founded until 1192. Cf. "Wiener-Neustadt," *Brockhaus Konversationslexikon* (15th ed.), Vol. XX.

[27] Cf. Otto of Freising's description of Hungary (*Gesta*, I, xxxii, 49 [31]).

pauperculam. Quod de illa superest, ut ita dixerim, pratum est nemorosum vel nemus[x] pabulosum. Bonis abundat quae sponte nascuntur, et ceteris est habilis si colonos haberet.[y] Non plana iacet, nec montibus asperatur; sed inter colles vineis et segetibus habiles rivis et fontibus lucidissimis irrigatur. Caret fluviis; sed nec[z] usque Constantinopolim exinde nobis navibus opus fuit. Haec ad quintam dietam, primam (sed modicam) ex hac[a] parte Graeciae civitatem Nit ostendit. Nit, Hesternit, Philippopolis, Adrianopolis, civitates quattuor[b] dietis[c] ab invicem dissidentes; et ab ultima usque Constantinopolim sunt quinque. Quae interiacent plana sunt villis et castellis omnibusque bonis redundantia. Dextra laevaque montes sunt, tam prope ut videantur et tam longe ut lata, dives et iocunda planities includatur.

Hactenus haec. Oportet autem nos ultro citroque progredi et reverti; multa enim scribenda se offerunt, sed non debet oratio rerum multiplicitate[d] confundi. Collateraliter incedunt causae, sed oportet servari consequentiam in sermone. Ecce enim rex et imperator occurrerunt mihi memoriae pariter Ratisbonae; sed, cum rex mihi sit principalis materia, me cogunt tamen de imperatore pauca inserere facta eorum communia. Nostrum[e] regem praecessit Alemannus loco temporeque:[f] noster processit in Pentecosten,[g] ille in Pascha; noster de beato Dionysio movit pedem, ille de Ratisbona. Hoc tamen nostro contulit quod ille praecessit, quia, cum in terra eius multi fluvii sint, super ipsos sine proprio labore et sumptu novos pontes invenit. Ut autem verum fatear, valde imperialiter egressus est, et navali apparatu et pedestri exercitu; et bene, habebat enim tunc Hungaros inimicos. Igitur imperator animosus na-

[x] nemo > nemus D1.	[c] dictis M; diebus W.
[y] habet M.	[d] multiplicate > multiplicitate D1.
[z] *om.* M.	[e] Vestrum > Nostrum Dx.
[a] hoc M.	[f] locoque tempore D; loco et tempore CM.
[b] sunt *inserted* CM.	[g] petecosten D.

[28] Presumably because supplies were abundant without the aid of supply ships.

[29] For Odo's technique of writing history see above, pp. xxiv ff.

[30] Conrad celebrated Easter in Bamberg, held court in Nuremberg, then proceeded to Ratisbon, where he stayed until the latter part of May. He then pitched camp on May 29 at Ardacker. See Otto of Freising, *Gesta*, I, xlvi, 64 (44).

[31] The relations between Germany and Hungary had been hostile indeed. Through the intercession of the duke of Bohemia, Boris, the pretender to the throne of Hungary, had obtained aid from Conrad against King Geisa (Otto of Freising, *Chronicon*, VII, 34). Thus in 1146 certain knights from the East March invaded Hungary and captured the stronghold of Bosau, which the king of Hungary purchased back. Enraged by this incident, Geisa

fodder-growing woodland, so to speak. It abounds in good things
which grow of their own accord and would be suitable for other
things if the region had cultivators. It is neither as flat-lying as a
plain nor rugged with mountains, but is located among hills which
are suitable for vines and grains, and it is watered by the very
clearest springs and streams. It lacks rivers; for that matter, all
the way from there to Constantinople we had no need of boats.[28]
On the fifth day's march the land reveals Nissa, the first (though
small) city in this part of Greece. The cities Nissa, Sofia, Philippopolis, and Adrianople are a four-day journey one from another,
and from Adrianople it is a five-day journey to Constantinople.
The plains between the towns are full of villages, fortresses, and
all kinds of resources. On the left and the right there are mountains, so near that you can see them and so far that a wide, rich,
and pleasant plain is enclosed by them.

So much for these things! It is necessary to go back and forth—
to progress and to turn back in my story—for although many
things present themselves for description, the account should not
be confused by the wealth of subjects. Many events happen at the
same time, but in discourse one must observe a sequence.[29] For instance, the king and the emperor both came to mind when I was
writing about Ratisbon; for, although the king is my main subject, their mutual experiences force me to include a few words
about the emperor. The German sovereign preceded ours in time
and place: our king set out at Whitsuntide, the German king in
the Easter season; our king departed from St. Denis, the German
king from Ratisbon.[30] The fact that the German king went first
gave our king the advantage that, although there are many rivers
in Germany, he found new bridges constructed over them without
any expense or exertion on his part. Now, to tell the truth, the
emperor set out in a most imperial fashion in respect to both fleet
and land forces; this was advisable, for at that time the Hungarians
were his enemies.[31] Thus, the spirited emperor, who was both

collected a large army, marched against the duke in September, and defeated him. Otto of
Freising, who tells this in the *Gesta*, I, xxxi, 48 (30) and xxxiii, 51 (32), adds that the defeat
had not yet been avenged by the Germans when he wrote.

Jaffé, *op. cit.*, p. 124, n. 7, illustrated the hostile fashion in which Conrad entered Hungary
by quoting Thwrocz: "He appeared as a pilgrim belonging to Hungary but not to Christ,
and there he did not exercise peace, but the wrath of a tyrant and robber instead."

valis et pedes, habens in navibus copiosum militem secum et iuxta se per terram equos et populum, sicut[h] oportuit et decuit principem ingressus est[i] Hungariam.[j]

Erat autem quidam Boricius nomine qui ius hereditarium[k] in regno illo clamabat et super [21r] hoc Stampas regi nostro litteras miserat, plenarie querimoniam exponentes et humiliter iustitiam postulantes. Hic, dum regi nostro veniret obviam litteras suas sequens, offendit[l] in quo confidere posset imperatorem. Causam igitur suam illi[m] exponit, multa promisit (immo, sicut audivimus, dedit) et ab eo spem sui iuris accepit. Rex autem Hungaricus, sciens se[n] posse vincere facilius auro quam ferro, multam pecuniam inter Alemannos effudit et eorum impetum[o] evasit. Boricius autem, spe frustratus inani, delitescens arte qua potuit, regis transitum expectavit et nescio qua intentione furtive[p] se Francis immiscuit. Dicitur[q] tamen hoc duos principes scisse et, gratia imperatoris Constantinopolitani, neptem cuius habebat, hunc illis[r] satis favorabiliter adhaesisse. Tali velamine tectus et tutus procedit cum exercitu per Hungariam.

Inter haec[s] rex Hungaricus, nostrum timens et venerans, legatis et muneribus eius gratiam conquirebat, sed interposito Danubio praesentiam devitabat. Optabat autem eius colloquium quem fama sibi commendaverat, res monstrabat, sed, cum navigare in nostram ripam timeret, humiliter supplicat regi ut ad suam ripam sua dignatione veniret. Rex igitur, cui mos erat dilectione et humilitate facile superari, ductis secum quibusdam episcopis et ducibus, eius paruit[t] voluntati. Deinde post oscula, post amplexus, statuunt pacem, firmant amorem et ut securi deinceps per Hungariam nostri peregrini transirent. Quo facto rex noster Hungarum laetum dimisit. Prosequuntur eum regia munera equorum, vasorum, et vestium,

[h] et *inserted* M.
[i] et C.
[j] bungariam > hungariam Dx.
[k] bereditarium > hereditarium Dx.
[l] ostendit DM > offendit D1CW.
[m] illi suam W.
[n] non D; *correctly deleted* CBMW.

[o] impetu > impetum Dx.
[p] furtivus W.
[q] discitur M.
[r] illic M.
[s] velamine . . . haec D2.
[t] ducibus eius pa- D2.

---

[32] Boris, who has been mentioned in the preceding note, was the son of King Coloman of Hungary and Euphemia of Kiev. See Otto of Freising, *Chronicon*, VII, 21. Encouraged by John Comnenus to combat his elder brother in order to seize the throne, he continued his plots against Bela II and Geisa II and was evidently killed in a Greek expedition against Hungary in 1155. See Chalandon, *Jean II Comnène*, pp. 54–63, 406–7, 413–14.

[33] Jaffé, *op. cit.*, p. 125, n. 8, supplements this statement by a quotation from Thwrocz:

sailor and foot soldier (seeing that he had a very large army in the fleet with him and the horses and the rank and file beside him on the shore), entered Hungary as behooved and became a prince.

There was, moreover, a certain man named Boris[32] who proclaimed a hereditary right to Hungary and who had sent letters to this effect to our king at Étampes, setting forth his complaint in full and humbly suing for justice. When coming to our king, following in the wake of his letters, he met the emperor, in whom he could trust. Therefore he set forth the case to him, promised him many things (indeed, as we have heard, gave him many things), and in turn received hope of gaining his right. But the king of Hungary, knowing that he could conquer more easily by gold than by force, poured out much money among the Germans and thus escaped an attack from them.[33] Now Boris, who had been deluded by vain hope, hiding away as best he could, awaited the passage of our king and, with some strategem or other in mind, stealthily joined the Franks. It is said that two princes[34] knew this, nevertheless, and that, because of the emperor of Constantinople whose niece he had married, Boris had joined the Franks with sufficient approbation on the part of those two. Protected and concealed by such shielding, he went through Hungary with the army.

Meanwhile the king of Hungary, fearing and revering our king, sought his favor by sending messengers and gifts, but he avoided crossing the Danube to meet him. He hoped for a conference with the man whom reputation had recommended to him (as the event showed), but, since he was afraid to cross to our side of the river, he humbly entreated the king to deign to come to his side. And so the king, whose wont it was to be won over easily by charity and humility, took along certain of his bishops and lords and gratified his wish. Then, after kisses, after embraces, they established a peace, strengthened their amity, and provided that from that time forth our pilgrims might pass through Hungary in safety. When he had accomplished this our king left the king of Hungary a happy man. Kingly gifts of horses, vases, and garments accom-

"from the kingdom of Hungary he wrung a sum of money that was by no means small, with the result that there was no church nor monastery in all Hungary from which money was not extorted and given to the crusading emperor out of fear."

[34] It is difficult to identify these two princes. Kugler suggests, however (*Studien*, p. 137, n. 74), that they were Conrad and Louis.

et parat adhuc rex Hungarus nostrum et eius optimates pro posse venerari, cum ecce intelligit inter Francos esse Boricium. Mittit ergo qui regi foedus novum dilectionis et pacis praetenderent et inimicum suum qui latebat in exercitu sibi tradi prece humili postularent. Hoc totum factum est nocte. Rex autem, totius duplicitatis ignarus, id penitus non credebat; sed tandem illis constanter hoc asserentibus et precantibus acquievit. Illi ergo laeti audacter amplius quam prudenter incedunt; nam ille, tumultu quaerentium a lecto excitus, nudus evasit; unde illi confusi redierunt [21v]. Fugitivus autem non tamen stupidus. Dum tendens ad fluvium tentoria exisset obvium[u] habuit armigerum super optimum equum cum quo pro equo animose confligit. Clamat armiger et resistit; et superat magis[v] clamore quam viribus; confluunt enim undique qui Boricium sicut latronem capiunt et verberatum, luto sordidum, nudum exceptis[w] femoralibus, regi adducunt. Omnes eum latronem putabant. Ipse vero regi prostratus, licet ignoraret linguam nostram et rex tunc interpretem non haberet, quaedam tamen verba nota barbaris vocibus inserens et suum nomen saepius iterans, quis esset aperuit. Mox igitur honeste induitur et in crastinum reservatur.

Hungarus autem rex, qui prope nos tentoria fixerat et Boricium iam expertus metuebat, loco vicinus et timore curiosus, ilico scivit quod gestum est. Hunc ergo a rege sicut ab amico et pro foedere amoris quasi ex debito requirit, et insuper ob hoc multa immo vix credenda promittit. Similiter prece et pretio sollicitat animos procerum; sed non valet extorquere a rege instantia precum aut munerum[x] nisi quod prius iudicasset communis sapientia sapientum.[y] Suum hunc fatebatur amicum, non tamen propter eum sibi facien-

---

[u] so D, *not* obviuum *as noted* W.   [x] numerum D.
[v] magis superat CM.   [y] sententia sapientum CM; sententia sapientium W.
[w] exe- > exc- D1.

panied him, and the king of Hungary further intended to reverence our king and his nobles insofar as he could, when, alas, he found out that Boris was with the Franks. He therefore sent men to propose a new treaty of friendship and peace with the king and to demand with humble supplication that his enemy, who was hiding in the army, be delivered to him. All this happened at night. However, the king, unacquainted with the extent of the duplicity, did not wholly believe the story; but at last he gave way to the messengers who were continually asserting it and beseeching his co-operation. Happy on this account, they proceeded more boldly than wisely; for Boris, roused from his bed by the noise made by those seeking him, escaped naked; and so they went away, their effort to no avail. Now, the fugitive was by no means stupid. When he had left the shelter of the tents, on the way to the river he encountered an esquire mounted on an excellent horse and struggled stoutly with him for the horse. The esquire cried out and resisted, and he prevailed more by his outcry than by his strength, for people appeared from every direction, and they seized Boris as if he were a robber and took him to the king, beaten, soiled with mud, and naked except for his breeches. Everyone thought he was a robber. But after he had thrown himself at the king's feet, even though he did not know our language and the king did not then have an interpreter, he, nevertheless, by mixing with his own language certain words we knew and by repeating his own name often, made known his identity. Presently, therefore, he was clad properly, and his case was reserved for the next day.

Now the Hungarian king, who had pitched his tents near us and who, as a result of his previous acquaintance with Boris, feared him, immediately found out what had happened, for he was close by and curious because of anxiety. He therefore demanded Boris from the king as from a friend and as if his surrender were obligatory according to their pact of amity; and in return he also made many promises which were hardly credible. Likewise, he stirred the minds of the nobles by his presence and presents; but neither the urgency of his supplications nor his gifts could obtain this request from the king before the council had rendered judgment. Our king said that the king of Hungary was his friend, but, nevertheless, that he must not do on behalf of the king anything

dum esse quod dedeceret peregrinum. Episcopi tandem et optimates alii convocati, discussa ratione, iudicaverunt ut rex regi pacem
servaret et viro nobili licet capto vitam servaret, quia scelus esset
utrumque et morti hominem vendere et amici sine ratione foedus[z]
rumpere. Ergo rex Hungarus, se nostris non credens sed tristis
abscedens, tutiora et remotiora sui regni requirit. Noster autem
Boricium[a] satis honeste secum habens de Hungaria educit.

Explicit Secundus

[z] foedera CM.   [a] boririum > boricium D1.

which ill became a pilgrim. Then, when the bishops and the other magnates had been assembled and the matter had been examined, they decided that their king should preserve peace with the Hungarian king and that he should protect the life of the nobleman, even though he was a captive, because it would be a crime either to sell a man to death or, without cause, to break a treaty with a friend. Therefore the king of Hungary, not trusting himself to us, but departing with some distress, sought safety in a more remote part of his realm. Our king, however, keeping Boris with him, with due honor took him out of Hungary.

End of Book Two

Incipit Tertius

Hucusque lusimus, quia nec damna pertulimus ex malitia hominum nec pericula timuimus de astutia subdolorum. Ex quo autem intravimus Bulgariam terram Graecorum, et virtus laborem pertulit et sensus exercitium. Ingressuri desertum in Brundusio paupere civitate victualibus onustamur[a] quae maxime Hungaria per Danubium ministravit. Erat ibi tanta navium multitudo quas Alemanni adduxerant ut domibus aedificandis et igni civibus in longum [22r] sufficerent. Harum minores nostri accipiebant, et, transducto amne, de quodam castro Hungariae non longe posito necessaria convehebant. Hic primo cupream[b] monetam staminas[c] offendimus, et pro una earum quinque denarios et pro duodecim solidis marcam tristes dabamus vel potius perdebamus. Ecce in introitu suae terrae Graeci periurio maculantur; debetis enim iam[d] dicta reminisci, illos scilicet pro suo imperatore forum idoneum et concambium nostris iurasse. Ceterum deserta transivimus terramque pulcherrimam et opulentissimam quae sine interruptione protenditur usque Constantinopolim intravimus. Hic primo coeperunt iniuriae fieri et inveniri; nam ceterae regiones, quae nobis necessaria competenter vendiderunt, nos omnino pacificos invenerunt. Graeci autem suas civitates et castella obserabant[e] et per murum funibus venalia submittebant. Sed nostrae multitudini non sufficiebat victus tali modo[f] ministratus. Peregrini ergo, in rerum abundantia penuriam non ferentes, praedis et rapinis sibi necessaria conquirebant.

Visum tamen est aliquibus hoc Alemannorum nos praecedentium culpa fuisse qui cum omnia praedarentur. Invenimus eos insuper

---

[a] honestamur W.
[b] c *over erasure of* o D1.
[c] estammas DW; et stammas CM; staminas Du Cange, *Glossarium.*

[d] enim iam D2.
[e] observabant CM.
[f] mora CM.

[1] Evidently a popular term among the Greeks for coins, the word means "stamped metal" pieces, which can be compared as a term with our "coppers" and "greenbacks." It is probable that it is part of the debased coinage issued by Manuel, who struck no gold coins during his reign, owing to the financial difficulties of the Empire. See F. Chalandon, "The Earlier Comneni," CMH, IV, xi, 348.

[2] See below, p. 67, for further information about the rate of exchange.

[3] Manuel had sent out proclamations saying that food supplies should be offered for sale along the routes by which the Westerners would cross the country. Nicetas, op. cit., pp. 80-83.

Beginning of Book Three

Thus far we were engaged in play, because we neither suffered injuries from men's ill will nor feared dangers arising from the cunning of crafty men. However, from the time when we entered Bulgaria, a land belonging to the Greeks, our valor was put to the test and our emotions were aroused. When about to enter the un-inhabited portion, we stocked ourselves in the poor town of Brandiz with provisions, the most of which Hungary supplied via the Danube. There the fleet which the Germans had brought and abandoned was so huge that for a long time it furnished the citizens with building material and firewood. Our men took the smaller types of these boats and, after crossing the stream, brought supplies from a certain Hungarian castle which was not far away. Here we first encountered the copper money "staminae,"[1] and for one of these we unhappily gave five denarii, or rather we lost a mark on twelve solidi.[2] Thus, at the entrance to their own land the Greeks stained themselves with perjury, for you should remember what has already been said, namely, that the messengers had sworn on behalf of their emperor to furnish us a suitable market and ex-change.[3] But we crossed the wasteland and entered the exeedingly beautiful and rich territory which stretches without interruption all the way to Constantinople. Here for the first time wrongs began to arise and to be noticed; for the other countries, which sold us supplies properly, found us entirely peaceful. The Greeks, how-ever, closed their cities and fortresses and offered their wares by letting them down from the walls on ropes.[4] But food furnished in such measure did not suffice our throng. Therefore, the pilgrims, unwilling to endure want in the midst of plenty, procured supplies for themselves by plunder and pillage.[5]

Some thought, however, that this state of affairs was the fault of the Germans who preceded us, since they had been plundering

[4] *Ibid.*, pp. 83–89, for another account of the Greeks who let down supplies on ropes.
[5] Disorderly conduct on the part of the French in Greek territory is shown by this passage and pp. 45, 57, 67, 97, below.

aliqua suburbia combussisse; nam quod aegre referendum est: Philippopolis extra muros nobilem burgum Latinorum habebat, qui
supervenientibus necessaria abundanter pretio[g] ministrabat. Ubi
cum tabernis insedissent Alemanni[h] malo auspicio adfuit ioculator
qui, licet eorum linguam ignoraret, tamen sedit, symbolum[i] dedit,
bibit; et post longam ingurgitationem serpentem quem praecanta-
tum[j] in sinu habebat extrahit et scypho[k] terrae imposito super-
ponit, et sic inter eos quorum mores et linguam nesciebat ceteris
lusibus ioculatoriis sese frangit. Alemanni, quasi viso prodigio,[l]
ilico cum furore consurgunt, mimum[m] rapiunt, et in frusta[n] discer-
punt; scelusque unius omnibus imputant, dicentes quod eos occidere
Graeci veneno volebant. Turbatur urbs tumultu suburbii, et dux
cum turba suorum ut sedaret turbam foras[o] inermis sed festinus
egreditur. Turbatus autem a[p] vino et furore, oculus Alemannorum
non arma videt, sed cursum undique[q] causa pacis. Accurrentibus
[22v] occurrunt irati, putantes a se homicidii vindictam exigi. Illi
autem fugientes in urbem recepti sunt. Tunc sumptis arcubus (haec
enim sunt arma eorum), denuo exeunt; fugant quos fugerant, occidunt, vulnerant; expulsisque omnibus de suburbio cessant. Ibi
multi Alemannorum occisi sunt, et maxime in hospitiis et pro pe-
cuniis suis in speluncis proiecti. Resumptis ergo animis et armis,
ut vindicarent suam verecundiam et aliorum necem, redierunt et
extra muros fere omnia combusserunt.

Nostris etiam erant importabiles Alemanni. Nam quadam vice
quidam nostrorum, regiae multitudinis oppressionem vitantes et
ideo praeeuntes, iuxta illos hospitati sunt. Itur ad forum ab utris-
que; sed Alemanni non patiebantur ut Franci aliquid emerent nisi

[g] abundanter pretio necessaria CM.
[h] om. W.
[i] symboium > symbolum D1.
[j] precantarum DW > precantatum D1.
[k] cito > cifo D1.
[l] prodigo D.

[m] numum > mimum Dx.
[n] frustra M.
[o] forus > foras D1.
[p] om. W.
[q] unde CM.

[6] Cinnamus, *Epitome rerum . . . gestarum*, (ed. by A. Meineke, CSHB, XXV), II, 13, states
that as long as the Germans were in the rugged section between the Ister River and Sofia
they were peaceful, but that when they came to the plains they began to plunder.

[7] That is, by the snake venom.

[8] Nicetas, *op. cit.*, pp. 80–89, reports that good relations obtained between Conrad and
Michael the Italian, the bishop of Philippopolis, although Conrad was likely to mistreat
the people who brought supplies to the camp whenever he did not have ready money. The
struggle which Odo describes appears to have arisen between the Greeks and the last part of
the German army after Conrad had left. When he returned to help settle matters, he was
placated by the bishop.

everything.[6] We found also that they had burned certain settle-
ments outside cities; for the following incident must unfortunately
be related. Outside the walls of Philippopolis was located a fine
settlement of Latins who sold a great many supplies to travelers.
When the Germans had got settled in the tavern, by ill chance a
juggler came in and, although ignorant of their language, nevertheless sat down, gave his money, and got a drink. After a prolonged guzzling he took a snake, which he had charmed and kept
in his inside pocket, and placed it on top of a goblet which he had
put on the floor, and thus, among people whose language and customs he did not know, he indulged in other jugglers' pranks. As
if they had seen an evil portent the Germans immediately rose up,
seized the juggler, and tore him to bits; and they attributed the
crime of one man to all, saying that the Greeks wished to poison
them.[7] The city was disturbed by the uproar in the outskirts, and
with a group of his men the governor came outside the walls, un-
armed, but in haste, to calm the crowd. Agitated by wine and
rage, however, the eyes of the Germans saw, not the situation in
regard to arms, but the fact that to keep the peace people were
rushing together from all sides. Angrily they rushed at those who
were approaching, thinking that they came to wreak vengeance
for the murder. In flight the Greeks now retreated to the city.
Then, taking up their bows (for these are their weapons), they
went forth again; they killed, wounded, and routed those whom
they had fled, and only when all had been driven from the settlement did they stop. Many of the Germans were killed there, especially those who had taken refuge in inns and, in order to protect
their money, in caves. When the survivors had recovered their
spirits and taken up arms again, they rallied in order to avenge
their own shame and the slaughter of their comrades, and they
burned nearly everything outside the walls.[8]

The Germans were unbearable even to us. One time, for instance,
some of our men who wished to escape the press of the crowd
around the king, and therefore went ahead, lodged near them.[9]
Both groups went to market; but the Germans did not allow the

[9] Bernhardi's location of this incident at Constantinople seems doubtful. See Bernhardi,
op. cit., pp. 620–21. The description appears rather to fit an unidentified place somewhere
between Philippopolis and Constantinople.

postquam ipsi exinde satis habuissent. Inde rixa, immo garritus, oboritur; ubi enim alter, alterum non intelligens, cum[r] clamosa voce impetit, garritus est. Franci ergo, percutientes et repercussi, de foro cum victualibus redierunt; Alemanni,[s] quia multi erant,[t] paucorum Francorum superbiam dedignantes, contra illos arma sumunt, furiose invadunt; illique similiter armati[u] animose resistunt. Sed Deus illud nefas nocte cito superveniente finivit. Nocte illa ignis eorum nec extingui potuit nec consopiri, quia mane debacchantes acrius surrexerunt; sed sapientes eorum, stultorum genibus provoluti, humilitate et ratione insaniam sedaverunt.

Sic Alemanni praecedentes omnia perturbant, et ideo Graeci subsequentem nostrum pacificum fugiebant. Conventus tamen ecclesiarum et clerus omnis, de civitatibus exeuntes cum iconiis[v] suis et alio Graeco apparatu, illum semper cum timore et honore debito suscipiebant. Dux quoque Hesternensis, cognatus imperatoris, in via regi semper adhaerens et pacem indigenis et ex parte forum fecit exhiberi peregrinis. Qui regi de victualibus satis honorifice serviebat;[w] sed ipse inde sibi parum vel nihil retinens, modo totum divitibus, modo pauperibus dividebat. Ideoque cum illo pax districtius servabatur, quia ibi minus necessitatis et amplius erat timoris; multae vero illum praecedebant acies et sequebantur, [23r] vel de foro si poterant, vel de praedis quia hoc poterant sibi abundantiam conquirentes.

Tandem venitur Philippopolis, ubi Alvisus venerandus Atrebatensis episcopus, dum legatione Constantinopolim fungeretur, octavo idus Septembris in sancta confessione obierat. Hic post longam aegritudinem dum inter festum sancti Bertini, cuius monachus fuerat, et nativitatem beatae Mariae acrius[x] urgeretur, obortis lacrimis (quarum gratiam semper habuerat), monachis suis et clericis convocatis dixit, "Carissimi, festum sancti Bertini honore debito celebretis.[y] Sed quia sollemnitati beatae Mariae vobiscum

[r] om. W.	[v] ieconiis D; icconiis W.
[s] autem *inserted* CM.	[w] serb- > serv[iebat] D1.
[t] erant *over erasure* D1.	[x] ar- > ac- D1.
[u] amati > armati Dx.	[y] celebratis M.

[10] Chalandon, *Jean II Comnène*, p. 294, identifies him as Michael Branas.
[11] September 6, 1147.
[12] September 5.
[13] See above, p. 22, n. 5.
[14] September 8.

Franks to buy anything until after they themselves had had all they wanted. From this situation arose a dispute, or rather a brawl; for, when one person accuses another in a very loud voice without understanding him, there is a brawl. Thereupon the Franks, after this exchange of blows, returned from market with their supplies; that is, the Germans, scorning the pride of the few Franks, because they themselves were many, took arms against them and fell upon them furiously, and the Franks, likewise armed, resisted spiritedly. But God put an end to the wicked encounter, for night fell rapidly. Their anger could neither be quenched nor lulled by that night, for in the morning they arose, raging more bitterly; but wise men among them, falling at the knees of the fools, calmed this rage by humility and reason.

Thus, the Germans disturbed everything as they proceeded, and the Greeks therefore fled our peaceful king, who followed after. Nonetheless, the congregations of the churches and the entire clergy always received him with due reverence and honor, issuing forth from their cities with icons and other Greek paraphernalia. Also, the duke of Sofia,[10] a kinsman of the emperor's who always kept close to the king during the journey, both established peace for the inhabitants and saw to procuring part of the market for the pilgrims. He served the king honorably in regard to provisions, but Louis, keeping little or nothing of this for himself, divided the entire amount, some with the poor, and some with the rich. And so peace was maintained more strictly with Louis, because he was less needy and commanded more respect than the others. But there preceded and followed him many divisions who gained plenty for themselves, either from the market, whenever that was possible, or from plunder, because they had the power to do that.

At last they came to Philippopolis, where, while on a mission to Constantinople, Alvisus, the venerable bishop of Arras, had died in holy confession on the eighth day before the Ides of September.[11] Here, between the feast of St. Bertin,[12] whose monk he was,[13] and the Nativity of the Blessed Virgin,[14] while in great discomfort after a long illness and with tears in his eyes (weeping had always furnished him solace), he said to his assembled monks and clerks, "Dearly beloved, celebrate the feast of St. Bertin with due honor. But because I shall not be with you on the festival of the Blessed

non interero, impendite mihi gratiam quam potestis, ut, praeoccu-
pantes eam, sumptis libris omne mihi servitium sollemniter de-
cantetis.'' Illi autem flebiliter obsequentes diei et noctis omne
servitium morosius decantarunt. At ille, quotienscumque illud
ave[z] singulare vel nomen Virginis audiebat, in ipso mortis articulo,
nisu[a] debili sed devoto surgebat. Post haec reddidit Virgini animam cuius ipse[b] tam devote iam tenebat memoriam. Corpus autem
eius extra urbem in ecclesia sancti Georgii ante altare venerandam
habuit sepulturam. Ad cuius tumulum rex postmodum veniens
illum obiisse doluit et cum suis episcopis et abbatibus ei lugubres
exsequias iteravit. Sciendum[c] est quod nos pro certo vidimus febri-
citantes prius subtus feretrum, deinde supra tumulum, obdormire,
postmodum de sua sanitate Deo et defuncto episcopo gratias agere.

His autem paululum intermissis, libet Alemannos Constantinopolim duci, immo etiam et transduci; debet enim res ordine quo
gesta est recitari. Incedunt igitur satis audacter sed minus sapienter, quia dum in terra illa ubique inveniunt opulentiam, et in ea
non habent temperantiam. Pedites eorum remanentes ebrii neca-
bantur, et inhumatis eorum cadaveribus omnia foedabantur, unde
Francis sequentibus minus nocebant armati Graeci quam occisi
Alemanni. Qui[d] venientes Adrianopolim invenerunt transitum
Constantinopolim partim resistendo, partim consulendo, prohibentes et apud sanctum Georgium [23v] de Sesto mare strictius et
solum fertilius asserentes; sed imperator eorum resistentes et con-
sulentes aequa lance vilipendit. Tendens ergo quo coeperat, in
medio fere itinere pratum invenit fluviolo quodam vel torrente irri-

---

[z] ave *over erasure of word beginning with g, possibly* glorie, D1.   [c] quoque *inserted* CM.
[a] nisi > nisu D1; nitu M.   [d] Illi vero CM.
[b] ipsa > ipse D2; ipsa M.

---

[15] The *Historia Monasterii Aquicincti*, MGSS, XIV, 588, gives Alvisus' epitaph.

[16] Cinnamus, *op. cit.*, II, 13–14, tells that Manuel heard of the disorder among the German pilgrims and sent his general, Prosuch, at the head of a force which had been assembled
quickly in order to follow the crusaders, observe their actions, and keep them from stray-
ing from the road on which they were travelling. This band of Greeks found that the
Germans were going slowly and wandering along the road without any formal order. The
death of the foot-soldiers mentioned by Odo may have been due to reprisals on the part of
the Greeks whom the crusaders plundered or to the activity of Prosuch's men.

[17] Kugler, *Studien*, p. 121, believes that the men who blocked the way to Constantinople
were Prosuch's army. Cinnamus, *op. cit.*, II, 14, says that Manuel sent Andronicus Opus to
adjust affairs with the Germans and to suggest the more direct route.

Virgin, grant me a favor which lies in your power; namely, anticipating the festival, take up your books and sing the entire service
to me as you would on the festival." Amid tears they gratified his
wish and slowly sang the entire service of the day and the night.
Now as often as he heard the one word "ave" or the name of the
Virgin, even in the very moment of death, he rose with a feeble
but devout effort. After this he gave up his soul to the Virgin,
whom he had remembered with such devotion. His body then received an honorable burial outside the city, before the altar of the
Church of St. George.[15] Afterward, when the king came to the
tomb, he grieved over the death of Alvisus and, with his bishops
and abbots, went through the sad ceremony for him again. I must
tell you that I myself really saw sufferers from fever sleeping first
beneath the bier and then, after his burial, above the grave and
later thanking God and the deceased bishop for their cure.

Now, after this brief interruption, I want to describe how the
Germans were led to Constantinople, nay, even across the sea; for
a story ought to be recounted in the order in which it has happened. As I was saying then, they proceeded boldly, but not wisely
enough, for, although they found plenty everywhere in that land,
they showed no moderation. Foot soldiers of theirs were killed
when they lagged behind drunk,[16] and, since the bodies were not
buried, all things were polluted, so that to the Franks who came
later less harm arose from the armed Greeks than from the dead
Germans. When the Germans came to Adrianople, they found
Greeks who prevented them from going to Constantinople, partly
by blocking the way, and partly by advising against that road and
assuring them that the sea was more narrow and the soil more fertile at St. George of Sestos.[17] But their emperor disparaged equally
those who blocked and those who advised against the passage.[18]
Thus, pursuing the course which he had undertaken, he found,
about midway in the journey, a meadow watered by a certain little

---

[18] Odo omits the incident told by Cinnamus, *ibid.*, II, 13, and Nicetas, *op. cit.*, pp. 83–89,
of the injured German noble who retired to a monastery in Adrianople after the departure of
Conrad and was burned in his lodging by some Greek guerrillas who wished to obtain his
money. When Frederick of Suabia heard this he returned to Adrianople and burned the entire monastery. Prosuch then intervened, and Frederick withdrew. Cinnamus, *op. cit.*, II,
14, adds that the Germans continued plundering after they left Adrianople and that Manuel
therefore garrisoned Constantinople and sent additional troops under Basil Tzicandyles to
join Prosuch.

guum et mari contiguo terminatum. Dum igitur ibidem fixis tentoriis pernoctaret, erupit pluvia super eos quidem, sicut audivimus,
modica sed in montibus tanta inundantia ut eos potius[e] raperet
quam aspergeret; torrens enim tumidus et rapidus, tentoria sibi
obvia et quicquid continebant involvens et rapiens, in mare vicinum
praecipitavit et ipsorum multa milia submersit.

Imperator autem et superstes multitudo, non sine dolore quidem
sed tamen velut sine damno tantum[f] malum perferentes, consurgunt
et, quasi audaciores redditi pro eventu, Constantinopolim veniunt.
Erat ante urbem murorum ambitus spatiosus et speciosus multimo-
dam venationem includens, conductus etiam aquarum et stagna
continens.[g] Inerant[h] etiam quaedam fossa et concava quae loco
nemorum animalibus praebebant latibula. In amoenitate[i] illa quaedam palatia nimia ambitione fulgebant[j] quae imperatores ad iocunditatem vernorum temporum sibi fundaverant. In hunc, ut verum
fatear, "deliciarum locum" Alemannus imperator irrupit, et, undique paene omnia destruens, Graecorum delicias ipsis intuentibus
suis usibus rapuit; imperiale namque palatium et singulare, quod
muris supereminet urbis, istum sub se habet locum et inhabitantium
in eo fovet aspectum. Tamen si tale spectaculum Graeco imperatori
stuporem attulit vel dolorem, repressit, et per suos Alemanni colloquium postulavit. Sed alius eorum ingredi civitatem, alius egredi
timuit aut noluit, et neuter pro altero mores suos aut fastus consue-
tudinum temperavit.

Rex interim Francorum, cui semper mos fuit regiam maiestatem
humilitate condire, imperatori Alemannorum cum multa prece
mandavit ut eum citra Brachium expectaret et quorum voluntas

[e] potius *in margin*; potius *in text over erasure* Dx.
[f] *om.* W, *although insertion of* tantum *is suggested in note.*
[g] continens *over erasure of* aquarum D1.
[h] inecant > inerant D1.
[i] ame- *over erasure, possibly of* anim *as in* animalibus *in line above* D1.
[j] fulgebunt > fulgebant Dx.

[19] This meadow is known as the plain of the Choerobacchi, and it is watered by the rivers Melas and Athyras. For other accounts of the disaster on September 8, cf. Otto of Freising (who was a witness), *Gesta*, I, xlvii, 65 (45); Cinnamus, *op. cit.*, II, 14; Nicetas, *op. cit.*, pp. 83–89; *Annales Herbipolenses*, MGSS, XVI, 4.

[20] This statement is substantiated by Cinnamus, *op. cit.*, II, 14, where, after hearing about the flood, Manuel is described as sending messengers to suggest to Conrad that the two emperors should confer about important matters. Conrad replied that Manuel should meet him on the way to Constantinople, and he made other stipulations which annoyed Manuel and caused him to abandon the negotiations.

[21] This park, called the Philopation, was located outside the wall of Constantinople, very close to the Golden Gate. Cinnamus, *op. cit.*, II, 14, describes it and says, much as

brook or freshet and bounded by the neighboring sea.[19] Then, while he was encamped there for the night, there broke above them, we have heard, a rain which was really moderate, but which formed such a huge flood in the mountains that it ravaged rather than sprinkled them; for the swift, swollen flood, seizing and rolling together in its course the tents and whatever they contained, cast them into the neighboring sea and drowned many thousands of the men.

The emperor and the surviving throng, however, enduring such a great misfortune, not without sorrow it is true, but yet as if without injury, rose up and, just as though rendered bolder by this event, came to Constantinople.[20] Before the city stood a spacious and impressive ring of walls enclosing various kinds of game and including canals and ponds. Also, inside were certain hollows and caves which, in lieu of forests, furnished lairs for the animals. In that lovely place certain palaces which the emperors had built as their springtime resort are conspicuous for their splendor. Into this "Place of Delights," to give it the proper name,[21] the German emperor burst and, destroying practically everything, under the very eyes of the Greeks seized their delights for his own uses,[22] for the imperial palace,[23] the only building which rises above the city walls, is actually directly above that place and affords a view of its inhabitants. Yet if that distressing sight caused the Greek emperor grief or amazement, he repressed the emotion, and he sent messengers to ask the German for a conference. But the German was afraid or did not wish to enter their city, and the Greek felt the same about leaving it, and neither modified his habits or his customary arrogance for the other.[24]

Meanwhile the king of the Franks, whose wont was always to season majesty with humility, enjoined upon the German emperor with urgent entreaty that he should wait for him on this side of

Odo does, that it may have been thus named because dwelling in it is pleasant. Odo knew the palace first-hand, for Louis VII was lodged there during his stay at Constantinople. Cf. Cinnamus, *ibid.*, II, 17.

[22] September 8/9. Kugler, *Studien*, p. 124, n. 35, thinks that Odo goes too far when he blames Conrad personally for the act. As we have seen in the case of Manuel, Odo is prone to this sort of identification.

[23] Blachernae.

[24] This negotiation is evidently the one referred to in n. 20, above. Cf. Kugler, *Studien*, pp. 124–25, n. 36, on this point.

eadem eundem laborem susceperat eodem consilio fruerentur. Ipse vero fervore quo coepit accelerat, et accepto a Graeco imperatore duce itineris (immo potius erroris et mortis) transmeat; et licet[k] [24r] ego[l] praescripserim, et verum sit, de illius exercitu infinitos iam obiisse, audivimus tamen a Graecis qui numerarunt transeuntes eum cum nongentis milibus[m] et quingentis sexaginta sex transfretasse. Venit ergo Nicomediam, ubi sui oborto scandalo schisma fecerunt. Imperator tetendit Iconium; frater autem eius, Otto[n] Frisingensis episcopus, et nobiles multi cum eo maritima tenuerunt. Flebiles eorum[o] eventus et celeres[p] loco et tempore referemus; sed ad nostros interim redeamus.

Venerandus Mettensis episcopus et frater eius, Renaldus comes[q] de Moncon, et Tullensis episcopus, Alemannos non ferentes, cum copioso exercitu adventum pacifici principis expectabant; sed Graeci quibus poterant iniuriis et maxime fori subtractione illos transfretare cogebant, dicentes se pactum cum eorum[r] imperatore firmasse quod nullum suorum ibi permitterent remanere. Regii vero

---

[k] ego *in small hand at edge* Dx.
[l] licet ego *at top of margin*; ego *in text over erasure of* licet Dx.
[m] militibus D.
[n] autem eius otto *over erasure of* autem eius D2.

[o] e- *over erasure* D1.
[p] sceleres D.
[q] *om.* W, *although note gives* Renaldus *this title.*
[r] corum M.

---

[25] The Bosporus is often called the Arm of St. George.

[26] The subject of the stay of the Germans at Constantinople and their crossing into Asia Minor is extremely confusing, because of our lack of adequate information. Conrad and Manuel, estranged by the incidents between the Germans and the Greeks on the way to Constantinople and the failure to carry out their negotiations, evidently did not meet. Among the conflicting evidence in the *Annales Herbipolenses, loc. cit.*, pp. 4–5, is the plausible account that Manuel ordered provisions to be furnished to the pilgrims according to the agreement, but that none of the pilgrims dared to enter the city. Cinnamus, *op. cit.*, II, 14, avers that since Conrad saw that Constantinople was well fortified and not at all terror-stricken by his arrival before the walls he despaired of making the city open to him and thus crossed to the suburb of Picridium. While the Germans were quartered there a clash between the Greek and German forces occurred, and shortly afterward Conrad crossed the Arm. Kugler contends in *Analekten* and *Neue Analekten*, both cited before, that this discouraging stay beside Constantinople made Conrad disgusted with the whole idea of the crusade and caused his unwise and hasty campaign in Asia Minor. Be that as it may, it is necessary to remember that the break between the two emperors was not complete, a fact which is indicated by the passage in the *Annales Herbipolenses* which has just been quoted, by the report that Manuel gave Conrad some swift horses as a gift (Cinnamus, *op. cit.*, II, 16) and that he furnished him a guide. Bernhardi, *op. cit.*, p. 618, explains these amenities by pointing out that at this time Roger of Sicily, against whom Conrad and Manuel were mutually allied, was attacking the Byzantine Empire.

[27] For a discussion of this number see Kugler, *Studien*, pp. 130–31, n. 50.

[28] Jaffé, *op. cit.*, p. 130, n. 28, has pointed out that the *Annales Zwifaltenses* place this incident at Nicaea, a location which is more logical geographically than Nicomedia. See below, p. 88, n. 3.

the Arm[25] and that those whose common will had undertaken a common task should also use a common plan of action. The German emperor, however, was hastening ardently toward the place for which he had set out, and when he had received a guide for the journey (or, rather, for wandering and death) from the Greek emperor, he went across.[26] Although I have written before, and it is true, that an infinite number of his men had already perished, we heard from the Greeks who counted them as they crossed that he went across with 900,566 men.[27] Accordingly, he came to Nicomedia,[28] where his men divided into groups because of a disagreement.[29] The emperor went to Iconium; his brother, Bishop Otto of Freising,[30] and many nobles took the shore route. We shall refer to their lamentable and swift misfortunes at the proper time and place; but in the meantime let us return to our men.

Since the venerable bishop of Metz[31] and his brother Renald, count of Monçon,[32] and the bishop of Toul[33] could not endure the Germans, they and their numerous army were awaiting the arrival of the peaceful prince; but by every possible outrage, especially by withdrawing market privileges, the Greeks forced them to cross, saying that they had made an agreement with the German emperor stipulating that they would not allow any of his men to

[29] The *Annales Palidenses*, MGSS, XVI, 83, explain this disagreement as another case in which there was friction between the royal party and the commoners. Reports were circulated to the effect that Conrad had observed that the foot soldiers were worn out from hunger, inexpert in war, less wary of danger than other members of the crusade, and had suffered a high mortality; that, therefore, he proposed to grant them gifts in order to allay their poverty and then to send them directly to Jerusalem. The people resented this plan and decided to make a man named Bernard their leader "saying, 'Since he is too proud to have us common people with him, we, too, refuse to follow him as king.' " In order to settle the disturbance Conrad agreed to this arrangement.

[30] Otto, bishop of Freising 1137-58, was the son of Leopold III of Austria and Agnes, daughter of Emperor Henry IV and former wife of Frederick I of Suabia. Educated at Paris, he became the outstanding western historian of his age because of his *Chronicon* and *Gesta Friderici*. For an excellent study of Otto see the introduction to *The Two Cities*, translated by C. Mierow.

[31] Stephen, bishop of Metz 1120-60, was the nephew of Calixtus II and the son of the count of Bar. For further information about him see GC, XIII, 744 ff.

[32] The life of Renald I, count of Monçon and Bar 1104-49, was filled with the turbulent activity which one conventionally ascribes to feudal barons. For details see *L'Art de vérifier les dates*, Part 2, Vol. XIII, pp. 429-32.

[33] Henry I, bishop of Toul 1126-65, was the brother of the count of Flanders. He had risen to his bishopric after being canon, archdeacon, and cantor of Toul, archdeacon of Metz, deacon of Verdun, archdeacon of Langres. See GC, XIII, 997 ff.

nuntii qui adhuc in urbe morabantur, hoc audientes et verum esse
credentes, litem illam tali pacto terminarunt ut illi transmearent
et forum idoneum in aliam partem expectantes haberent. Quo
facto, pauci Franci qui supervenerant remanserunt; quos cum alios
sequi monerent, cogerent, nec impetrarent, immensam multitudinem Pincenatorum et Cumanorum ad eos debellandos miserunt qui
etiam in desertis Bulgariae per insidias de nostris plurimos occide-
runt. Illi autem quendam terrae tumulum ascendentes et in eo se
bigis et quadrigis saepientes viriliter[s] restiterunt. Ibi nostri primam perpessi sunt penuriam, quia forum non habebant, nec illi ab
impugnatione cessabant. In urbe vero regii nuntii tarde licet hoc
scientes imperatorem adeunt nimia commotione furentes;[t] cognito
enim doloso scelere, de his qui transierunt[u] pridie conqueruntur et
maxime de his qui in urbe Christianorum[v] ab infidelibus impugnantur. Tunc imperator, quasi aliter Pincenatos[w] inhibere[x] non posset,
iubet nostros accedere propius et subtus se ad pedem palatii hospitari, et mercatum[y] praeberi. Igitur illi audito nuntio claustra sua
qualiacumque exeunt, et, quod[z] iussi fuerant, quasi nihil timentes
incedunt, cum ecce illos Pincenatorum alii persequuntur, [24v] alii
locum illorum occupare nituntur.[a] Illi autem celeriter et viriliter
revertentes[b] et persequentibus [et] locum suum[c] occupantibus animose resistunt.[d] Ibi multi pedites ut expeditius fugerent suarum
rerum proicientes aliqua perdiderunt. Tunc quidam nuntiorum
ardentius inflammati—Evrardus[e] videlicet de Britolio et Manasses

[s] viruiter > viriliter D1.
[t] ferentes CM.
[u] tranfierunt > transierunt D1.
[v] two crude dots above c in christianorum and below -r in impugnantur may suggest change in word order: qui in urbe christianorum impugnantur ab infidelibus Dx; not adopted CMBW.
[w] picenatos D.

[x] -ib- over erasure D1.
[y] mercatim > mercatum D1.
[z] quo CM.
[a] m > ni D1.
[b] v over erasure D2.
[c] " in margin, probably stopping point of scribe or corrector.
[d] restiterunt CM.
[e] -dus over erasure D1.

[34] Leo, abbot of St. Bertin, Bartholomew the chancellor, Evrard of Barres, Manasses of Bulles, Anselm the seneschal of Flanders, and others.

[35] Probably the men who had traveled fast in order to avoid the congestion around the king. See above, p. 43.

[36] Chalandon considers these acts on the part of the Patzinaks and Cumans reprisals for the pillaging of the Franks. See *Jean II Comnène*, p. 294.

[37] I have been able to find little information about Evrard of Breteuil. The fact that he was a member of the royal guard (see below, p. 123) and took part in this embassy indicates that he was a noble of some importance. Luchaire, *op. cit.*, p. 104, records his name, together with that of his father Galeran and (probably older) brother Ivette, as occurring on a charter issued in 1138; and he mentions him as a witness to a charter issued by Louis in Paris just

remain behind. Now, when the royal messengers,[34] who up to this time had been waiting in the city, heard this and believed it true, they put an end to the dispute by concluding an agreement that these forces should cross over and have a suitable market while waiting for the others. After this agreement had been put into practice, the few Franks who had preceded the army remained in the city;[35] when the Greeks warned and urged them to follow the rest and did not prevail, they sent to dislodge them a huge band of the Patzinaks and Cumans, who had already killed a great many of our men by ambush in the uninhabited parts of Bulgaria.[36] Climbing onto a certain mound of earth and barricading themselves with two- and four-horse carts, however, the Franks resisted valiantly. There our forces first endured want, because they had no market and the enemy did not cease attacking. Now, in the city the royal Frankish messengers, learning tardily of this affair, went to the emperor in great rage and excitement; for, having heard of this wily crime, they complained on behalf of those who had crossed the sea the day before and especially on behalf of those who were assailed by infidels in a Christian city. Then the emperor, as if unable to stop the Patzinaks in any other way, gave orders for our forces to draw near and to lodge at the foot of the palace and for a market to be established for them. Consequently, when the Franks heard this message they came out of their barricade, such as it was, and, because they had been ordered to go, marched ahead as if devoid of fear, when, behold, some of the Patzinaks pursued them and the rest tried to seize their stronghold. Returning swiftly and courageously, they heroically resisted both those pursuing and those engaged in occupying their position. There many foot soldiers lost some of their equipment, flinging it away in order to flee the more swiftly. At that time certain of the messengers who were very deeply enraged—Evrard of Breteuil[37] and Manasses of Bulles[38] and Anselm, the seneschal of Flanders,[39]

before the crusaders set out (*ibid.*, p. 163). Despite Odo's assertion that he was the brother of William III of Warenne, I find no evidence of such a relationship.

[38] Manasses of Bulles is another member of the royal guard about whom little is known. See below, p. 123.

[39] Anselm, seneschal of Flanders 1145–47, was also chatelain of Ypres 1130–47. For the scanty information available on this subject see H. Nowé, "Les Sénéchaux du comté de Flandre aux XIe and XIIe siècles," in *Mélanges offerts à Henri Pirenne* (Brussels, 1926), I, 335–43.

de Bullis et Ansellus[f] dapifer Flandrensis et quidam alii—iudicantes melius honeste pati mortem suam quam turpiter videre suorum, armantur, civitatem exeunt, iunguntur suis, et participes efficiuntur discriminis. Magister vero Templi, dominus[g] Evrardus de Barris, et Bartholomeus cancellarius, Archembaldus Burbonensis, et quidam alii imperatorem aggredientes, eum quem tunc viribus superare non poterant ratione vicerunt. Iurat ille se hoc nescisse; suis petit veniam; nostrosque facit iuxta palatium hospitari; et omni propulsa inquietudine[h] mercatum facit praeberi.

Esset nuntiis satisfactum nisi probarent scelus ex scelere; didicerunt enim eum cum Turcis pacem habere, et qui regi scripserat ad debellandas gentes incredulas secum ire et se de illis novam et gloriosam victoriam habuisse certum[i] erat cum eisdem indutias duodecim annorum firmasse. Augebatur etiam ex hoc et declarabatur perfidia, quod per regnum eius sola incedebat multitudo secura; episcopus enim Lingonensis et comes Warenensis et quidam alii qui ad arma sibi praeparanda ciborumque viaticum Constantinopolim paucos praemiserant, magna rerum damna pertulerant et suorum vulnera mortesque dolebant. Et hoc non[j] semel accidit; ex quo enim terram ipsius intravimus suorum latrocinia, quia viribus erant impares, perpessi sumus. Esset hoc forsitan tolerabile, et poterat dici mala quae pertulimus malis quae fecimus meruisse, nisi blasphemia iungeretur. Nam si nostri sacerdotes missas super eorum altaria celebrabant, quasi essent profanata lustrando et abluendo postea expiabant. Habent omnes divites capellas proprias, picturis, marmore, et lampadibus sic ornatas, ut [25r] unusquisque eorum

---

[f] -sel- *over erasure* D1.　　　　　[i] cervim > certum D1.
[g] domnus M.　　　　　[j] Et hoc non *crowded into space originally occupied by* et n D2.
[h] et *over erasure* D1.

---

[40] Evrard des Barres, preceptor of the Templars 1143–47, was master of the order 1147–49. During the crusade he was very helpful to Louis in matters of discipline (see p. 000, below) and finance (see the letter of Louis to Suger and Raoul of Vermandois, RHGF, XV, 501). When he returned to France he became a monk of Clairvaux. In 1174 he died. *L'Art de vérifier les dates*, Part 2, Vol. V, pp. 339–40.

[41] Cinnamus, *op. cit.*, II, 11, refers to a peace which Manuel made with the Turks. Chalandon, *Jean et Manuel Comnène*, pp. 244–47, dates the treaty in 1147. Odo's allusion seems to be based on the letter which Manuel wrote to Louis in 1146 (RHGF, XVI, 9), saying that although his realm had not been prepared for war and had been as if at peace with the Turks, he was willing to make use of the forces at hand and to enter the conflict, inasmuch as the Turks had broken the peace.

It must be remembered, however, that a reorganization of Islam had taken place after this letter. According to William of Tyre (Babcock and Krey, *op. cit.*, Vol. II, p. 166),

and some others—, thinking it preferable to suffer an honorable death themselves than basely to watch their men die, seized arms, went out from the city, joined their men, and took part in the conflict. Then the Master of the Temple, Lord Evrard of Barres,[40] Bartholomew the chancellor, Archibald of Bourbon, and some others went to the emperor and by reasoning vanquished him whom they could not then overcome by force. He swore that he had not known of this incident; he begged indulgence for his men, and he had the troops lodged next to the palace. And when all unrest had been dispelled, he had a market furnished.

This outcome would have satisfied the messengers if they had not judged one crime in the light of another; for they learned that the emperor had an agreement with the Turks and that the very man who had written to our king that he was going to accompany him in fighting the infidels and had won a recent and renowned victory over them had actually confirmed a twelve-year armistice with them.[41] Also, his treachery was increased and made manifest by the fact that only a great number could get through his realm in safety; for the bishop of Langres and the count of Warenne[42] and certain others, who had sent a few men ahead to Constantinople to provide arms and food for the journey, had suffered a considerable loss of possessions and were mourning their wounded and dead. And this did not happen just once; for from the time when we entered his territory we endured the robberies which his people perpetrated on us because our strength did not equal theirs. Perhaps this condition would have been bearable, and it could have been said that we deserved the evils which we suffered on account of the evils which we had committed, if blasphemy had not been added. For instance, if our priests celebrated mass on Greek altars, the Greeks afterwards purified them with propitiatory offerings and ablutions, as if they had been defiled. All the wealthy people have their own chapels, so adorned with paintings, marble,

when the Sultan of Iconium learned that Conrad and Louis were on the way East he called for aid from the remotest parts of the Orient. See also Cahen, *La Syrie du Nord*, pp. 374–79. Such an Islamic movement would be known to Manuel and be a factor in his making a treaty with the Turks.

[42] William III, count of Warenne and earl of Surrey 1138–48, the son of William II of Warenne and Isabel of Vermandois, was a loyal supporter of Stephen of England. For the circumstances of his death see below, p. 123. A summary of his life can be found in the article "William de Warenne" in DNB.

merito diceret, "Domine, dilexi decorem domus tuae," si lampas
in eis orthodoxae fidei coruscaret. Sed pro nefas! audivimus scelus
eorum morte luendum, quia quotienscumque nostrorum conubia
contrahunt,[k] antequam conveniant eum qui Romano more baptiza-
tus est, rebaptizant. Alias haereses eorum novimus, et de more
sacrificii et de processione Spiritus sancti. Sed nihil horum nostram
paginam sordidaret nisi nostrae materiae conveniret. His enim de
causis nostrorum incurrerant odium, exierat namque inter laicos
etiam error eorum. Ob hoc iudicabantur non esse Christiani, caede-
sque illorum[l] ducebant pro nihilo et a praedis et rapinis difficilius
poterant revocari.

Sed revertamur ad regem qui, licet fere diebus singulis novos
imperatoris nuntios habeat, causatur tamen moras suorum, quia
quid cum eis agatur ignorat. Bona semper nuntiant, nunquam
ostendunt; et minus creduntur quia omnes eundem adulationis
semper habent prooemium. Polychronias eorum suscipit sed vilipendit (sic enim vocantur reverentiae quas non solum regibus sed
etiam quibuslibet suis maioribus exhibent, caput et corpus sub-
missius inclinantes vel fixis in terram genibus vel etiam sese toto
corpore prosternentes). Interdum imperatrix reginae scribebat et
tunc Graeci penitus frangebantur in feminas; omne virile robur et
verborum et animi deponentes, leviter iurabant quicquid nos velle
putabant, sed nec nobis fidem nec sibi verecundiam conservabant.
Generalis est enim eorum[m] sententia non imputari periurium quod
fit[n] propter sacrum imperium. Nec me putet aliquis odiosum genus
hominum[o] persequi et odio eorum fingere quem[p] non vidi. Requisi-

---

[k] contrabunt M.
[l] q; ĪĪĪĪ *over erasure, perhaps of* quas D2.
[m] eorum enim CM.

[n] sit M.
[o] homnium > hominum Dx.
[p] quae CM.

---

[43] Psalms 26:8.

[44] The Greek Church permitted its members to partake of both the bread and the wine
in the Eucharist; it taught that the Holy Ghost proceeded from the Father alone, rather
than from the Father and the Son.

[45] Literally this word means "long live" in salutations like "Long live the king!"

[46] Bertha, who was known in Constantinople as Irene, was the daughter of the count of
Sulzbach, an important Bavarian noble, and a sister of Gertrude, the wife of Conrad III.
Betrothed to Manuel before the death of John Comnenus, she was married in 1146. See
Otto of Freising, *Chronicon*, VII, 28, and *Gesta*, I, xxiv, 37 (23), J. McCabe, *The Empresses
of Constantinople* (London, 1913).

[47] Wilken, *op. cit.*, III, 137, thinks that these letters were not written by the empress and
he cites the phrase "tunc Graeci penitus frangebantur in feminas" as support. As has been
indicated above, p. xxiii, Kenneth Setton has suggested that a lacuna occurs here, due to a

and lamps that each magnate might justly say, "O Lord, I have cherished the beauty of Thy house,"[43] if the light of the true faith shone therein. But, O dreadful thing! we heard of an ill usage of theirs which should be expiated by death; namely, that every time they celebrate the marriage of one of our men, if he has been baptized in the Roman way, they rebaptize him before they make the pact. We know other heresies of theirs, both concerning their treatment of the Eucharist and concerning the procession of the Holy Ghost,[44] but none of these matters would mar our page if not pertinent to our subject. Actually, it was for these reasons that the Greeks had incurred the hatred of our men, for their error had become known even among the lay people. Because of this they were judged not to be Christians, and the Franks considered killing them a matter of no importance and hence could with the more difficulty be restrained from pillage and plundering.

But let us return to the king, who, although he received new messengers from the emperor nearly every day, nevertheless complained about the delay of his own ambassadors, because he did not know what had happened to them. The Greeks always reported good news, but they never showed any proof of it, and they were the less believed because on every occasion all used the same prefatory flattery. The king accepted, but considered of slight value, their *polychroniae*[45] (for that is the name of the gestures of honor which they exhibit, not only toward kings, but even toward certain of their nobles, lowering the head and body humbly or kneeling on the ground or even prostrating themselves). Occasionally the empress[46] wrote to the queen.[47] And then the Greeks degenerated entirely into women; putting aside all manly vigor, both of words and of spirit, they lightly swore whatever they thought would please us, but they neither kept faith with us nor maintained respect for themselves. In general they really have the opinion that anything which is done for the holy empire cannot be considered perjury. Let no one think that I am taking vengeance on a race of men hateful to me and that because of my hatred I am inventing a Greek whom I have not seen. Whoever has

revision which removed all outstanding accounts of Eleanor from the history. Such a revision would be a cutting out of offending passages rather than a careful reworking and remolding of the material.

tus[q] enim quicumque Graecos noverit fatebitur quia quando timent
nimia sua deiectione[r] vilescunt et quando praevalent gravi subditorum oppressione superbiunt. Ceterum multo studio consulendo
laborabant ut rex ab Adrianopoli ad sanctum Georgium de Sesto
gressum diverteret et ibi celerius et utilius transfretaret. Rex autem
noluit incipere quod Francos audiebat numquam fecisse. Igitur
eisdem vestigiis, sed non eisdem auspiciis, Alemannos [25v] subsequitur praecedentes, et, cum ad unam dietam Constantinopolim
propinquasset, suos nuntios habuit obvios, rumores de imperatore
quos iam ex parte retulimus reportantes. Tunc fuere qui regi con-
sulerent retrocedere et terram opulentissimam[s] cum castellis et urbi-
bus capere et interim regi Rogerio,[t] qui tunc imperatorem maxime
impugnabat, scriberet et, eius adiutus navigio, ipsam Constantinopolim[u] expugnaret. Sed vae nobis,[v] immo Petri apostoli subditis
omnibus, quod non praevaluerunt voces eorum! Processimus igitur, et nobis appropinquantibus civitati, ecce omnes illius nobiles
et divites tam cleri quam populi catervatim regi obviam processerunt et eum[w] honore debito susceperunt, rogantes humiliter ut ad
imperatorem intraret et de sua visione et collocutione illius deside-
rium adimpleret. Rex autem, eius timori compatiens et petitioni
oboediens, cum paucis suorum intravit et eum in porticu palatii
satis imperialiter obvium habuit. Erant fere coaevi et coaequales,
solis moribus et[x] vestitu[y] dissimiles. Tandem post amplexus et
oscula mutua[z] habita, interius processerunt ubi positis duobus sedi-
libus pariter subsederunt. Circumstante autem corona suorum,
loquuntur per interpretem. Requirit imperator esse regis et volun-

[q] r *over* e D1.
[r] diectione > deiectione Dx.
[s] opulis- > opulentissimam D1.
[t] rog- *over erasure* D1.
[u] constantinopoum > constantinopolim D1.

[v] vobis > nobis Dx.
[w] cum M.
[x] *om.* M.
[y] vestibus CM.
[z] mutuo CM.

[48] Bédier, *op. cit.*, IV, 131, points out that the road on which Louis traveled was supposed
to have been the route taken by Charlemagne as well as by the members of the First Crusade.
See the *Gesta Francorum et aliorum Hierosolymitanorum*, RHCHO, III, 121: "Those very powerful knights went . . . along the route which Charlemagne, the wonderful king of France,
had formerly taken to Constantinople."
[49] See above, pp. 51–53.
[50] Prominent among them was Godfrey of Langres.
[51] In the late summer of 1147 Roger's fleet sailed from Otranto to Corfu, where he managed to set up a garrison. From this base he pillaged Negropont and Cerigo, then proceeded
up the Gulf of Corinth and took Thebes and Corinth. Cf. Otto of Freising, *Gesta*, I, xxxiv,
53 (33); *Annales Cavenses*, MGSS, III, 192; *Historia ducum Veneticorum*, MGSS, XIV, 75; Nicetas,
op. cit., pp. 83–89.

known the Greeks will, if asked, say that when they are afraid
they become despicable in their excessive debasement and when
they have the upper hand they are arrogant in their severe violence
to those subjected to them. However, they toiled most zealously
in advising the king to turn his route from Adrianople to St. George
of Sestos and there to cross the sea the more swiftly and advantageously. But the king did not wish to undertake something which
he had never heard that the Franks had done.[48] Thus, by the same
paths, but not with the same omens, he followed the Germans who
had preceded us, and when a day's journey from Constantinople
met his own messengers, who told him the stories concerning the
emperor which we have already related in part.[49] There were
those[50] who then advised the king to retreat and to seize the exceedingly rich land with its castles and cities and meanwhile to
write to King Roger, who was then vigorously attacking the emperor,[51] and, aided by his fleet, to attack Constantinople itself.
But, alas for us, nay, for all St. Peter's subjects, their words did
not prevail! Therefore, we proceeded, and when we approached
the city,[52] lo, all its nobles and wealthy men, clerics as well as lay
people, trooped out to meet the king and received him with due
honor, humbly asking him to appear before the emperor and to
fulfil the emperor's desire to see and talk with him.[53] Now the
king, taking pity on the emperor's fear and obeying his request,
entered with a few of his men and received an imperial welcome
in the portico of the palace. The two sovereigns were almost identical in age and stature, unlike only in dress and manners. After
they had exchanged embraces and kisses, they went inside, where,
when two chairs had been arranged, they both sat down.[54] Surrounded by a circle of their men, they conversed with the help of
an interpreter. The emperor asked about the king's present state

[52] October 4. Cf. the letter which Louis wrote to Suger from Constantinople (RHGF,
XV, 488): "with every kind of joy and good fortune we came to Constantinople on the
Sunday before the feast of St. Denis."
[53] Cinnamus, op. cit., II, 17, says that all the trusted men and the chief officers of the empire
were along the king's path, and they took him to the palace with the greatest honor.
[54] This account differs somewhat from that of Cinnamus, ibid. The Greek writer pictures
a more formal audience in which Louis was brought to the place where Manuel was seated
on his throne and allowed to sit on a little stool while conversing. This was an honor,
however, because the members of the retinues were forced to stand throughout the conversation.

tatem, optans ei quae Dei sunt, quae sua sunt repromittens. Utinam
sicut honeste sic[a] vere! Si gestus corporis, si alacritas faciei, si
verba cordis intima demonstrarent, circumstantes[b] illum nimio
affectu regem diligere comprobarent; sed tale argumentum proba-
bile[c] est, non necessarium. Post haec[d] sicut fratres ab invicem
discesserunt, et regem foras ad palatium in quo erat hospitatus im-
perii nobiles conduxerunt.

Explicit Tertius

---

[a] sive M.   [c] probib- > probile D1.
[b] crigstantes . . . ni- D1.   [d] baec > haec Dx.

and his wishes for the future, wishing for him the things which are God's to give and promising him those within his own power. Would it had been done as sincerely as it was gracefully! If his gestures, his liveliness of expression, and his words had been a true indication of his inner thoughts, those who stood nearby would have attested that he cherished the king with great affection; but such evidence is only plausible, not conclusive. Afterwards they parted as if they were brothers, and the imperial nobles took the king away to the palace which had been designated as his lodging.[55]

End of Book Three

---

[55] In the Philopation. See Cinnamus, *ibid*.

Incipit Quartus

Constantinopolis, Graecorum gloria, fama dives et rebus ditior, ad formam veli navalis in trigonum ducitur. In interiori angulo sanctam Sophiam habet et palatium Constantini, in quo capella est quae sacrosanctis reliquiis honoratur. Duobus autem lateribus mari

[1] Millingen, *Byzantine Constantinople*, p. 2, describes the site as a promontory which is actually a trapezium, but is generally called a triangle because of the comparative shortness of the eastern side. It is about four miles long and one to four miles wide, and the surface is broken up into hills and plains.

[2] For details about Santa Sophia see W. R. Lethaby and H. Swainson, *The Church of Sancta Sophia Constantinople* (London, 1894). More recent is the article by W. Emerson and R. L. Van Nice, "Haghia Sophia Istanbul: Preliminary Report of a Recent Examination of the Structure," *American Journal of Archaeology*, XLVII (1943), 403–36.

[3] The Great Palace, built by Constantine the Great at the east of the Hippodrome, was the official residence of the emperors from his time to that of Alexius Comnenus. For a con-

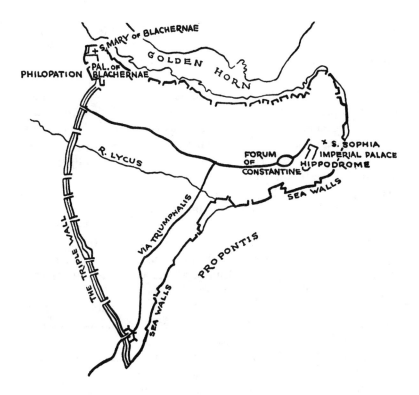

Beginning of Book Four

Constantinople, the glory of the Greeks, rich in renown and richer still in possessions, is laid out in a triangle shaped like a ship's sail.[1] In its inner angle stand Santa Sophia[2] and Constantine's Palace,[3] in which there is a chapel that is revered for its exceedingly holy relics.[4] Moreover, Constantinople is girt on two sides by the sea; when approaching the city we had the Arm of St. George[5] on the right and on the left a certain estuary, which,

temporary account of its size and luxury see Constantine Porphyrogenitus, *op. cit.* A good modern book is Ebersolt, *Le Grand Palais de Constantinople et le Livre des cérémonies.*

[4] Among the most precious relics were those of the Passion: the Holy Lance, the Holy Cross, the Crown of Thorns, the Nail of the Crucifixion, the Shroud, and the Stone from the Tomb. J. Ebersolt, *Sanctuaires de Byzance* (Paris, 1921), pp. 17-30.

[5] The Bosporus.

praecingitur; venientes ad urbem Brachium sancti Georgii ad dexteram et quendam profluvium qui de ipso procedens ad quattuor fere
milia tenditur [26r] habebamus ad laevam. Ibi palatium quod
dicitur Blasserna fundatur quidem in humili, sed sumptu et arte
decenti proceritate consurgit et triplici confinio triplicem habi-
tantibus iocunditatem offerens mare, campos urbemque visibus
alternis despicit. Exterior eius pulchritudo fere incomparabilis[a]
est, interior vero quicquid de illa dixero superabit. Auro depingi-
tur undique variisque coloribus, et marmore studioso artificio
sternitur area; et nescio quid ei[b] plus conferat pretii vel pulchritu-
dinis, ars subtilis vel pretiosa materia. Latus tertium de trigono
civitatis campos habet, sed duplici muro munitur et turribus qui a
mari usque ad palatium fere duobus milibus tenditur. Hic nec ro-
bore firmus est nec turres in altum subrigit; sed urbs, sicut aestimo,
in sua multitudine et antiqua quiete confidit. Infra muros terra
vacua est quae aratra patitur et ligones, habens hortos omne genus
olerum[c] civibus exhibentes. A foris subterranei conductus influunt,
qui aquas dulces civitati largiter tribuunt.

Ipsa quidem sordida est et fetida multisque in locis perpetua
nocte damnata; divites enim suis aedificiis vias tegunt sordesque et
tenebras pauperibus et hospitibus derelinquunt; ibique[d] caedes ex-
ercentur et latrocinia et quae tenebras diligunt alia scelera. Quoniam autem in hac urbe vivitur sine iure, quae tot quasi dominos
habet quot divites et paene tot fures quot pauperes, ibi sceleratus
quisque nec metum habet nec verecundiam, ubi scelus nec lege
vindicatur nec luce venit in palam. In omnibus modum excedit;
nam sicut[e] divitiis urbes alias superat, sic etiam vitiis. Multas
quoque habet ecclesias sanctae Sophiae magnitudine impares non

---

[a] ini- > inc- D1.
[b] quid ei quid ei > quid ei Dx.
[c] omne genus hortos holerum > hortos omne genus holerum Dx.

[d] Ibi CM.
[e] sic CM.

---

[6] The Golden Horn.

[7] The section where this palace stands was originally outside the walls. It was located
on a hill, which was partly built up so that it furnished a suitable platform or terrace for
the buildings. Deriving much importance from its site near the shrine of the Theotokos of
Blachernae and its easy access to the country, the palace came into special favor at the
time of the Comneni. Manuel repaired and adorned it until it gained the title of "The New
Palace." Millingen, *op. cit.*, pp. 128–30.

[8] Constantinople had in the Theodosian Walls a very elaborate system of defense: a moat
61 feet wide and *ca.* 22 feet deep, an outer terrace 61 feet wide, an outer wall 27½ feet higher
than the terrace and from 2 to 6½ feet thick, an inner terrace from 50 to 64 feet broad, and

after branching from the Arm, flows on for about four miles.[6] In that place the Palace of Blachernae, although having foundations laid on low ground, achieves eminence through excellent construction and elegance and, because of its surroundings on three sides, affords its inhabitants the triple pleasure of looking out upon sea, fields, and city. Its exterior is of almost matchless beauty, but its interior surpasses anything that I can say about it. Throughout it is decorated elaborately with gold and a great variety of colors, and the floor is marble, paved with cunning workmanship; and I do not know whether the exquisite art or the exceedingly valuable stuffs endows it with the more beauty or value.[7] The third side of the city's triangle includes fields, but it is fortified by towers and a double wall which extends for about two miles from the sea to the palace. This wall is not very strong, and it possesses no lofty towers; but the city puts its trust, I think, in the size of its population and the long period of peace which it has enjoyed.[8] Below the walls lies open land, cultivated by plough and hoe, which contains gardens that furnish the citizens all kinds of vegetables. From the outside underground conduits flow in, bringing the city an abundance of sweet water.[9]

The city itself is squalid and fetid and in many places harmed by permanent darkness, for the wealthy overshadow the streets with buildings and leave these dirty, dark places to the poor and to travelers; there murders and robberies and other crimes which love the darkness are committed. Moreover, since people live lawlessly in this city, which has as many lords as rich men and almost as many thieves as poor men, a criminal knows neither fear nor shame, because crime is not punished by law and never entirely comes to light. In every respect she exceeds moderation; for, just as she surpasses other cities in wealth, so, too, does she surpass them in vice. Also, she possesses many churches unequal to Santa Sophia

an inner wall which was loftier and thicker than the outer wall. The weakest spot, as Odo discerned, was in the suburb of the Blachernae, which had been included in the city after the system of walls had been laid out. For more technical details, see Millingen, *op. cit.*, pp. 51–58.

[9] Water was brought to the city by aqueducts which had been laid through the moat and walls, and it was stored in immense underground reservoirs located for the most part in the center of the city, around or beneath Santa Sophia. Fifty-eight of these reservoirs exist at the present time. R. Byron, *The Byzantine Achievement* (New York, 1929), p. 247. See also Emerson and Van Nice, *loc. cit.*

decore, quae sicut sunt admirabiles pulchritudine sic[f] sunt etiam numerosis sanctorum pignoribus venerandae. Ad has intrabant qui poterant, alii curiositate videndi, alii devotione fideli.

Rex quoque duce imperatore loca sancta visitavit et revertens cum eo, victus precum instantia, comedit. Convivium illud sicut gloriosos convivas habuit, sic apparatu mirifico,[g] dapum deliciis, voluptuosis iocorum plausibus aures et os et [26v] oculos satiavit. Timebant ibi[h] regi suorum multi;[i] ipse vero, qui Deo commiserat curam sui, fide et animositate penitus nil timebat; non enim cito credit sibi noceri qui nocendi non habet animum.

Licet Graeci nullum argumentum perfidiae demonstrarent, credo enim illos non tam sedulum exhibuisse servitium si bona cogitarent. Suas vero dissimulabant iniurias post Brachii transitum exigendas. Nec imputabatur eis si portas urbis multitudini obserabant, quia multas eorum domos et oliveta combusserant vel penuria nemorum vel insolentia et ebrietate stultorum. Faciebat eis rex aures, manus, et pedes saepius detruncare, nec sic poterat eorum vesaniam refrenare. Immo erat necessarium alterum e duobus, vel multa milia simul occidere vel eorum mala plurima tolerare. Forum igitur satis abundanter nobis afferebat navigium,[j] et ante palatium vel etiam[k] in tentoriis habebamus congruum, si duraret, concambium, minus quam duobus denariis staminam[l] unam et earum triginta (tres solidos) propter marcam. Postquam vero tribus diebus urbem transivimus, pro una quinque vel sex denarios et pro duodecim solidis marcam unam perdebamus.

Ceterum dum rex venientes per Apuliam[m] expectat,[n] inter Brun-

---

[f] sicut > sic Dx.
[g] mirifice M.
[h] illi M.
[i] multi suorum CM.
[j] afferebat navigium *over erasure and crowded* D1.

[k] vel etiam *over erasure* D1.
[l] stammam DCM.
[m] apuliam DCM > apuleam D1.
[n] expectaret D.

---

[10] As was true for the Germans (see above, p. 50, n. 26), the gates of the city were closed, and the pilgrims were forced to remain outside the walls. In the case of the French, however, the king and some of his retinue were admitted.

[11] Cinnamus, *op. cit.*, II, 17, says that soon after his arrival Louis went with Manuel to the palaces in the southern part of the city to see the things there which excite admiration and to make a pilgrimage to the very holy relics of the Passion.

[12] Constantine Porphyrogenitus, *op. cit.*, II, 15, depicts the ceremonies and banquets which the emperors of Constantinople tendered to their official guests. Despite the fact that this book dates from the tenth century and is written about the Great Palace, D. C. Hesseling in *Essai sur la civilisation Byzantine* (Paris, 1907), pp. 180–81, assures us that the ceremony observed by the royal court continued to be essentially as described by Constantine.

[13] This lack of discipline may be laid in part to the character of the army, which was composed of many noncombatants who had no idea of formal discipline; of personal bands

in size but equal to it in beauty, which are to be marveled at for their beauty and their many saintly relics. Those who had the opportunity entered these places,[10] some to see the sights and others to worship faithfully.

Conducted by the emperor, the king also visited the shrines[11] and, after returning, when won over by the urgency of his host's requests, dined with him. That banquet afforded pleasure to ear, mouth, and eye with pomp as marvelous, viands as delicate, and pastimes as pleasant as the guests were illustrious.[12] There many of the king's men feared for him; but he, who had entrusted the care of himself to God, feared nothing at all, since he had faith and courage; for one who is not inclined to do harm does not easily believe that anyone will harm him.

Although the Greeks furnished us no proof that they were treacherous, I believe that they would not have exhibited such unremitting servitude if they had had good intentions. Actually, they were concealing the wrongs which were to be avenged after we crossed the Arm. However, it was not held against the Greeks that they closed the city gates to the throng, since it had burned many of their houses and olive trees, either for want of wood or by reason of arrogance and the drunkenness of fools. The king frequently punished offenders by cutting off their ears, hands, and feet, yet he could not thus check the folly of the whole group. Indeed, one of two things was necessary, either to kill many thousands at one time or to put up with their numerous evil deeds.[13] As I was saying, a ship supplied us an ample market, and in front of the palace and even in the tents we had a rate of exchange which would have been adequate if it had lasted; namely, less than two denarii for one stamina and a mark for thirty staminae (three solidi). But after we had traveled three days beyond the city we paid five or six denarii for one stamina and lost a mark on twelve soldi.

Now while the king was awaiting the forces coming from

attached to knights, barons, and chiefs rather than to the king directly; and finally of the lords themselves, who acted in an individualistic fashion rather than as officers subordinate to the king. That this state of affairs was recognized is shown by the reorganization of the troops by the Templars in Asia Minor (see pp. 125 ff., below).

[14] In this rapid rise in favor of the Byzantines the rate of exchange tripled and thus returned to the figure which the crusaders had found prevailing at the entrance to Greek territory. See above, p. 41. Chalandon, *Jean II Comnène*, pp. 298–99, n. 2, has tabulated the change.

dusium et Dyrrachium transfretantes, sollemnitas beati Dionysii accidit, quam ipse veneratione qua debuit celebravit. Novit hoc imperator, colunt etenim Graeci hoc festum, et clericorum suorum electam multitudinem, dato unicuique cereo magno variis coloribus et auro depicto, regi transmisit; et sollemnitatis gloriam ampliavit. Illi quidem a nostris clericis verborum et organi genere dissidebant, sed suavi modulatione placebant; voces enim mixtae, robustior cum gracili, eunucha videlicet cum virili (erant enim eunuchi multi illorum), Francorum animos demulcebant. Gestu etiam corporis decenti et modesto plausu manuum et inflexione articulorum iocunditatem visibus offerebant. Referimus imperatoris obsequia ut pateat[o] dolus ipsius qui praetendebat affectum quem solemus amicis praecordialibus demonstrare et gerebat animum quem non [27r] possemus nisi mortibus nostris placare. Certe nemo Graecos cognosceret nisi experimento vel spiritu prophetiae!

Episcopus vero Lingonensis eorum fidem improbans, contemnens obsequia, prophetans mala quae postea sensimus, urbem capi suadebat. Muros fragiles, quorum magna pars ante nostros oculos[p] corruit, inertem populum, sine mora vel labore ruptis conductibus dulces aquas posse subtrahi comprobabat. Dicebat vir ille, prudens animo sacer religione,[q] quod capta illa civitate non esset necessarium alias expugnare, quia gratuitum possidenti caput earum praeberent obsequium. Addebat etiam quod ipsa rem Christianitatis non habet, sed nomen, et, cum deberet per se Christianis auxilium ferre non alios[r] prohibere,[s] ante paucos annos imperator Antiochenum principem aggressus est expugnare. "Prius cepit[t] Tarsum et Mamistram[u] et castella plurima terramque latissimam, expulsisque catholicis episcopis urbium et haereticis substitutis, obsedit Antio-

---

[o] patebat *crowded*; pateat Dx.
[p] *om.* CM.
[q] religione sacer CM.
[r] non illo non M.

[s] per (?) > pro Dx.
[t] coepit CM.
[u] Manustram CM.

---

[15] Those of the counts of Maurienne and Auvergne and the marquis of Montferrat. See below, p. 79.

[16] October 9.

[17] In speaking of the Greeks and of Manuel Odo very often reports actions and then interprets them most adversely. For a discussion of this see above, p. xxii, n. 56.

[18] This is in great contrast to Cinnamus' description of the awe with which Conrad examined the defenses of Constantinople and then withdrew. See Cinnamus, *op. cit.*, II, 14.

[19] Otto of Freising, *Chronicon*, VII, 28, describes the expedition of John Comnenus against Raymond of Antioch in 1142-43. See also Nicetas, *op. cit.*, pp. 51-55; William of Tyre in Babcock and Krey, II, 83 ff., 94 ff.

Apulia, when they were crossing between Brindisi and Durazzo,[15] the feast of St. Denis occurred,[16] and he celebrated it with proper veneration. Since the Greeks celebrate this feast, the emperor knew of it, and he sent over to the king a carefully selected group of his clergy, each of whom he had equipped with a large taper decorated elaborately with gold and a great variety of colors; and thus he increased the glory of the ceremony. These clergy certainly differed from ours as to words and order of service, but they made a favorable impression because of their sweet chanting; for the mingling of voices, the heavier with the light, the eunuch's, namely, with the manly voice (for many of them were eunuchs), softened the hearts of the Franks. Also, they gave the onlookers pleasure by their graceful bearing and gentle clapping of hands and genuflexions. We recall these favors on the part of the emperor so that there may be manifest the treachery of him who simulated the friendship which we are accustomed to show only to our most intimate friends, while he harbored a feeling which we could not have appeased save by our very death. Surely no one could understand the Greeks without having had experience of them or without being endowed with prophetic inspiration.[17]

Distrusting their pledge, scorning their favors, and foretelling the injuries which we afterwards endured, the bishop of Langres, however, urged us to take the city. He proved that the walls, a great part of which collapsed before our eyes, were weak, that the people were inert, that by cutting the conduits the fresh water supply could be withdrawn without delay or effort.[18] He, a man of wise intellect and saintly piety, said that if that city were taken it would not be necessary to conquer the others, since they would yield obedience voluntarily to him who possessed their capital. He added further that Constantinople is Christian only in name, not in fact, and, whereas for her part she should not prevent others from bringing aid to Christians, her emperor had ventured a few years previously to attack the prince of Antioch.[19] He said: "First he took Tarsus and Mamistra and numerous strongholds and a broad expanse of land, and, after expelling the Catholic bishops in the cities and replacing them with heretics,[20] he besieged Antioch.

[20] That is, bishops of the Greek Orthodox Church. For a description of the formation of the Latin Church in Antioch in 1100, see Cahen, *op. cit.*, pp. 308–26; 331 ff.

chiam. Cumque deberet sumptis Christianorum copiis paganorum viciniam propulsare, illorum auxilio nisus est Christianos extermi- nare. Deus autem, horum cognitor, iudex et vindex, voluit ut ipse sibi toxicatam sagittam infligeret et modico vulnere vitam indig- nam finiret. Iste vero qui nunc regnat, heres questus et criminis, sicut iura ecclesiarum sibi retinet et alia quae pater impie conquisi- vit, sic ceteris inhiat quae ipse concupivit, et iam principi[v] extorsit hominium[w] et, erigens altare contra altare, patriarcha Petri de- specto, in urbe statuit suum. Sit vestri iudicii utrum illi parcere debeatis quo regnante cruci Christi et sepulcro nihil tutum, quo destructo nihil contrarium.''

Cum perorasset episcopus, placuit[x] aliquibus quod dicebat. Plu- res autem quibus displicuit haec et similia respondebant: ''De fide istorum non possumus iudicare legis ignari. Quod autem impugna- vit Antiochiam malum fuit, potuit tamen causas habere iustitiae quas nescimus. Certum vero est regem nuper cum papa locutum fuisse et super hoc nec praeceptum eius nec consilium accepisse. Visitare sepulcrum Domini cognovimus[y] nos et ipse et nostra cri- mina, praecepto summi [27v] pontificis, paganorum sanguine vel conversione[z] delere. Nunc autem urbem Christianorum ditissimam expugnare possumus et ditari, sed caedendum est et cadendum. Si ergo caedes Christianorum peccata diluit, dimicemus. Item si nos- tris mortuis non nocet ambitio, si tantum valet in itinere pro adqui- renda pecunia interire quantum summi pontificis oboedientiae et voto nostro intendere, placent divitiae; sine timore mortis discri- mina subeamus.''

Talis erat eorum altercatio et favebant sibi de iure assertores utriusque sententiae. Credo tamen quod vicisset episcopus nisi

---

[v] principis DC > principi D1; principibus M.   [y] convenimus CM.
[w] hominum D.   [z] conversi[one] *over erasure* D1.
[x] perorasset episcopus pla *over erasure* D2.   [a] -lerent *over erasure* D1.

---

[21] 1143. Cf. Babcock and Krey trans. of William of Tyre, II, 121–29.

[22] The expedition set out in 1144; Raymond, count of Antioch (1136–49), probably moved by the capture of Edessa, opened negotiations in 1145. After making an apology to the tomb of John Comnenus he paid homage to Manuel as a vassal of the Byzantine Empire. Cf. Cinnamus, *op. cit.*, II, 3.

[23] Among these must have been Arnulf of Lisieux, who disagreed constantly with Godfrey. See above, p. 22, n. 8.

[24] Eugenius had promised remission of sins ''to those who will decide to undertake and to perfect such a holy and exceedingly necessary task and work of devotion''; he further de- scribed this sort of pilgrim: ''one who will enter upon the exceedingly holy journey de-

And although it was his duty to ward off the nearby infidels by uniting the Christian forces, with the aid of the infidels he strove to destroy the Christians. Nevertheless, God, who knows, judges, and avenges such things as these, willed that he should wound himself with a poisoned arrow and end his shameful life as the result of that slight wound.[21] However, just as the present ruler, the heir of that lamentable crime, keeps for himself the ecclesiastical domains and other property which his father acquired by wickedness, just so he gazes longingly at the rest of the territory which his father wanted and already has exacted the prince's homage[22] and, setting up one altar against another, has established his own patriarch in the city, scorning Peter's patriarch. Let it be your decision whether you ought to spare the man under whose rule the cross and sepulcher of Christ are not at all safe and after whose destruction nothing would be hostile to them."

When the bishop had finished speaking, his remarks found favor with some. Many with whom he did not find favor, however, replied with words such as the following:[23] "Without knowledge of the law we cannot judge about their good faith. The fact that he attacked Antioch was evil, but he could have had justifiable reasons which we do not know. It is certainly true that the king recently conferred with the pope and that he was not given any advice or command concerning this point. He knows, and we know, that we are to visit the Holy Sepulcher and, by the command of the supreme pontiff, to wipe out our sins with the blood or the conversion of the infidels.[24] At this time we can attack the richest of the Christian cities and enrich ourselves, but in so doing we must kill and be killed. And so, if slaughtering Christians wipes out our sins, let us fight. Again, if harboring ambition does not sully our death, if on this journey it is as important to die for the sake of gaining money as it is to maintain our vow and our obedience to the supreme pontiff, then wealth is welcome; let us expose ourselves to danger without fear of death."

Such was their contention, and the supporters of each side defended themselves ably. Nevertheless, I believe that the bishop

---

voutly and either travel to the end or die on the way." RHGF, XV, 430. Godfrey's opponents skillfully utilized the contrast between these words of the pope and the bishop's excellent military advice.

Graeci magis praevalerent[a] dolis quam viribus. Qui nostras moras[b]
habentes suspectui, urgere transitum non audebant, forum tamen
ex parte subtrahentes, rumoribus Alemannorum nostros ad transitum concitabant. Primo retulerunt Turcos copiosum exercitum
congregasse[c] et Alemannos de illis sine damno suorum quattuorde-
cim milia peremisse. Post diem alteram feliciori eventu infaustum
transitum amplius persuadebant; dicebant enim Alemannos perve-
nisse Iconium et ante adventum illorum eiusdem civitatis perterri-
tum fugisse populum. Et quoniam ipsi festinant in antea, imperatorum[d] alter alteri scripsit ut veniat et quod sine suo labore
conquisitum est defendendo possideat. His stimulis exercitus agi-
tur et de mora regis commurmurat dum quidam lucris eorum,
quidam laudibus invidebant. Victus ergo rex et Graecorum monitis
et suorum querelis, antequam venirent quos expectaverat transfre-
tavit; et imperator sicut hoc ardenter voluit sic velociter navium
copiam praeparavit.

Rex autem citra[e] Brachium[f] fecit dies quinque[g] partem sui exercitus expectando et ultra similiter quinque Graecorum versutias tolerando. Habent illi locum quem expectaverant, et audent detegere
quae cogitaverant, tamen nostrorum vesaniae dederunt eis velamina
suae nequitiae; unde dictum est a pluribus quod nobis fecerunt non
esse malitiam sed vindictam. Ex parte iudicat qui rem novit ex
parte, sed non potest facere rectum iudicium, qui causam ex integro
non cognoscit. Illi enim offendi poterant, [28r] non placari. Ecce
pertransivimus, et nos naves cibariae cum cambitoribus subsequun-

b -as *over erasure* D1.   f C *suggests*: Hic deest transit vel quid simile; *such an insertion is not*
c -sse *over erasure* D1.   *necessary, however, with the reading* citra.
d imperator CM.   g quindecim D (*this occurs again in the same sentence*); cf. *n.* 29, *below.*
e cum CM.

25 That is, the Greeks feared that the Franks would join forces with Roger of Apulia
against Constantinople. This fear was increased by the fact that Louis was waiting for
the forces who had traveled via Sicily.

26 Manuel.

27 That the Greeks spread such rumors is very likely. It is interesting to notice that they
incorporated their idea of having the Westerners give up any conquered territory to the
Greek emperor. That part of the report has a decidedly Greek tinge and should have made
the Franks suspicious if they had been in closer contact with the imperial army and realized
how poor had been the relations between the two emperors at Constantinople. William of
Tyre, translated by Babcock and Krey, II, 169, reports these rumors as taking place
after Conrad's defeat. This is probably caused by a misunderstanding of Odo or a similar
account.

28 *Ca.* October 16 or 17.

would have won out if the Greeks had not gained the upper hand more by treachery than by force. Since they considered our delay suspicious,[25] they did not dare to urge us to cross over, but, while taking away part of our market, they also incited us to cross by circulating rumors about the Germans. First they said that the Turks had assembled a huge army and that the Germans had killed 14,000 of these men without experiencing any loss. Two days later they further persuaded us to make the unfortunate crossing by reporting a happier event; for they said that the Germans had reached Iconium and that before they arrived the terrified populace of this city had fled. And since the Germans were hastening ahead, the one emperor wrote to the other, saying that he[26] should come and by maintaining the defense should take possession of what had been conquered without effort on his part.[27] The army was aroused by these goads, and they murmured against the king's delay, for some envied the Germans' wealth and others their fame. Thus overcome, both by the advice of the Greeks and the complaints of his own men, the king crossed before the arrival of those he was awaiting;[28] and the emperor prepared a fleet with speed which equaled his great eagerness for this move.

Now the king spent five days[29] on the nearer side of the Arm, awaiting part of his army, and also five days on the other side,[30] enduring the craftiness of the Greeks. They now had the opportunity which they had anticipated, and they dared to disclose their schemes, but our men's folly allowed them to conceal their wickedness; thus many have characterized the Greeks' actions toward us as revenge, not malice. The man who knows a case partially makes a partial judgment, but the man who does not know the entire case cannot make a just judgment. Actually the Greeks could be injured, but not appeased. And so we made the crossing, and food ships, with money changers aboard, followed us. The money

[29] Although the manuscript reads *quindecim*, Kugler, *Studien*, pp. 146–47, n. 106, points out correctly that since Louis' letter to Suger from Constantinople shows that they arrived on October 4 and since the date of the eclipse during which they marched forth into Asia Minor was October 26, the Franks were in the neighborhood of Constantinople for 23 days. Of these he thinks that Louis spent thirteen days in his official stay at Constantinople, five additional days awaiting the people coming from Apulia, and five days on the coast of Asia Minor before he began to march.

[30] These references to "the nearer side" and "beyond" appear to have been written from the point of view of the reader in France.

tur. Sternunt gazas in littore; fulgent auro tabulae, vasisque argenteis quae a nostris emerant onustantur.[h] Veniunt de exercitu qui
cambiunt necessaria, iunguntur et illis qui ambiunt non sua. Igitur
una die Flandrensis quidam, dignus flagris et flamma, cernens immensas divitias et immoderata cupiditate caecatus, clamat "Havo!
havo!"[i] rapiens quod cupivit; et audacia[j] pariter et praedae pretio
sibi similes ad nefas animavit. Et quoniam ubique stulti erant[k]
(in concambio enim quot otiosi[l] tot stulti), corruunt ubique qui
pecunias in promptu habebant. Crescit clamor et[m] furor, corruunt
exedrae, conculcatur aurum et rapitur. Metu mortis cambitores
fugiunt spoliati,[n] navesque suscipiunt fugitivos; et subductae
littori referunt ad urbem qui cibos emebant nostrorum plurimos.
Verberantur isti et spoliantur. Civitas quoque quos hospites habuit
quasi hostes spoliavit.

Fiunt haec nota regi, succensusque ira, requirit maleficum; qui,
a comite Flandrensi redditus, in prospectu civitatis ilico est suspensus. Deinde festinat quaerendo perdita, reddentibus donando veniam, celantibus comminando[o] similem poenam; et ne suam praesentiam timerent[p] vel erubescerent, iussit ut episcopo Lingonensi
omnia redderent. Revocantur in crastinum qui pridie fugerant, et
quod se iurare poterant perdidisse plenarie rehabebant. Requirebant plurimi amplius quam deberent; sed rex maluit quod defuit de
suo restitui[q] quam pacem sui exercitus violari.

Quo facto, eligit qui suos et quae perdiderant ab imperatore
requirerent et exercitui forum reducerent, Arnulfum Luxoviensem,[r]
episcopum eloquentia et religione praeclarum, et Bartholomeum
cancellarium. Et quoniam rex urgebat, qui semper festinus erat

[h] honestantur CM.	[n] sporiati > spoliati Dx.
[i] haro M.	[o] *second* n *over erasure* D1.
[j] audacio > audacia D1.	[p] timeb- > timer- D1.
[k] eunt CM.	[q] restui D.
[l] occisi CM.	[r] luxorvensem > luxoviensem D1.
[m] *om.* CM.	

---

[31] Du Cange, *op. cit.*, considers that this word comes from L. *habere* and Fl. *have* (wealth);
this derivation would accord with the fact that the robber was Flemish. Migne identifies
havo with *haro*, which was used in raising a hue and cry.

[32] Theobald, count of Flanders 1127–68, gained that position by enlisting the aid of the
communes of Flanders against William Clito, who died defending his position. The crusade
of 1147 was one of his four trips to the East. For further information about his life see
H. Pirenne, *Histoire de Belgique* (Brussels, 1902), I, 183–85.

[33] This solution of the difficulty shows the weakness of Louis' discipline in the army.
His generosity at this time and later (pp. 125, 137, below) resulted in many urgent demands

changers displayed their treasures along the shore; their tables
gleamed with gold and were groaning with the silver vessels which
they had bought from us. From the army came people who were
bartering for necessities, and they were joined by men who coveted
the supplies of others. One day, therefore, a certain Fleming, fit
to be scourged and burned in Hell, seeing the great wealth and
blinded by immoderate greed, cried, "Havo! havo!"[31] seizing
what he wished. And by his boldness, as well as by the value of
the loot, he incited men like himself to crime. And since there
were fools on every side (for in money changing there are as many
idlers as fools), those who had money on hand rushed away in all
directions. The noise and confusion increased, the stalls came falling down, the gold was trampled on and seized. In fear of death
the despoiled money changers fled, and, as they fled, the ships took
them on board; and when the ships left they brought back to the
city many of our people who were aboard purchasing food. Those
men were beaten and plundered. Also the city plundered her guests
as if they were enemies.

These circumstances were made known to the king, and, in-
flamed with wrath, he demanded possession of the criminal, who,
when surrendered by the count of Flanders,[32] was hanged right on
the spot, within full view of the city. Then the king made haste
to search for the lost goods, to pardon those who returned them,
to threaten those concealing them with punishment like the Fleming's; and, so that they might not be frightened or shamed by his
presence, he ordered them to return everything to the bishop of
Langres. On the morrow the money changers who had fled the
day before were recalled, and they got back in full what they could
swear they had lost. Most of them asked more than they ought;
but the king preferred to restore the missing articles from his own
property rather than to disturb the peace of his army.[33]

Following this restitution he chose as envoys, who were to demand from the emperor the return of Louis' men and their goods
and the restoration of a market to the army, Arnulf of Lisieux, a
bishop very eminent because of his eloquence and piety, and
Bartholomew the chancellor. And since the king, who was always

on Suger for money. See, for example, the letters written by Louis from Hungary, Constantinople, and Antioch, RHGF, XV, 487–88, 499–501.

errata corrigere,[s] satis mane transfretaverunt et aedituum gratia
palatium intraverunt, sed loqui cum idolo[t] nequiverunt. Illo die
fuit alter alteri pro solatio, intuitus picturarum pro cibo et, instanti
nocte, marmoreum pavimentum pro culcitra vel lecto. Sequenti
vero die, cum profanus [28v] ille circa tertiam surrexisset, vocati
veniunt ante illum, sobrii et insomnes, suam legationem absolven-
tes et de satisfactione suorum et de querela nostrorum; fecissetque
eum episcopus satis tractabilem prudenti eloquentia et suavi, si
posset serpens ille ab aliquo incantari; sed aspidis more surdus et
veneno turgidus, mutatus est ab illo quem antea viderant, immo
detectus quem sub doli tegmine prius non cognoverant. Tamen
instat episcopus, et ex parte praevalet; habet forum exercitus, et
peregrinis suis rebus perditis patet egressus. Dicit ille se adhuc cum
rege locuturum et cito nuntios praemissurum. Urget episcopum
regredi privata necessitas, ne cum eo faceret triduanum ieiunium.

Ille bonum adhuc simulat ut amplius noceat, exhibens forum—
sed parce, locuturus cum rege—sed tarde. Dum ergo mittit nuntios
et remittit plures dies pertranseunt, et Franci quod ad viam[u] prae-
paraverant comedunt. Volebat regem ad suum palatium regredi;
rex in sua ripa[v] vel in mari ex aequo[w] colloquium fieri. Tandem
quod caute distulerat per nuntios revelavit; et regis cognatam,
quam regina secum habebat, cuidam nepoti suo[x] coniugem sibique
baronum hominium requisivit. Ob hoc duces itineris et ubique
forum et concambium competens promittebat. Ubi hoc non haberent[y] praedarentur; si castrum vel civitas negarent huiusmodi cape-
rentur, sed[z] sumptis spoliis sibi vacuae dimitterentur. Offerebat

[s] erat errata corrigere *over erasure* Dx.   [w] ex equo CM.
[t] ioolo > idolo Dx.   [x] suo nepoti CM.
[u] viani > viam D1.   [y] har- > hab- D1.
[v] in suam ripam DCM.   [z] si CM.

[34] Again, on p. 91, Manuel is referred to as "the idol." This term probably results from
the fact that the Byzantine emperor, clothed in his elaborate jeweled vestments, treated as
a representative of Christ and as a sacred priest, and surrounded by extreme adulation and
ceremony, may have reminded Odo of an idol worshiped by the Greeks.
[35] Cf. Psalms 58:4.
[36] That Manuel desired this homage from the time when he first heard of the crusading
movement we know by his statement to Eugenius (see above, p. 10, n. 31) that he wished to
treat the crusaders as Alexius had treated them.

quick to correct mistakes, urged them on, they crossed early in the morning and were admitted to the palace by the doorkeepers, but they were not able to speak with the "idol." [34] On that day the envoys had to solace each other; looking at pictures took the place of food, and at night the marble pavement was a substitute for a mattress or bed. On the following day, however, after that impious man had risen at about the third hour, when at his summons they came into his presence without having eaten or slept, they carried out the aim of the embassy concerning both the reparation to his men and the complaint of ours; and with wise and gentle eloquence the bishop would have rendered the emperor tractable if that serpent could have been charmed by anyone; but, deaf and swollen with poison as an adder, [35] he had changed from the man whom they had seen before, or, rather, the man stood revealed whom they had not known previously because he was hidden behind a veil of deceit. Nevertheless, the bishop was insistent, and he prevailed in part; the army obtained a market, and a way of departure lay accessible to the pilgrims who had lost their goods. The emperor said that he would still confer with the king and would soon dispatch messengers. Then the bishop's own need forced him to withdraw before he should have to fast for the third day in the emperor's palace.

The emperor still feigned kindness in order to be the more harmful, supplying a market—but a scanty one; intending to confer with the king—but too late. Thus, while he sent messengers to and fro more days elapsed, and the Franks ate the food which they had set aside for the journey. The emperor wanted the king to return to the palace; the king wanted the conference to take place on his side of the water or on the sea, where they would be on an equal footing. At last the emperor revealed by messenger the stipulations which he had cautiously deferred. He demanded two things: a kinswoman of the king's, who accompanied the queen, as wife for one of his nephews, and the homage of the barons for himself. [36] In return he promised guides and fair exchange and markets everywhere. Where they did not have these advantages the Franks might plunder; if a castle or a town refused aid of this kind, it might be seized, but, after it was plundered, it was to be released to him unoccupied. To the king, moreover, he offered

insuper regi munera digna rege et baronibus singulis suae congruentia dignitati.

His auditis, fuit iterum opus morarum, tum quia comes Morianensis et marchisus de Monteferrato (avunculi regis), Alvernensis comes, et plures alii quos expectabamus ultra urbem in conspectu nostro tentoria fixerant; tum quia barones de imperatoris quaestione dissentiebant. Graeci autem, qui solebant urgere transitum, prohibendo tardabant. Igitur egregii milites per montana dispersi, morae providentes et itineri, praedis replent exercitum Graecorum damno. Suis ementes navigium, offerunt igitur quod prohibuerant, traductique,[a] recipiunt quos expectaverant. Interea, [29r] dum quod requirebat imperator in dubio est, Perticensis comes Robertus, regis germanus, cognatam suam reginae clam subripit se cum quibusdam baronibus illius subducens hominio et cognatam suam nepotis eius matrimonio. Sic praecedit Nicomediam, et rex cum[b] episcopis et aliis baronibus imperatoris discutit causam. Dicebant quidam et maxime Lingonensis, "Ecce impius patefacit quod ante celaverat. Vestrum requirit hominium, quorum servus potuit extitisse, promittens turpiter quod victoria debuit acquisisse. Nos autem, carissimi, praeferamus commodis honestatem; obtineamus viribus quod ipse quasi cupidis et timidis pollicetur. Turpe est enim in praesenti tam gloriosum habere dominum et infideli facere hominium."

Alii vero, quorum numerus et ratio superavit, huiusmodi respondebant, "Et consuetudine post regem plures dominos habere possumus quorum feodos possidemus, sed illi fidem principaliter observamus. Si iudicamus hoc esse turpitudinem, deleamus consuetudinem. Nunc autem imperator, sibi timens, nostrum requirit hominium.[c]

---

[a] transductique M.   [b] Sic . . . cum D2.   [c] hominum M.

[37] Amadeus II, count of Maurienne, was the son of Humbert II of Maurienne and Gisèle of Burgundy. He went to Italy with Henry V in 1111 and was made a count of the Holy Roman Empire. Despite the enmity of his sister Adelaide of Savoy, who wished to obtain his land, he was friendly to his nephew Louis VII. While on the crusade he died at Nicosia in Cyprus on May 1, 1148. See L'Art de vérifier les dates, Part 2, Vol. XVII, pp. 163–64.

[38] William III, count of Montferrat, the son of Marquis Rainier of Montferrat and Gisèle of Burgundy, was a very zealous partisan of Conrad III and Frederick I. He was the father of William Long-Sword and the grandfather of Baldwin V of Jerusalem. See L'Art de vérifier les dates, Part 2, Vol. XVII, pp. 213–16.

[39] William VIII, count of Auvergne 1145–55, was forced from that position by his uncle William IX and assumed the title of William I, dauphin of Auvergne and count of Pui. He died in 1169. See L'Art de vérifier les dates, Part 2, Vol. X, pp. 136-37, 157–58.

[40] Wilken, op. cit., III, 151, suggests that Manuel kept back his demands on the French

kingly gifts, to each of the barons gifts appropriate to his estate.

After they had heard these conditions it was again necessary to delay, first because the count of Maurienne[37] and the marquis of Montferrat[38] (the king's uncles), the count of Auvergne,[39] and many others whom we were awaiting had camped outside the city, where we could see them; then, because the barons disagreed over the emperor's request. Moreover, the Greeks, who usually pressed people to cross, retarded the crossing by devising hindrances.[40] Therefore, eminent knights scattered throughout the mountains, providing for us during the delay and the journey, and by raids they replenished the army, to the loss of the Greeks. In buying a vessel for their followers they thus furnished what the Greeks had withheld, and, sailing across the Arm, they welcomed the men whom they had awaited. Meanwhile, when the emperor's demands were hanging fire, Robert, count of Perche,[41] the king's brother, secretly abducted his kinswoman from the queen's retinue, thereby releasing himself and certain barons from paying homage to the emperor and his relative from marrying the emperor's nephew. Thus he proceeded to Nicomedia, and the king discussed the emperor's offer with the bishops and the rest of the barons. Some said, and especially the bishop of Langres, "See! that wicked man is disclosing what he previously concealed. He asks homage from you, whose subordinate he might have been, promising basely what victory ought to have gained. However, dearly beloved, let us place honor before convenience; let us acquire by force the advantages he promises us as if we were timid and greedy men. When we already have such a noble lord, it is certainly disgraceful to do homage to an infidel."

Others, however, whose number and reasoning prevailed, replied in this fashion: "After the king we can, according to our custom, have many lords of whom we hold fiefs, but we maintain loyalty to him first and foremost. If we think this shameful, let us destroy the custom. Now, however, the emperor fearing for

until this last band of crusaders had come to Constantinople, so that he might use them as hostages.

[41] Robert I, count of Dreux 1132–84, also bore the title count of Perche because of his marriage in 1144 to Harvis of Evreux, the widow of the count of Perche. He was the third son of Louis VI. For further information see *L'Art de vérifier les dates*, Part 2, Vol. XI, pp. 459–63.

Si ergo turpe est nos ab eo timeri, si est inhonestum quod minoribus facimus nos facere imperatori, dimittamus. Si vero metus imperatoris vel mos nostrae consuetudinis nec regi facit iniuriam nec nobis verecundiam, acquiescamus nostrae consuetudini. Pro nostro commodo illius parcamus formidini. Velimus commoda providentes itineris necessitati. Nemo nostrum novit hanc terram; igitur opus est duce. Contra paganos properamus; Christianorum utamur pace.''

Dum haec aguntur omnes fere quos rex expectaverat transfretarunt; quorum nomina mihi dolor est recitari, quia mortes eorum immaturas aspexi (et esset forsitan legenti taedium qui quaerit utilitatis vel probitatis exemplum). Et quoniam solus imperator erat ulterius causa morandi, imperat rex castra moveri. Quod ille audiens, praemissis nuntiis, post eum properat, determinans quoddam castrum eorum colloquio; in quo sibi cavit vicini maris adunato navigio. Rex autem Alemannorum aemulus, quorum bonam famam laetus audierat, et similem festinanter quaerebat nec morari voluit nec colloquium respuit. Igitur exercitu pro- [29v] cedente[d] revertitur ducens secum baronum gloriam et militum multitudinem expeditam. Aegre tamen ferebat quod ille suorum hominium requirebat, sed Dei servitio putabat esse utile quod promittebat. Si Christianus esset illud sine aliqua exactione deberet, sed dicebat quod nostram gentem iam expertam suo regno timeret, et esset ante illos quicquid foret eis utile fugiendum si non eum facerent tali satisfactione securum. Rex autem contra paganos de festinatione succensus, ad illius voluntatem rigorem sui animi maluit inclinare quam Dei servitium aliqua occasione tardare.

Convenientes igitur pactiones prius exponunt, videlicet quod ei rex nec castrum nec civitatem quae sui iuris essent auferret. Satis

---

[d] praecedente CM.

[42] See above, pp. 41, 45, 57, 67, 79.

his own interests asks homage from us. If, therefore, it is shameful for us to be feared by him, if it is dishonorable to do for the emperor what we do for lesser lords, let us abandon the idea. If, however, the emperor's fear and our customary usage neither injures the king nor disgraces us, let us observe our custom. Let us dispel his fear in order to gain advantages for ourselves. As we look ahead to the exigencies of the journey, we want supplies. None of us is acquainted with this territory; therefore we need a guide. We are marching against the pagans; with Christians let us be at peace."

During this discussion nearly all the men the king had awaited crossed the Arm; to mention their names causes me grief, for I saw their untimely death (also the list would probably be tedious for the reader who is looking for an instance of usefulness or worth). And since only the emperor was causing further delay, the king gave orders to break camp. Hearing this, the emperor after sending messengers ahead hastened after the king, appointing a certain castle for their conference; and there he provided for his own safety by assembling a fleet on the sea nearby. Now the king, who was emulating the Germans of whose good repute he had been glad to hear, and immediately seeking a like reputation for himself, did not want to delay, but he did not refuse the conference. While the army advanced, therefore, he returned, taking along his chief barons and a troop of light-armed knights. Although he could hardly endure the emperor's demand for homage from his men, he thought, nevertheless, that his acquiescence would be advantageous to the service of God. If the emperor had been a Christian, he would have been under obligation to serve God without making any demands for himself; but he said that he feared our people, of whom he had already had experience in his realm,[42] and that if they did not reassure him with such guarantee he would have them deprived of all advantages. Since the king was excited about speeding against the pagans, moreover, he preferred to alter his firm purpose to fit in with the emperor's will, rather than to retard the service of God in any way.

On meeting, therefore, they first set forth the agreements, that is, that the king should not take from the emperor any stronghold or town which was under his jurisdiction. This reasonable and mod-

est haec rationalis[e] et modesta petitio quam subsequitur aeque
liberalis sed fallax promissio; ut enim paci regiae imperialis[f] gratia
responderet, adiecit quod duo vel tres optimatum suorum cum rege
procederent quem recto itinere conducentes forum competens ubique
ministrarent. Ubi autem hoc deesset, praedationes castrorum et
urbium captiones sine querela toleraret, si, sumptis spoliis, terra
illa[g] vacua remaneret. Tunc[h] temporis rex Rogerius Apuliensis
illum[i] importune et feliciter impugnabat et locis pluribus expugna-
bat.[j] Contra quem si regem nostrum sibi sociare potuisset, omnem
illi thesaurorum copiam effudisset;[k] sed cum eum nequiret ad hoc
flectere vel assidua prece vel incredibili promissione, de supradictis
alter alteri mutuo sese foedere sociavit. Deinde sumpto baronum
hominio et rege cum illis donis satis imperialibus honorato, hic
post exercitum properavit. Ille sacrilegus, novo periurio macula-
tus, exuto timore remansit, forum longo tempore necessarium paucis diebus exhibens et promissos duces itineris nunquam reddens.

Illo die sol vidit scelus quod ferre non potuit, sed ne videretur
illud aequare proditioni Dominicae, servivit mundo dimidius et
dimidius se abscondit. Cum igitur exercitus dimisso rege procede-
ret et solem in forma dimidii panis magna diei parte conspiceret,
verebatur ne ille qui super alios fide lucebat, dilectione fervebat,
spe superna tenebat proditione Graecorum aliqua portione sui lumi-
nis [30r] privaretur. Sed aliud accidit aeque dolendum; imperator
enim Alemannorum,[l] a duce suo proditus et in concavis montibus
clam relictus, multis suorum iaculis Turcorum confossis milibus
retrocedere compulsus est, sicut postea referemus. Quod postquam

---

[e] rationalibus CM.
[f] imperiralis D.
[g] illi C.
[h] Tunc *over erasure* D1.

[i] -is ill- *over erasure* D1.
[j] -bus ex- *over erasure* D1.
[k] effundisset > effudisset Dx.
[l] Alemannus W.

[43] See above, p. 59, n. 51.

[44] Kugler, *Studien*, pp. 146–47, believes that Louis' refusal to ally himself with Manuel
against Roger annoyed Manuel so much that he never sent the guides and soon stopped
sending supplies.

est request was followed by an equally generous, but false, promise; for in order to grant a favor which would form a counterpart to the king's agreement of peace the emperor added that two or three of his chief barons should go along to guide the king on the right route and to furnish a suitable market everywhere. When a market should be unavailable, however, he would willingly allow them to plunder castles and seize cities, if, when the spoils had been taken, the land should remain unoccupied. At that time King Roger of Apulia was attacking the emperor insistently and successfully and was conquering many places.[43] If the emperor could have gained our king as his ally against Roger, he would have lavished on him all the wealth in the treasury; but since he could not thus influence him, either by continuous requests or a promise in which faith could not be put, they entered upon an alliance concerning the aforesaid provisions. Finally, when homage had been exacted from the barons, when the king and the barons had been honored with gifts which were imperial in their generosity, Louis hastened after his army. The impious emperor, sullied with a new breach of faith, but relieved from fear, stayed behind, procuring for only a few days the market which was needed for a long time and never sending the guides which he had promised.[44]

On that day the sun saw a crime which it could not endure, but, so that this crime should not seem equal to the betrayal of the Lord, half of the sun gave light to the world and only half hid itself.[45] Thus, when the army was proceeding without the king and saw the sun shaped like a half loaf of bread for most of the day, it feared that the king, who above all others shone with faith, glowed with charity, and attained celestial heights because of hope,[46] had been deprived of some part of his light by the treachery of the Greeks. But something else, equally lamentable, happened; for the German emperor, betrayed and secretly abandoned in narrow mountain passes by his guide, had been forced to withdraw after many thousands had been killed by Turkish arrows, as we shall record hereafter.[47] Because we later learned its meaning, we

---

[45] For a very complete résumé of the literature pertaining to the eclipse see Bernhardi, *op. cit.*, p. 635, n. 18.

[46] This is evidently a reminiscence of the "faith, hope, and charity" of I Corinthians, 13:13.

[47] See below, pp. 89 ff.

didicimus quid significaret, caeleste prodigium rectius exposuimus, dicentes nostrum regem et Alemannum esse unum[m] solem, quoniam unius fidei lumine coruscabant, et hunc lucere dimidium et dimidii circuli radios abscondisse, quando, rege fervore solito tenente cursum, Alemanni retrocedebant.

Explicit Quartus

---

[m] unum esse CM.

have explained the heavenly phenomenon more correctly, saying that our king and the German emperor were one sun, since they shone with the light of one faith, and that half of the sun shone and half hid its rays because the Germans retreated while the king was proceeding with customary zeal.

End of Book Four

Incipit Quintus

Constantinopolis superba divitiis, moribus subdola, fide corrupta; sicut propter suas divitias omnes timet, sic est dolis et infidelitate omnibus metuenda. Si autem careret his vitiis, aere temperato et salubri fertilitate soli et transitu facili ad fidem propagandam posset locis omnibus anteferri. Habet enim Brachium sancti Georgii, quod fecunditate[a] piscium mare est et salsedine, fluvius quantitate, qui possit in die septies vel octies ultro citroque sine periculo navigari.

Ultra Romania est, terra latissima montibusque saxosis asperrima, meridiana sui[b] parte pertingens usque Antiochiam et in orientali habens Turciam. Quae cum tota esset iuris Graecorum,

[a] fer- > fec- D1.   [b] sua W.

ROUTE OF LOUIS VII..........
ROUTE OF CONRAD III_____
LOUIS VII & CONRAD III___.___

Beginning of Book Five

Constantinople is arrogant in her wealth, treacherous in her practices, corrupt in her faith; just as she fears everyone on account of her wealth, she is dreaded by everyone because of her treachery and faithlessness. If she did not have these vices, however, she would be preferable to all other places because of her temperate climate, rich fertility of soil, and location convenient for propagating the faith. In fact she commands the Arm of St. George, which is at one and the same time a body of water teeming with fish and salt and a stream so small that it can safely be crossed seven or eight times in one day.

Romania, a land which is very broad and exceedingly rugged with stony mountains, lies beyond, extending to Antioch on the south and bordering Turkey on the east. Although all Romania

hanc ex magna parte Turci possident, illis expulsis, aliam destruxe-
runt; ubi vero Graeci adhuc munitiones obtinent redditus partiun-
tur. Tali servitio retinent quod Francorum virtus, quia[o] Ierosoly-
mam conquisierunt, liberavit; et perdidisset omnia populus iners,
sed aurum auro redimens, diversarum gentium conductis militibus
se defendit. Semper tamen perdit (sed multa possidens, non potest
omnia simul), non enim sufficiunt alienae vires propriis destituto.
Quod nobis Nicomedia prima monstravit; quae sentibus et dumis
consita, ruinis sublimibus antiquam sui gloriam et praesentium
dominorum probat inertiam. Frustra iuvabat eam quidam maris
profluvius qui de Brachio consurgens post dietam tertiam in ea
terminatur.[d]

Ab hac viae tres dirigunt Antiochiam, quantitate dispares et
qualitate dissimiles. Quae vergit ad sinistram brevior est. Si
obstacula non haberet, et tribus hebdomadibus finiretur; sed post
dies duodecim praetendit [30v] Iconium, soltani[e] sedem, nobilissi-
mam civitatem, et post quinque alios, praeteritis[f] Turcis, terram
Francorum. Robustus ergo[g] exercitus, fide munitus et multitudine,
ista contemneret si non[h] nivibus montium in hieme terreretur. Quae
dexteram[i] tenet pacatior est et abundantior; sed marinis anfractibus
triplicem moram facit viantibus, habens fluvios et torrentes timen-
dos in hieme loco nivium et Turcorum. Media vero partis utriusque
commodis et dispendiis temperatur, breviori longior sed tutior,
longiori brevior et tutior sed pauperior. Igitur Alemanni qui nos
praecesserant facto schismate, plures cum imperatore ad sinistram
partem[j] sinistro auspicio per Iconium[k] tetenderunt; reliqui[l] vero
cum fratre illius ad dexteram versi sunt, consequentes omnia sini-
strorsum.[m] Nobis autem sors media cecidit, utriusque lateris infor-

[o] qui CM.
[d] terminantur C.
[e] solistam D; solistani CMW; *we should expect*
   soltani.
[f] civitatem . . . perterritis *crowded* D2; praeterritis MW
[g] autem CM.

[h] sed CM.
[i] dexteram *over erasure* D1.
[j] partes D.
[k] phiconium > per hiconium Dx.
[l] reuqui > reliqui D1.
[m] sinistrosum M.

---

[1] With the aid of the crusaders Alexius had regained Nicaea, Smyrna, the west and south
coasts of Anatolia as far as Antioch.

[2] The use of mercenaries had long been established among the Byzantines.

[3] Odo makes one of his rare geographical mistakes in locating the three routes at Nicomedia
instead of at Nicaea. The same confusion occurs above on p. 50, n. 28.

[4] See above, p. 51.

was formerly under Greek jurisdiction, the Turks now possess a
great part and, after expelling the Greeks, have devastated another part; but where the Greeks still hold castles the two peoples
divide the revenues. In such subjection the Greeks retain the territory the Franks procured because they went in quest of Jerusalem;[1]
and the lazy people would have lost all if they had not defended
themselves by importing knights from various nations, thus compelling gold to redeem gold.[2] Nevertheless, they always lose (but
since they possess much they cannot lose all at once), for mercenaries do not suffice a people without forces of its own. Nicomedia
first showed us this; set among thorns and brambles, her lofty ruins
testify to her former glory and her present masters' inactivity. In
vain does a certain estuary of the sea, which terminates in the city
three days after rising in the Arm, offer her the advantage of good
transportation.

From this city[3] three routes, unequal in length and unlike in
character, lead to Antioch. The one bearing to the left is the
shorter. Had it no drawbacks, it could be traveled in three weeks;
but after twelve days it arrives at Iconium, the Sultan's very fine
capital, and then, five days after passing the Turks, at the land of
the Franks. Now a strong army, secure in its faith and numbers,
would discount all that if it were not alarmed in winter by the
snow-clad mountains. The road bearing right is richer and more
peaceful; but, in following the broken coastline, it delays travelers
thrice over, since it crosses rivers and rushing streams which are as
much to be feared in the winter as are the snow and the Turks on
the first road. The middle route, however, is tempered by the advantages and disadvantages of the other two, since it is longer,
but safer, than the shorter route, and shorter and safer, but poorer,
than the longer route. Therefore the Germans who had preceded
us had separated.[4] Led by the emperor, the majority took the left-
hand route through Iconium, by ill luck;[5] with the emperor's
brother, however, the rest turned to the right, pursuing a course
which was unfortunate in every respect. Now the middle lot,
which mitigates the disadvantages of the other two, fell to us.

[5] Conrad explained the reason for his route to Wibald of Corvey, saying that he wished
to finish the expedition quickly and therefore took a short cut through the mountains which
the guides showed them. See RHGF, XV, 533.

tunio temperato. Cum igitur ad sinistram relicta Nicaea super
lacum ipsius sederemus, Graecorum[n] rumoribus stimulati post
Alemannos properare et prosperari,[o] ecce[p] viri nobiles ab eorum[q]
imperatore post regem missi supervenerunt, qui nobis illos refugisse
Nicaeam contra nostrum votum[r] et aestimationem flebiliter retulerunt.

Audientes hoc nostri cum stupore dolent et cum dolore stupent
tam robustum exercitum tam[s] subito defecisse et inimicos Dei et
nostros de nostris sociis tam leviter triumphasse.[t] Requiruntur illi
ordinem, modum, seu causam[u] tanti infortunii; sed omnia haec
forsitan dicuntur[v] improprie, siquidem confusio non habet ordinem, nec[w] excessus modum, nec[x] causam illud quod ratio aliqua
non praecedit. Habuit[y] tamen finem et principium malum utrumque, sicut hi qui casum illum potuerunt evadere docuerunt. Satis
iuste primo erant accusatores sui ipsorum, quod nimium in propriis
viribus confidebant qui Deum saepius et solito amplius offendebant.
Deinde Constantinopolitanum[z] idolum execrabantur, qui, cum dedisset eis viae conductorem et traditorem, quantum in ipso fuit
Christianorum fidem stravit, paganismum stabilivit, animos illorum timidos animavit, fervorem nostrorum[a] frigidavit. Ducti enim
Nicaeam a duce suo, iussi sunt octo dierum cibariis onustari, tali
viatico Iconium perventuri. Finitis autem diebus et escis, putabant
[31r] viam similiter finiendam; sed de illius infinitate obsessi montibus et eorum scopulis, immensi[b] possent capere coniecturam.[c]
Tamen a duce (immo a[d] truce) suo seducti, amplius de crastino in
crastinum usque in tertium patiuntur, et in montes invios longius
intruduntur. Tandem credens adhuc vivum exercitum iam sepul-
tum, proditor ille nocte per compendia sibi nota fugit, et ad praedam Turcorum maximam multitudinem convocavit. Diluculo igitur in sequenti, cum more solito signiferi[e] praevium suum, iam
irati in eum, quaererent nec invenirent, Turcos subito vident scopu-

[n] r- > g- D1.
[o] properari CM.
[p] om. CM.
[q] i- > e- D1.
[r] votum nostrum CM.
[s] om. W.
[t] t over erasure D1.
[u] seu c- over erasure of sine D1.
[v] et inserted CM.

[w] non > nec Dx.
[x] non > nec Dx.
[y] -buit . . . principium D2.
[z] constantinopolim > constantinopolitanum D1.
[a] fervorum nostrorum > fervorem nostrorum D1.
[b] immersi CM.
[c] comecturam > coniecturam Dx.
[d] om. CM.
[e] signiferi over erasure D1.

Thus, when, goaded on by Greek rumors to overtake and to take over in the Germans' footsteps, we had left Nicaea behind on the left and were camping beside the Nicene lake, suddenly there arrived German nobles[6] who had been sent after the king by their emperor and dolefully reported that, contrary to our desire and belief, the Germans had fled back to Nicaea.

On hearing this our men were grieved with stupefaction and stupefied with grief that such a strong army had failed so suddenly and that our enemies and God's had triumphed so easily over our allies. The Germans were asked about the order, method, and cause of such a great misfortune; but perhaps all of those inquiries were made improperly, since confusion actually has no order, aberration no method, and the unreasonable no cause. Nevertheless, each evil had a beginning and an end, as those who managed to escape that calamity told us. Rightly enough, they first accused themselves, because, trusting too much in their own powers, they were offending God more often and to a greater extent than usual. Then they cursed the idol of Constantinople,[7] who, by giving them a treacherous guide, had done as much as he could to prostrate the Christian faith, strengthen paganism, encourage the timid pagans, and cool our ardor. For, when conducted to Nicaea by their guide, the Germans were ordered to supply themselves with provisions for eight days; and on such provisions they were to reach Iconium. When the days and the food had come to an end, they thought that the road must end, too; but, hemmed in by mountain peaks, they could only hazard guesses as to where the route would stop. Yet, led farther astray by their leader (nay, rather, their bleeder), they suffered from morrow to morrow until the third day, and they pushed farther into the pathless mountains. Finally, believing that the army had been buried alive, the traitor fled at night by certain shortcuts which he knew, and he summoned a huge crowd of Turks to the prey. Therefore, at the dawn of the next day, when the standard-bearers, who were angry at him already, were looking as usual for their guide and did not find him, they suddenly saw that the Turks had occupied the mountain peaks; they were espe-

[6] Among them was Frederick of Suabia, according to William of Tyre, Babcock and Krey, *op. cit.*, II, 173.
[7] See above, p. 76, n. 34.

los montium occupasse; dolentes maxime quem quaerebant[f] sine sui sceleris digna mercede fugisse.

Fiunt haec nota imperatori tam relatione suorum quam solis. Consulit itaque in illo articulo sapientes suos, sed tarde, quia non erant de malo bonum sed de malis levius electuri. Procedendum erat vel recedendum, sed processum fames prohibebat et hostis et incognita montium labyrinthus, recessum aeque fames et opprobrii metus. In hoc tamen erat spes aliqua evadendi, sed cum turpitudine; in alio certa mors sine utilitate[g] vel laude. Quid igitur faciet virtus ieiuna? Fugiet in Dei servitio quae non solet in suo? Item procedit incassum ilico moritura, quae adhuc servire Deo poterit conservata? Mallet certo[h] mortem gloriosam quam turpem vitam, sed si utramque maculat turpitudo,[i] melius est strenuis actibus turpiter conservari quam turpiter sine correptione finiri. Tali consideratione cedentes, Alemanni faciunt quod non solent; recessum damnantes, iudicio concedentes pro tempore correctionis, intuitu faciunt quod possunt, volunt quod debent. Armantur itaque omnes ad tolerantiam contra famem (habentes ad esum fessos et morientes equos) et quidam comes egregius, Bernardus nomine, solus[j] cum suis ad militiam contra persequentes inimicos.[k] Dum sic redeunt ordinati, augent dietas cibos quaerentes, et minuunt vires labor et esuries. Turci vero paulatim eos temptabant, et, debilitate cognita,

[f] quem querebant D2.
[g] veritate CM.
[h] certe CM.
[i] turpito > turpitudo D1.

[j] quemdam comitem egregium bernardum nomine solum CM.
[k] W *suggests:* quaedam deesse videntur; *this is not true, however,* if armantur *is carried over to this clause also.*

[8] Odo's account of this entire incident, hinging as it does upon the treachery of the guide, is similar to that of William of Tyre, translated Babcock and Krey, II, 168–72. It is not borne out, however, by the evidence furnished by Conrad to Wibald (RHGF, XV, 533). From this letter we learn the following important facts: that Conrad took a short-cut in order to bring the expedition to a quick conclusion (not that he was led astray by the will of the guides); that the Germans assembled the provisions that were available (not that they were limited by the guides to the specific amount that would provide for eight days); that he does not mention the departure of the guides, evidently thinking it an incident of minor importance; that he does not, therefore, link the appearance of the Turks with activity on the part of the guides. Cf. Bernhardi, *op. cit.,* pp. 629–33, on this topic. Inasmuch as Conrad was actually present throughout and it would have been easy for him to explain the defeat by shifting the blame to the Greek guides, his account seems preferable. Odo got his material second-hand, and William's information was even further removed from the source, because he wrote after a considerable length of time. According to Cinnamus, *op. cit.,* II, 16, the Turks were the forces of Mamplanes the Persian. William of Tyre, *op. cit.,* II, 172, names the Turkish satrap Paramus as commander.

[9] It is at this point that Cinnamus, *ibid.,* tells of a struggle between the Turks and the Germans, during which the German cavalry charged their foes violently, the Turks feigned flight until they had tired the Germans and drawn them away from the rest of the army

cially grieved that the man whom they sought had fled without receiving a reward befitting his crime.[8]

These facts were made known to the emperor, not only by the return of his men, but also by the light of the sun. Therefore in that extremity he consulted his council, but it was too late, because they had to choose, not good from evil, but the lesser of two evils.[9] They had to advance or retreat, but hunger and the enemy and the unknown mountain labyrinth kept them from advancing; and hunger and fear of dishonor kept them from retreating. In retreat, nevertheless, there was some hope of escape, though with shame; in advance, death without profit or honor was certain. What, therefore, will their starving valor do? Shun, in the Lord's service, what they are not accustomed to shun in their own? Will they who could serve the Lord if preserved, advance to die then and there in vain? Certainly they would prefer a glorious death to a base life, but if baseness stains both alternatives it is better to be saved basely by prompt action than to die basely, though without reproach. Yielding to this consideration, the Germans did what they usually do not; condemning the retreat, but agreeing to it, since the time called for reformation,[10] they therefore did what they could, they wished what they ought.[11] And so all were armed to endure hunger (since they had merely the feeble and dying horses to eat), and only a certain Count Bernard[12] and his men were armed to combat the pursuing enemy. While they retired thus in order, the people increased the length of the journey by trying to acquire food, and exertion and hunger diminished their strength. The Turks tested the crusaders gradually, however, and,

and then killed many of them. Kugler, *Studien*, p. 154, n. 19, considers that Conrad's silence on this point in the letter to Wibald is compensated for by his description of the suffering of the crowd on foot at this time. The skirmish related by Cinnamus is typical of the encounters between the crusaders and Turks (cf. the retreat of the Germans to Nicaea and the instructions which the Templars gave to the Franks in the Laodicea neighborhood, pp. 95 and 125, below); and it would be a more urgent reason for the retreat than would hunger and fear of the Turks, an enemy whom they had not yet met in battle.

[10] Hebrews 9:10.

[11] Conrad tells Wibald (*loc. cit.*, XV, 533) that he grieved over the death of his people and at the request of all the princes and nobles led his army toward the sea, so that it might be refurbished, preferring to keep it intact for greater events than to triumph over the archers with a victory which would be so bloody for the Germans.

[12] Count Bernard of Plötzkau, a Saxon noble. I have not been able to find further information about his life. For other accounts of this incident see *Annales Palidenses, loc. cit.*, XVI, 82–83; *Annales Magdeburgenses, loc. cit.*, p. 188.

de die in diem acrius infestabant. Tandem comes illustris, laude dignus et luctu, dum fessos expectat, dum supportat debiles, [31v] exercitus quendam montem pertransiit,[1] et ipse nocte superveniente ultra remansit. Quem ibidem Turci a longe circueunt[m] et sagittant et sine damno suorum occidunt levius quam sperabant;[n] carebat enim vir ille[o] arcubus et balistis, famesque et labore abstulerat veloces equos[p] armatis.[q] Nolebant Turci manu ad manum congredi; nec ille habebat arma quibus a longe posset defendi; nec armatos in hostes ferre poterant equi ieiuni. Plangenda nimis est iuventus agilis, quae, saepius[r] extracto gladio, vervecum pelles habens pro scuto, dum velociter et audacter currit in hostem in medio itinere offendit mortem volantem. Dum papa sanctus accipitres et canes prohibuit armisque militum et vestibus modum imposuit, sicut iussit sapienter et utiliter, sic qui eius imperio non consensit stulte et inutiliter. Sed aeque utinam pedites instruxisset, retentisque debilibus, fortibus quibusque pro pera gladium et pro baculo arcum dedisset; quia semper debiles et inermes suis sunt onus hostibus praeda.

In crastinum comes[s] requiritur, qui ad defensionem suorum ultro se solebat offerre, et discitur illum sero ad exercitum non venisse sed in via cum suis Turcorum iaculis interisse. Plangunt omnes mortem illius, de cuius viribus et consilio plurimum confidebant, et quia mors similis imminet[t] universis. Armantur itaque omnes qui poterant, et, fame et hoste solito acrius debacchante, properant. Turci enim iam nihil a longe metuunt, ubi arcus non esse et equos veloces agnoscunt. Ergo non solum postremos urgebant, sed etiam primos et medios sagittabant. Non possum describere damna itineris in quo ipse imperator vulneratus est[u] duabus sagittis; ubi prope-

---

[1] pertransit W.	[q] et labore . . . ar *crowded* D2.
[m] circuunt D1.	[r] u- > se- D1.
[n] sperant CM.	[s] comes *over erasure of* omnes D1.
[o] ille vir CM.	[t] immineret CM.
[p] equos veloces CM.	[u] *om.* CM.

---

[13] Cf. Eugenius' letter to Louis (RHGF, XV, 430). The Pope urged Louis to see that his men provided themselves with arms, horses, and other equipment with which they might fight the enemy, rather than with costly or finely cut garments, dogs, falcons, and other things which give luxurious pleasure.

[14] *Annales Palidenses, loc. cit.*, p. 83, state that Conrad had been wounded in the head by an arrow and was incapacitated for a long time.

as their weakness became apparent, molested them the more cruelly
from day to day. At last, while the distinguished count, to be
praised and to be lamented, was attending the weary and support-
ing the weak, the army crossed a certain mountain, but he remained
on the other side, since it was almost night. Then and there the
Turks from afar surrounded him and shot arrows and, without
damage to themselves, killed him more easily than they had hoped;
for that man had neither bows nor arbalests, and hunger and toil
had deprived his knights of swift horses. The Turks did not wish
to engage in a hand-to-hand struggle; he did not have weapons
with which a long-range attack could be warded off; and the fam-
ished horses could not carry his knights against the enemy.
Greatly to be lamented is the fate of these active youths who,
midway in their course, encountered winged death instead of the
enemy against whom they were running swiftly and boldly with
oft-drawn swords and using sheep-skins for shields. When the
Holy Father forbade dogs and falcons and restricted the nature of
knights' arms and clothing,[13] men who did not concur with this
command acted with a lack of wisdom and utility which equaled
the presence of wisdom and utility in his command. But, would
that he had instructed the infantry in the same way and, keeping
the weak at home, had equipped all the strong with the sword instead of the wallet and the bow instead of the staff; for the weak
and helpless are always a burden to their comrades and a source of
prey to their enemies.

The next day they looked for the count, who often defended his
people without the aid of others, and they learned that he had not
been late in coming to the army, but that on the way he and his
men had perished at the hands of the Turkish bowmen. Since they
relied greatly on his strength and wisdom and since a similar death
was threatening them all, everyone lamented his death. All who
were able took arms, and they hastened on, pursued more fiercely
than ever by hunger and by the enemy. Actually, since they knew
that the crusaders had no bows or swift horses, the Turks no longer
stayed away fearfully. Then they not only harassed the rear guard
but even shot arrows into the vanguard and the center of the army.
I cannot describe the losses on that journey, during which the emperor himself was wounded by two arrows[14] and where, while the

rantibus aliis remanent debiles, et in turba media pluvia sagittarum
necat inermes. Sic tandem venere Nicaeam morientes. Ibi currunt[v]
ad escas famelici quas, sicut in tali necessitate poterant, nimium
caras vendebant Graeci, spathas[w] et loricas requirentes non aurum,
ut penitus nudarent exercitum. Cuius pars maxima, viribus con-
sumptis et rebus perditis, repatriare volens, Constantinopolim[x]
ivit; sed antequam[y] possent habere vel forum vel transitum, eorum
plus quam triginta milia, sicut audivimus, [32r] fames occidit.
Imperator vero, solatio destitutus humano et praesumens adiutorium de divino, constanti animo tendit post regem, ad Dei servitium eius expetens societatem. Quem ab eo praemissi nuntii super
lacum Nicaenum, sicut praedictum est, invenerunt, et ei quae
descripsimus retulerunt, rogantes ut occurrat obviam subsequenti
praestaturus opem et consilium indigenti. Rex autem damnum
socii sicut proprium doluit, et cum multo baronum comitatu eius
personae et precibus libenter et celeriter obviavit. Amplexantur
igitur alter alterum, et infigunt oscula quae rorabant lacrimae pie-
tatis. Tandem statuunt ut[z] rex imperatorem ad castrum quod
Lupar dicitur expectaret et ille post[a] istum, sumptis in Nicaea
cibariis, festinaret.

De hinc coeperunt Graeci nostris forum subtrahere, sed illi non
poterant videre[b] opulentiam et esurire. Dispersi ergo plurimi,
rapiebant quod libentius emerent, et alii praedas emebant ab eis
quasi iustiores si quoquo modo de suo viverent. Sic veniunt ad
Lupar, ubi ex condicto Alemannos expectant; quos subsequentes
"ut residuum bruchi locusta comederet" cotidie Graeci rebus et
vita spoliabant. Tandem fessus imperator et eques cum non possent
evadere licet pauci essent inimici, armis viriliter resistendo descen-

---

[v] *so* D, *not* cucurrunt *as noted* W.   [z] quod W.
[w] poterant . . . spatas *over erasure and much crowded* D2.   [a] post *over erasure* D1.
[x] Constantipolim D.   [b] videre poterant W.
[y] sed antequam *much crowded* D2.

[15] Probably on November 2 or 3. With his customary thoroughness, Bernhardi, *op. cit.*,
p. 639, n. 22, gives bibliographical references for this arrival.

[16] The nature of this rather extravagant tale is indicated by "we have heard."

[17] The phrase "the king of the Franks came to our camp without our knowledge" in
Conrad's letter to Wibald, *loc. cit.*, p. 534, has been explained by Kugler, *Studien*, p. 157,
n. 29, not as a contradiction of Odo's tale of the German messengers, but as an indication
that Conrad did not know that Louis was so near him at that time. William of Tyre's account is similar to Odo's. See Babcock and Krey, *op. cit.*, II, 173.

[18] Conrad described the aid which Louis gave him (the letter to Wibald, *loc. cit.*, p. 534)

rest were hastening on, the weak remained behind and, in the midst of the tumult, a rain of arrows killed these defenseless men. Thus at last the dying Germans came to Nicaea.[15] There the starving people rushed for food, and the Greeks, as they could in such time of need, sold it very dear, demanding in payment cuirasses and swords instead of gold, in order to strip the army bare. Wishing to return home, the greatest part of the army, with strength exhausted and possessions lost, went to Constantinople; but before the men could obtain either a market or a means of crossing, hunger killed more than 30,000, we have heard.[16] But the German emperor, deprived of human comfort and trusting in divine aid, hastened after the king with a constant heart, to seek comradeship in the service of God. The messengers sent ahead by him encountered the king at the Lake of Nicaea, as has been said already, and they told him the events we have described, asking him to go to meet the emperor, who was following, and to be ready to give aid and advice to him in his time of need.[17] Now the king mourned his ally's injury as if it were his own and, with a great train of barons, swiftly and gladly came to him and heard his requests.[18] Then they embraced each other and exchanged kisses which tears of pity bedewed. At last they decided that the king should wait for the emperor at the castle of Lupar[19] and that the emperor, after acquiring supplies in Nicaea, should hasten after the king.

From this time on the Greeks began to withdraw our market, but the Franks could not bear to see plenty and be in want. Scattering over the countryside, therefore, a great many of them seized what they would rather have bought, and others bought this booty from them, as though they were more righteous if they lived at their own expense in any way. Thus they came to Lupar, where by agreement they awaited the Germans; these, as they followed, the Greeks despoiled daily of life and possessions,[20] "just as the locust consumes what the wingless locust has left."[21] At last the exhausted emperor and his knights, unable to escape, even though their enemies were few, with courageous resistance went wretch-

as respectful kindness and the offer of money and other possessions. The Frankish nobles also participated in this offer.

[19] Lopadium.

[20] Evidently a reprisal for Frankish plundering.

[21] Joel 1:4.

derunt in via misere procedentes animosius tolerando. Pauperes vero, qui non impediebantur ad fugam sarcinis, post regem properant, non timentes cupidos gratia paupertatis.

Imperator etiam illi per nuntios supplicat ut cum militari manu in obviam cito recurrat vel eorum cadavera sepelire vel semivivis vitae particulam custodire. Igitur conestabulus Ivo de Niella, Suessionensis comes, ad hoc urgente rege festinando laboravit, sed fessos Alemannos Graecis fugientibus sine labore liberavit. Et certe, sicut ipsi postea referebant,[c] nisi conestabulus tam cito venisset, omnes in horam et locum mortis inciderant. Heu quam miseranda fortuna Saxones Batavosque truces et alios Alemannos quos, in antiquis historiis legimus, quondam Romanam fortitudinem timuisse, nunc[d] dolis Graecorum inertium tam miserabiliter interisse! Referetur [32v] quoque suo tempore Francorum occasus, et erit intolerabilis geminus luctus; et habebunt gentes utraeque quod semper defleant, si filii mortes parentum non vindicant. Dat autem nobis qui pertulimus Graecorum scelera divina iustitia spem vindictae[e] et quod nostrae gentes non solent verecundas iniurias diu ferre. His interim maestos animos consolamur et, ut sciant posteri Graecorum dolosa facinora, nostra infortunia prosequemur.

Imperatore igitur ad regis tentoria conducto et in partem alteram cuiusdam fluminis hospitato, rex eundem navibus transiit et ad illum consolandum, animosus et pius, virilis et flebilis, pedes venit. Quem ille, sicut naufragus portum tenens, verba eius nimis gratanter suscepit, et ab eo quibus egebat valde humiliter postulavit. Eventus[f] suos sic incipiens satis constanter exposuit: "Domine rex, quem natura mihi vicinum praestitit et cognatum et Deus servavit in necessitate patronum, referre vobis meos casus me non oportet, quia supervacuum est monstrare alicui quod iam videt. Mali quidem sunt; sciatis autem quod inde non irascor Deo sed mihi;[g] Deus enim iustus, ego vero et populus meus stulti. Cum de meo regno

---

[c] ferebant CM.

[d] nec D. *This is evidently another example of the confusion of the abbreviation of* nunc *and* nec *on the part of the scribe. Cf. also p. 90, notes w and x.*

[e] divin- > vind- D1.

[f] que *inserted* CM.

[g] mer > mihi D1.

---

[22] Ivo of Nesle was count of Soissons 1146–78. For further information see *L'Art de vérifier les dates*, Part 2, Vol. XII, pp. 257–59.

[23] Pages 113 ff.

[24] Typical of the spirit of the age is the fact that, despite the account of the disorder and rashness of the Germans, Conrad recounts his folly and that of his people in terms of their

edly along the road, advancing only by enduring bravely. However, the poor, whose flight was not hindered by baggage, hastened
after the king, not fearing the greedy, for they were poor.

In a message the German emperor now asked the king to meet
him swiftly with a military force that would bury the German
dead and preserve the small spark of life remaining in those who
were still partly alive. Therefore, at the urgent request of the king,
Constable Ivo of Nesle,[22] count of Soissons, hastened to the task,
and, by putting the Greeks to flight, easily freed the exhausted
Germans. And truly, as the Germans later said, if the count had
not come thus swiftly, all of them would have encountered the
hour and the place of their death. Alas, what a pitiable fortune
that the fierce Saxons, Batavians, and other Germans whom, as we
read in ancient histories, Roman valor formerly feared, had now
perished so miserably because of the treachery of the indolent
Greeks! At the proper time the fall of the Franks will also be
recorded,[23] and the twofold grief will be unbearable; and both nations will always have something to bewail if the sons of these
men do not avenge their parents' death. To us who suffered the
Greeks' evil deeds, however, divine justice, and the fact that our
people are not accustomed to endure shameful injuries for long,
give hope of vengeance. Thus we comfort our sad hearts, and we
shall follow the course of our misfortunes so that posterity may
know about the Greeks' treacherous actions.

Therefore, when the emperor had been escorted to the king's
camp and lodged on the bank of a stream, the king crossed the
stream by boat and, spirited yet pious, vigorous yet tearful, went
on foot to comfort him. The emperor received his words with joy,
just as a shipwrecked man on reaching port, and he asked him most
humbly for the things which he needed. Beginning thus, he disclosed his own vicissitudes calmly: "O Lord King, whom nature
has appointed to be my neighbor and friend and whom God has
preserved to protect me in time of need, it is not meet for me to
relate my misfortunes to you, because it is superfluous to show
anyone what he sees already. They are evil indeed, but know that
I am not therefore angry at God, but at myself; for God is just,
but I and my people are foolish.[24] When I conducted a numerous

relation to God, not to man.

numerosum exercitum et pecuniosum educerem, si bonorum Largi-
tori dignas gratias redderem, forsitan qui dederat conservasset.
Intraturus barbaras regiones, si de praesenti vitam corrigerem et
de praeterito pia satisfactione deflerem, Deus correpta vitia non
punisset. Cum de Turcis victorias praesumebam, si de meo numero
non tumerem,[h] sed in Deo exercituum humiliter spem haberem,
Deus non inventam contumaciam non domasset. Adhuc tamen sua
gratia sanus sum, et divitias habeo, et in voluntate sui servitii
persevero, credens quia de tot periculis dives et incolumis non
exissem nec vos in mortis articulo ad meum suffragium invenissem
nisi me Deus adhuc valere aliquid in suo servitio providisset. Nolo
itaque deinceps a vestra societate seiungi nec, susceptus, primus vel
ultimus collocari, quia non possem hostes obvios propulsare nec
sequentes sine damno mediorum sufferre. [33r] His exceptis, quo
volueritis mea tentoria collocentur. Rogo autem ut de vestris
sociis meus numerus augeatur.''

   Cum haec interpretante Mettensi episcopo recenti dolore anxius
perorasset[i] et ad fletum viscera[j] omnium commovisset, rex episcoporum et baronum consilio suos avunculos Morianensem comitem
et marchisum de Monteferrato suosque cognatos Mettensem episcopum et fratrem eius comitem Renaldum et quosdam alios sibi sociavit; et ut e vicino posset ab illo consilium capere ambos simul
hospitari[k] debere iudicavit.

Explicit Quintus

---

[h] timerem D.   [j] via scera M.
[i] perforasset > perorasset Dx.   [k] hospa- > hospi- Dl.

and wealthy army from my realm, if I had rendered the proper thanks to the Giver of good things, perhaps He would have preserved His gift. When on the point of entering foreign countries, if I had corrected my present mode of life and in pious reparation had bewailed my past, God would not have punished my reprehensible faults. When reckoning on victories over the Turks, if I had not been puffed up on account of my large army, but had placed my hope humbly in the God of hosts, God would not have subdued an arrogance, which would not have existed. By His grace, nevertheless, I am still safe and have wealth; and I persevere in the desire to serve Him, because I believe that I would not have survived so many dangers rich and unharmed and would not have received aid from you at the very moment of death if God had not foreseen that I would still be of some worth in serving Him. Therefore I do not wish to be separated from your company hereafter or, when accepted by you, to be stationed either first or last, because I could not ward off the enemies in front or withstand those following us without injuring the soldiers in the middle line. With these exceptions, let my tents be pitched wherever you wish. I ask, however, that my numbers be supplemented by comrades of yours.''[25]

When, distressed by fresh grief, the emperor had finished speaking, with the bishop of Metz as interpreter, and had moved the hearts of all to tears, the king, on the advice of the bishops and the barons, associated with the emperor his two uncles, the count of Maurienne and the marquis of Montferrat, and his relatives,[26] the bishop of Metz and his brother, Count Renald, and certain others; and, so that he might conveniently make plans with the emperor, he decided that he and the emperor should be lodged together.

End of Book Five

---

[25] Bernhardi, *op. cit.*, p. 645, n. 29, advances the attractive hypothesis that this speech of Conrad's is genuine because it lacks the rancor which Odo invariably displays toward the Greeks. Cf. above, p. xxi.

[26] All were nephews of Calixtus II.

Incipit Sextus

Rex igitur, imperatorem diligens pro persona penes,[a] praeferens pro aetate, venerans pro fortuna, castra movit et post festum beati Martini ad castrum quod dicitur Eseron venit. Ego vero interim, dum recens est dolor, dum adhuc obsequii regii recordatur, regem adeo; iniurias quas beato Dionysio[b] faciebat de castro Estufin[c] et Hescelingis expono et excommunicationem quam de hoc papam audierat in Pascha facere ad memoriam reduco. Ille vero, exultans quod occasionem haberet suo patrono serviendi, non differt; sed ilico iubet sibi possessores horum monstrari. Cui ego respondi quod ipse imperator in castro turrem unam habebat et dux Fridericus aliam, qui praesens aderat, et cetera singulariter possidebat. Hoc audito requirit utrumque per se, per suos, prius privatim, deinde publice; pro se rogat, pro Deo placando et glorioso martyre hortatur, ex hoc familiares imperatoris sollicitans et sollicitando frequentans. Ille vero prius dubia respondebat, quia regem cessare ab incoepto taedio fatigatum sperebat; sed ipse ab honesta et religiosa postulatione non destitit donec ille quam irrevocabilis ab errore et quam ingratus esset beneficiis patefecit. Quamvis hoc non sit de nostra materia, pater Sugeri, tamen congruit ut sciatis quatinus pro illo qui vos praesens honorat et absens diligit devotius supplicetis.

Ceterum rex ex[d] proposito Philadelphiam properabat; et erat usque illuc[e] plana[f] via octo dierum sed plenarie victualia[g] non habebat. Quod intelligens imperator, cum rex praesens et barones

[a] pene sibi CM.
[b] *so* D, *not* Dioniosio *as noted* W.
[c] estusin D.
[d] ceterum rex > ceterum rex ex D1.

[e] *so* D, *not* illa *as noted* W.
[f] plena M.
[g] *so* D, *not* victalia *as noted* W.

---

[1] Sometime after November 11.
[2] The town of Esslingen in Suabia and Estusin (Königsberg) in Alsace were claimed by St. Denis because Fulrad, the fourteenth abbot of the monastery, had built and endowed cloisters in both places. Cf. Wilken, *op. cit.*, p. 175, n. 36. I have not found any special promulgation of the pope in relation to St. Denis and these possessions. Perhaps Odo was referring to some general pronouncement about the alienation of property.

Beginning of Book Six

Thus the king, esteeming the emperor as a personage, honoring his years, and respecting him because of his ill fortune, broke camp and arrived at the castle of Esseron after St. Martin's day.[1] But in the meantime, while the emperor's grief was fresh, while he still was mindful of the king's good offices, I went to the king; I disclosed how the emperor was injuring St. Denis in regard to Esslingen and the castle of Estusin, and I reminded him of the excommunication as punishment for such deeds which he had heard the pope promulgate on Easter.[2] Now the king, rejoicing at the opportunity of serving his patron saint, did not delay; on the contrary, he ordered that the holders of those places be indicated to him then and there. I replied that the emperor himself was holding one tower in the castle and that Duke Frederick,[3] who was also with us, held the other and had taken exclusive possession of Esslingen. On hearing this the king himself, and then his men, besought both Conrad and Frederick, first privately and then in public; importuning the emperor's friends and renewing his insistence about the matter, he asked it as a favor for himself, he urged it as a means of pleasing God and the glorious martyr. First, however, the emperor replied ambiguously because he hoped that the king would give up the undertaking if irked and wearied; but the king did not abandon his honorable and pious demand until the emperor showed how ungrateful for help he was, and how irrevocable from error. Although this is not part of our theme, Father Suger, it is proper for you to know that you may pray devoutly for him who, when present, shows you deference and, when absent, fosters your interest.

Now the king was hastening to Philadelphia, as he had planned, and toward that place there led a wide road which could be traversed in eight days but was not abundantly furnished with supplies. Knowing this, the emperor made a speech before the king

---

[3] For the life of Frederick of Suabia (Emperor Frederick I, 1152–90), see Otto of Freising, *Gesta;* Giesebrecht, *op. cit.*, Vols. V–VI; H. Prutz, *Kaiser Friedrich I* (3 vols.; Danzig, 1871–74).

adessent, de hoc sermonem habuit [33v] in quo nobis de sua fortuna, forsitan nescius, plenis phialis propinavit. "Sicut virtutis est," ait, "gesta fortia imitari,[h] sic prudentiae est de alieno infortunio cautum reddi.[i] Cum ego nuper exercitum haberem cui nulla gens incredula restitisset,[j] victus fame, cessit his quos habens victualia domuisset. In hoc autem nobis duobus est aequa conditio. Sicut non timetis gentis alicuius potestatem, sic non habetis iacula contra famem. Ecce vobis proponitur duplex via, una brevior sed egena, altera longior opulenta; sed certe melius est in opulentia diu honeste vivere quam cito turpiter in egestate perire; et[k] mora melior quae robustum[l] exercitum in abundantia servat quam illa quae fessum vel famelicum recreat. Unde vobis consulo quatinus maritima retineatis[m] et robus vestrae militiae ad Dei[n] servitium, licet tardius veniat, conservetis."

Annuit itaque rex sermoni magis verisimili[o] quam veraci; damna et pericula ilico perpessurus et ad Demetriam civitatem maritimam quo pars exercitus quae rectam viam tenuit die venit dimidia vix die tertia perventurus. Deviavit enim in quaedam concava, offendensque montium scopulos, dum eos circuit vel ascendit, non accedit quo volebat sed alternis vicibus inferno et sideribus propinquabat. Mane tertio vidimus villulam habentem rusticos socios beluarum, quorum unum fugientibus aliis cepimus; eiusque beneficio[p] eodem die ad nostros socios, de nobis[q] valde timentes, ante Demetriam[r] educti sumus. Primam vero iacturam et maximam fecimus in hos montes, mortuisque[s] summariis auro et argento, armis et vestibus valde[t] ditavimus Graecos silvestres, damnum hoc quia evasimus aequanimiter patientes; inerat enim ibi torrens sinuosus et rapidissimus quem oportebat in die novies vel octies transvadare,[u] qui, si modica pluvia paulo amplius tumuisset, nemo posset

[h] mutari D.
[i] reddit > reddi Dx.
[j] -so- > -sti- D1.
[k] est M.
[l] r- *over erasure of* ex- D1.
[m] teneatis CM.
[n] di > de D1.
[o] verissimi D.

[p] venen- > benefi- D1.
[q] de nobis de nobis > de nobis Dx.
[r] demetrias > demetriam Dx.
[s] mortuisque armis > mortuisque Dx.
[t] auro et ar- *written;* armis et vestibus valde *added* D1, *who began to write* arg-, *changed* g *to* m.
[u] transvadere M.

[4] Psalms 23:5.

and barons in which, perhaps unwittingly, he gave us to drink of the cup running over,[4] his own misfortune. "Just as a strong man," he said, "should imitate brave deeds, a wise man should be made wary by the misfortune of another. Although recently I had an army which no pagan race could have resisted, that army, when conquered by hunger, yielded to those whom it would have mastered had it been furnished with supplies. Now, in this our situation is the same. Although you do not fear the power of any people, yet you likewise do not have arrows which can subdue hunger. Behold, two roads are open to you; of these one is shorter, but meagerly supplied, the other longer, but abundantly supplied; yet surely it is better to live honorably for a long time amidst plenty than to perish swiftly and shamefully in want; and better is the delay in the midst of plenty, during which an army keeps strong, than that which revives a weary and starving army. Therefore I advise you to keep to the shore route and to preserve your knights' strength for the service of God, even though that service be somewhat delayed."

Accordingly, the king heeded this speech,[5] which was more plausible than true; for he was destined immediately to endure perils and injuries and with difficulty to arrive on the third day at the port of Edremid, where the part of the army following the direct route arrived in half a day. In fact, he wandered from the route into certain valleys and, while climbing or skirting the mountain crags which he found blocking the way, did not arrive where he wished, but alternately approached heaven and hell. Early on the third day we saw a hamlet of rustics, the companions of wild beasts, and we seized one, while the others fled; with his help we were led that same day toward Edremid, to our comrades who had been exceedingly anxious about us. We suffered our first and greatest loss among those mountains, and, as our pack animals died, we greatly enriched the Greek forest dwellers with gold and silver, arms and garments; this loss we bore patiently because we had escaped with our lives; for in that district there was a winding, exceedingly swift torrent which we had had to cross eight or nine times every day, and, if it had swollen a little more, even with a moderate rain, no one could have advanced or retired, but each

[5] That is, he chose the coast road rather than the more direct one to Philadelphia.

procedere vel redire, sed erat necesse[v] quemque in loco suo lugendo
peccata vitae terminum expectare.

Post haec sumus redditi marinis anfractibus, saxosos montes et
arduos fere cotidie inventuri et torrentium [34r] defossos alveos
quos erat labor etiam vacuos pertransiri[w] et si nivibus vel imbribus
augerentur, non esset possibilis eorum rapacitas ab equite vel pedite
transnatari. Ibi multas urbes destructas invenimus et alias quas
ab antiqua latitudine supra mare Graeci restruxerant,[x] munientes
eas muris et turribus. Ab his escas habebamus, cum labore quidem
propter nostrae multitudinis[y] importunitatem et nimis care propter
illorum cupiditatem. Sed dicet forsitan aliquis qui non interfuit
has debuisse capi et quod haberi non poterat iusto pretio gratis
rapi. Sed illi turres habebant et muros duplices ad tutelam et in
mari naves ad fugam. Quis igitur fructus si nostri mora, periculo,
et labore harum aliquam expugnassent et cives, sumptis urbis spoliis, aufugissent? Villarum quoque[z] animalia in montibus abscon-
debant, et villani,[a] domibus vacuatis, de navibus escas ad suum
libitum caras vendebant, et pauperes in tam longo itinere auro et
argento, armis et vestibus spoliabant. Illi autem, si quando naves
poterant invenire, naufragio postposito[b] duplici, intrabant, ruituri[c]
quocumque illos Graecorum fraus[d] vel hiemis tempestas vellet
deferre. Alii, quos conditio damnaverat servituti, ducebant levius
in eorum servitio remanere. Ne praetereundum nos in hac via,
stupentibus indigenis, contra morem tres fluvios facile transva-
dasse, et unumquemque post nostrum transitum ilico pluviis inundasse. Unde habebatur pro miraculo contra solitum nobis imbres
et hiemem pepercisse.

Sic tandem praeteritis Smyrna et Pergamo[e] venimus Ephesum,
quae inter ruinas antiquae gloriae venerandas sui status habet re-
liquias beati Iohannis sepulcrum in quodam terrae tumulo contra
paganos muro circumdatum. Ibi rex imperatoris nuntios cum litte-

---

[v] -sse *over erasure* D1.
[w] pertransuri DW.
[x] restraxerant > restruxerant D1; restrinxerant CM.
[y] multu- > multi[tudinis] D1.
[z] quorum > quoque D1.

[a] et villam D; ut villani CM.
[b] postpositio M.
[c] ituri CM.
[d] fraudes CM.
[e] perm > perg D1.

---

[6] Chalandon, *Jean II Comnène*, p. 306, concludes from the tenuous evidence of the peasants
selling food from ships and of some pilgrims sailing away that the Greek fleet was following
the army along the coast in order to supply food.

[7] William of Tyre reports that Count Guy of Ponthieu fell ill and died at Ephesus and
was buried in the vestibule of the church there. See Babcock and Krey, *op. cit.*, II, 174.

would have had to await the end of his life, grieving for his sins where he was.

After this we returned to the winding coast line, to encounter nearly every day steep, stony mountains and the deep channels of mountain torrents, which were difficult to cross even when dry and if filled with snow or rain possessed swift currents which neither horse nor infantry could swim through. There we found many cities in ruins and others which the Greeks had built up from the ancient level above the sea, fortifying them with walls and towers. From these cities we obtained food, with difficulty, indeed, because of the insolence of our mob, and too dearly, because of the inhabitants' greed. Now, perhaps someone who was not present may say that these cities should have been captured and that goods which could not be obtained at a fair price should have been seized without any payment. But the inhabitants had towers and double walls to protect them and ships in the harbor to enable them to flee. What would have been gained, therefore, if our men, at the cost of delay, danger, and hardship, had attacked a city and the citizens had fled, taking the spoils with them? Also the Greeks hid their farm animals in the mountains, and after the peasants had left their homes they sold food from on board ships as dearly as they pleased and, during the exceedingly long journey, plundered the poor of gold and silver, arms and clothing. Whenever the pilgrims could find ships, however, they embarked, without regard for the twofold danger, ready to rush wherever the Greeks' trickery or the winter storm might drive them.[6] Others, whom circumstances had condemned to servitude, considered it easier to stay behind in service to the Greeks. I should not omit the fact that on this journey, to the amazement of the natives, we had crossed three rivers with ease and that immediately after we crossed each had been flooded with rain. Therefore it was considered miraculous that, contrary to the ordinary course of events, the rains and the winter had spared us.

Thus, at last, after passing Smyrna and Pergamon we came to Ephesus, which, among the ruins of her ancient glory, has the venerable relics of her former state, the tomb of St. John, located on a certain mound of earth and surrounded by a wall erected in order to keep out the pagans.[7] There the king encountered messen-

ris habuit, qui contra eum Turcos supra numerum congregatos dicebant et ipsum refugere in illius castella suadebant. Cum vero rex Turcorum metum et imperatoris gratiam aequaliter contempsisset, obtulerunt alias sputo simili dignas, exponentes quae rex ibi[f] fecerat damna et quod non posset suos homines retinere deinceps [34v] a vindicta. His sine rescriptione despectis, processit, volens in valle Decervion nativitatem Domini celebrare;[g] et Alemannus, poenitens quod Constantinopolitanum imperatorem non viderat, apud eum reversus est hiemare.

In vigilia itaque natalis Domini fixis tentoriis in valle praediviti, Turci Graecis ductoribus nostris equis pascentibus primas insidias tetenderunt. Quibus egregii milites animose et provide resistentes, de capitibus eorum laeti primitias habuerunt et illo terrore festis diebus pacem fecerunt. In his dum divinis laudibus intendimus et quieti, aer obscurior, quasi vellet ante nostrum iter[h] divina providentia desecari[i] (qui Deo volente non fuit nobis postea usque Satelliam vel frigore horridus vel pluviis nebulosus), imbres emisit quibus rivi vallium[j] inundabant et montes nivibus albescebant. Post quartum denique diem aquarum, decursis tumoribus et aere serenato, fugatis nubibus,[k] rex, torrentibus timens intercipi si vel nives liquescerent vel aliae[l] imbres defluerent, vallem deserit Ephesinam, sumptis victualibus, properans Laodiciam.

Erat in hac via inter montes arduos Maeander, fluvius profundus et latus de aquis propriis sed tunc inflatior alienis. Hic cuiusdam vallis amplitudinem alveo suo mediam dividit et utramque[m] ripam copiosae multitudini perviam facit. In his Turci sese diviserant,[n]

[f] sibi CM.	[k] imbribus CM.
[g] celebran- > celebrar- D1.	[l] alto CM.
[h] os CM.	[m] statimque CM.
[i] defecari D.	[n] diviserunt M.
[j] vallum M.	

---

[8] Kugler, *Studien*, p. 166, explains these letters on the ground that the Turks had been encouraged by their victory over the Germans and had pushed beyond the borders to mass against the Franks; that the Greeks of Asia Minor, who had been enraged by the crusaders' behavior, were ready to help the Turks.

[9] A valley located in the neighborhood of Ephesus.

[10] Conrad reports to Wibald that they got as far as St. John (Ephesus) without any difficulty and were planning to celebrate Christmas there. However, Conrad and many others became ill, and since he failed to recuperate quickly he was unable to proceed with Louis, even though the Frankish king waited for him as long as he could. When the Greek emperor heard this, he and his empress approached Conrad very quickly. Cf. Conrad's letter to Wibald, *loc. cit.*, p. 534. Cinnamus, *op. cit.*, II, 18, attributes Conrad's departure to the facts that the French jeered at the Germans and that the emperor feared he would be inferior to the Franks. *Gesta Ludovici*, RHGF, Vol. XII, chapter 10 (printed at the bottom of the pages

gers bringing letters from the Greek emperor, who said that in-
numerable Turks had assembled to combat the king and urged him
to take refuge in the imperial castles. Then, since the king equally
disdained fear of the Turks and the emperor's favor, the messengers
presented other letters, worthy of like scorn, which set forth the
injuries done there by the king and the fact that the emperor could
not thereafter restrain his men from vengeance.[8] Without deigning
to reply to these letters, the king proceeded on his way, for he
wished to celebrate Christmas in the Valley of Decervion;[9] and,
since the German emperor regretted that he had not seen the emperor of Constantinople, he returned to spend the winter with
him.[10]

Therefore, on Christmas Eve, when our tents had been pitched
in the very fertile valley, Turks under Greek leadership tried for
the first time to take us unaware by attacking our horses as they
grazed. Resisting courageously and prudently, the excellent
knights joyfully obtained the first fruits of victory by killing some
of the Turks, and they effected peace for the holy days. Then,
while we were intent upon resting and praising the Lord, the dark-
ened sky, as if wishing to be cleansed by divine agency before we
advanced (for by the will of God the weather thereafter was not
unpleasantly cold or cloudy and rainy until we came to Adalia),
loosed heavy rains, which made the streams in the valleys overflow
and the mountains grow white with snow. At last, after the
fourth rainy day, when the torrents had ceased and the sky had
become clear, now that the clouds had been swept away, the king,
fearing to be cut off by freshets if the snow melted or if other rains
fell, left the valley near Ephesus and, after acquiring provisions,
pushed on to Laodicea.

Among the steep mountains on this route flowed the Maeander,
a river which ordinarily was deep and wide, but at that time was
swollen with water from other streams. Its channel divides in half
the width of a certain valley and makes both banks very accessible
to a large crowd. On these banks the Turks had arranged their

of the *Grandes chroniques*) also imputes Conrad's departure to the disadvantage of his present
situation. Manuel's change of heart since Conrad's stay at Constantinople may have been
caused by the fact that he no longer feared Conrad, since the latter's power was broken,
that he still wished to separate the crusading forces, and that he feared the anti-Greek party
in the French army.

putantes hos sagittis procedentem exercitum infestare illosque vada
fluminis tumida° prohibere et utrosqueᵖ quando nostris cederent
de refugio�q montium tutosʳ fore. Venientes huc, invenimus Turcorum manipulos montium scopulos occupasse aliosque se in plano ad
temptandum exercitum obiecisse et reliquos se ultra fluvium ad
prohibendum transitum conglobasse. Rex autem, sarcinis suis et
debilibus in medio congregatis, primos et ultimos et latera tegit
armatis, sic procedens tutus sed parum proficiens duabus dietis.
Astu enim non viribus retardabant cum collaterales inimici, ad
fugam docti et faciles et ad persequendum protervi. Cum igitur
illis proterve infestantibus et docte et leviter refugientibus pacem
non posset habere nec pugnam, transire [35r] volebat, sed nesciebat
vadum in fluvio; Turcisque prohibentibus, non poterat temptari
sine periculo. Circa meridiem vero secundae diei, Turcorum pars
una (sicut condixerant) post exercitum, alia supra fluvium, ubi
nostrisˢ erat ingressus facilis et in partem illorum egressus difficilis,
congregantur. Deinde tribus suorum transmissisᵗ qui contra nostros sagittas mitterent, illis iacientibus ambae partes clamore una-
nimi tonuerunt, illique via qua venerantᵘ refugerunt. Sed egregii
comites Henricus, filius comitis Theobaldi, et Flandrensis Theo-
dericus et Guillelmus Matisconensis post illos more turbinis irrue-
runt ripamque arduam sagittarum pluviam et Turcorum copiam
dicto citius penetrarunt. Rex quoque fortuna simili, a tergo sagit-
tantibus laxatis loris obvians, fugavit, secuit, et quibus equorum
velocitas dedit suffragium in concavos montes retrusit. Sic uterque
nostrorum impetus cito et facile de cadaveribus partis utriusque
campos usque ad latibula montium seminavit. Ibi quidam amira-
dus captus est, et, adductus regi, auditus est et occisus.

Erat in praesenti quaedam civitatula imperatoris, Antiochiae

° timida M.   ˢ abbreviation mark added Dx.
ᵖ utrosque erased, rewritten with greater economy of space D1.   ᵗ tru- > tra- D1.
q refugio over erasure D1.   ᵘ poterant CM.
ʳ tuto > tutos Dx; large space.

¹¹ Henry, count of Meaux at this time and count of Champagne and Brie 1152–81, was
the son of Theobald IV of Champagne and Matilda of Carinthia. Louis expressed the affection and respect which he felt for the young count in a letter to Theobald, in which he
described the incident that Odo tells of here. See RHGF, XV, 502. Another interesting
letter which concerns Henry on the crusade is that written by St. Bernard to Manuel, recom-
mending the young man very highly and asking the emperor to knight him. See RHGF,
XV, 607–8. For the later life of Henry see L'Art de vérifier les dates, Part 2, Vol. XI, pp. 368–70.
¹² William IV was count of Mâcon and Vienne 1125–ca.1156. For further information see
L'Art de vérifier les dates, Part 2, Vol. XI, pp. 21–23.

forces in groups, thinking that some should harass the advancing army with arrows and others should block the river's swollen fords and that in case of retreat both parties would be safe, since the mountains provided a refuge. When we arrived there, we discovered that Turkish maniples had seized the mountain crags and that other Turks had stationed themselves in the plain in order to assail the army and that the rest had massed on the other bank of the river to prevent us from crossing. After grouping his baggage and the disabled in the center line, however, the king covered the van, the rear, and the flanks with armed men and thus proceeded safely, but not very advantageously, for two days. Actually the enemies' harassing the flanks of the army hindered him by cunning, not by strength, for they were skilled and agile in flight and bold in pursuit. Thus, since he could neither have peace nor join battle with them, as they assaulted boldly and retreated skillfully and easily, he wanted to cross the river; but he did not know where the ford was, and, with the Turks blocking the way, the crossing could not safely be attempted. Around noon on the second day, however, one party of Turks assembled behind our army, as they had planned, another up the river, where the entrance was easy for us and the exit, in the face of the other Turks, difficult. Then they dispatched three men to shoot arrows at us, and while they were shooting, both groups roared in simultaneous din and the archers fled by the road on which they had come. But the excellent counts, Henry, son of Count Theobald,[11] and Theoderic of Flanders and William of Mâcon,[12] rushed after them like whirlwinds, scaled the steep bank, and penetrated the rain of arrows and the Turkish throng more swiftly than can be told. Also the king, by similar good fortune, when riding at top speed against the Turks who were shooting arrows from the rear, put them to flight, divided their forces, and pushed back into the cavernous mountains those whose swift horses enabled them to escape. Thus, each of our attacks swiftly and easily sowed the fields all the way to the mountain dens with corpses from both Turkish divisions. A certain emir was captured there and, when taken before the king, was questioned and put to death.

Near at hand was a certain little town of the emperor's, called Antiochetta, which furnished refuge to the fleeing pagans. Thereby

nomen habens diminutivum, quae paganis fugientibus patuit ad refugium. In quo ille de doloso proditore se in apertum transtulit inimicum. Hanc expugnasset rex ut reclusos caperet fugitivos, sed paene sibi deerant victualia, et in villa paupere nulla caperet spolia.

Certe fuerunt qui dicerent album quendam militem ante nostros ad transitum fluminis, quem non viderunt prius vel postea, se vidisse et primos ictus in proelio percussisse. In hoc ego nec fallere vellem nec falli; scio tamen quod in tali districto tam facilis et tam celebris victoria, non nisi divina virtute, fuisset, nec adversae multitudinis ferrea pluvia sine morte vel vulnere cecidisset; dante nobis Deo victoriam sine damno, nisi Milo de Nogentiaco in flumine suffocatus obisset.

In nostra via habebant Turci cum Graecis terrarum terminos, et nos utrosque sciebamus[v] unanimes inimicos. Illi ergo suos plangentes mortuos, alios convocant e vicino,[w] ad vindictam die septima numerosius et audacius reversuri;[x] [35v] nosque die tertia venimus Laodiciam, stolida praesumptione securi. Nunc venit in memoriam comes ille[y] Bernardus qui cum imperatore revertens de Iconio pro fratribus suis animam suam posuit, quia hic eum Frisingensi[z] episcopo, fratre imperatoris,[a] alius comes eiusdem nominis et fortunae simili proditione interiit; dux enim huius urbis cum deberet illos educere de montanis, per loca invia superduxit eos Turcorum insidiis, ubi comite occiso cum pluribus, qui potuerunt evadere latitando fugierunt.[b] Dux autem et Graeci quos duxerat[c] cum[d] Turcis spolia diviserunt. Ille idem, vel timens regem pro suo scelere vel nocere volens alio genere, urbem quibusque utilitatibus[e] vacuavit, fraudemque[f] devitans iam cognitam, aliam aeque nocivam[g] cogita-

[v] nobis *inserted* M.
[w] vicinio M.
[x] reversuris CM.
[y] *erasure between* ille *and* bernardus Dx.
[z] quia . . . fri D2.
[a] imperatore D.

[b] fugerant CM.
[c] duxerant M.
[d] -x au . . . cum D2.
[e] utilitatibus > utilibus Dx.
[f] frudemque C.
[g] nocuuam > nocivam Dx.

[13] Here, as in the case of the Greeks who made reprisals against the crusaders, Odo errs in holding Manuel answerable for actions of which he was probably unaware and for which he was certainly not responsible.

[14] Visions of this kind were not unusual in holy wars. Cf. this incident, for example, with the aid which Saint James of Compostella gave at the battle of Clavijo and Saint George at Cerami. For these and similar incidents see Erdmann, *op. cit.*, pp. 254–61.

[15] I have not been able to find any more material about him.

[16] January 3 or 4.

[17] Pages 93 ff. above.

[18] Otto of Freising had gone from Nicaea west along the coast of the Aegean Sea (cf.

the emperor transformed himself from a wily traitor to an avowed enemy.[13] The king would have attacked the town in order to seize the fugitives hidden there, but he had hardly any food supplies and he could not seize any spoils from the poor little town.

Actually there were people who said that they had seen ahead of us at the ford a certain white-clad knight, whom they had not seen before or since, and that he had struck the first blows in the battle.[14] As to this, I should not wish to deceive anyone or to be deceived; but I do know that in such straits such an easy and brilliant victory would not have occurred except by the power of God, nor would the rain of iron from the opposing army have fallen without causing death or wounds; yet God gave us a victory without any loss except for Milo of Nogent,[15] who drowned in the river.

Along our route the Turks and the Greeks together held the boundaries, and we knew that both were our common enemies. The Turks, mourning their dead, summoned comrades from the neighborhood, making ready to return for revenge on the seventh day in greater numbers than before and with more boldness; and we arrived at Laodicea on the third day,[16] careless because of our stubborn self-confidence. At this point I am reminded of that Count Bernard who when returning with the emperor from Iconium laid down his life for his brethren,[17] because here at Laodicea with the bishop of Freising, the emperor's brother, another count of the same name and fate died by similar treachery; for, although the commandant of this city should have led the Germans out of the mountains, he brought them through out-of-the-way places into a Turkish ambush, and, after the count and many of his men had been killed there, those who could escape fled and hid.[18] Moreover, the commandant and his Greek followers divided the spoils with the Turks. That same officer, either fearing the king on account of his crime or wishing to work harm in another way, emptied the city of every commodity and, while avoiding an act of treachery which was already known, designed another equally

above, pp. 51, 89), probably turning east at the valley of Hermes or the valley of Ephesus and proceeding up the Maeander, arriving in the neighborhood of Laodicea at the end of 1147. Here, hard pressed by the Turks, he lost Bernard of Carinthia and part of his army. Turning back toward the coast, he arrived at a city east of Adalia, where he suffered a severe attack at the end of February and sustained great losses. Kugler, *Studien*, pp. 158–60.

vit. Sciebat impius quod usque Satelliam, quousque postea plus-quam quindecim dietas fecimus, non possent alibi[h] victualia[i] inve-niri, et esset necessarium cunctos fame mori si cibi non possent ab urbe vacua vel emi pretio vel viribus extorqueri.

Rex autem super hoc consulit episcopos et alios optimates. Qui quamvis nemo dubitaret de illius prudentia, nisi ipse, semper tamen ordinabat multorum consilio res communes, et erat equidem pru-dens humilitas si se solum pluribus iuvenem senibus, aestimationem suam expertorum usibus postponebat; et quod posset ut dominus, quod sciebat ut sapiens, liberalitas fuit quod subditis deferebat. Illi autem qui solebant de causis aliis disputare et de coniecturis[i] diversarum rationum (quandoque subtilitate superflua)[k] dissentire modo stupebant non invenientes idoneam rationem in isto articulo, et dolebant quod non videbant exitum de communi periculo. Re-quirebant cibos in urbe de industria vacuata, potentes viribus ad tollendum et rebus divites ad emendum; sed quia non est ibi quod quaeritur, utrumque ad haec[l] habetur incassum. Consulunt[m] tamen fugitivos cives per montium devia quaeri et, firmata pace, cum venalibus illos reduci. Quo facto ex parte; illi[n] enim inventi sunt, non reducti.

Processimus, in hoc perdita una die, Turcos et Graecos habentes in nostro itinere praevios et sequentes. Erant ibi montes, adhuc de cruore Alemannorum madidi, et parebant idem[o] ibi[p] qui eos occiderant inimici. [36r] Unde[q] rex incassum doctior,[r] videns ho-rum agmina et aliorum cadavera, ordinat acies in quo Gaufridus de Rancone rancorem meruit sempiternum, quem ipse cum suo avunculo Morianensi comite miserat primum. Circa meridiem secundae diei mons execrandus faciliorem transitum habebat, quem

[h] alicubi CM.
[i] vicctualia > victualia Dx.
[j] comecturis > coniecturis Dx.
[k] superflua *much crowded* D2; *partially erased note in margin calling attention to it.*
[l] hoc CM.
[m] consultum CM.

[n] quo . . . il- D2; *note in margin referring to it.*
[o] et . . . idem D2.
[p] *om.* CM.
[q] *om.* CM.
[r] doctior D.

---

[19] Odo's interpretation of Otto's defeat and the evacuation of Laodicea is strongly colored by his anti-Greek bias.

[20] As has been said above, p. 97, n. 20, and p. 109, the Greeks had been enraged by the crusaders' plundering. Thus, it is not unlikely that some had joined forces with the Turks.

[21] That is, Otto of Freising's army. See p. 113.

[22] Geoffrey of Rancon (d. 1198), one of the principal barons of Poitou, began his pleasant

injurious. The wretch knew that all the way to Adalia, where we arrived more than fifteen days later, no provisions could be found anywhere else and that all must starve unless food could be bought for a price, or seized forcibly, from the evacuated city.[19]

Now the king consulted the bishops and other barons on this question. Although no one except himself doubted his wisdom, he nevertheless always conducted affairs of common interest according to the advice of many people, and his humility was wise indeed in that he subordinated himself, the one to the many, the young man to the old, and his own opinions to the knowledge of experienced men; and what he as lord could do, what he as wise man knew, it was his generous practice to refer to his subjects. However, the men who were used to arguing about other cases and to disagreeing in their opinions about different plans (sometimes with useless subtlety) were amazed at not finding the proper plan at that moment, and they were grieved because they did not see a way out of the common danger. They tried to find food in a city which had purposely been emptied; yet because what they wanted was not available, although they were strong enough to seize it and rich enough to buy it, either course of action was considered useless. Nevertheless, their advice was that fugitive residents should be sought out in the mountain by-paths and that after peace had been established they and their wares should be brought back. And this was done in part; for the residents were found, but not brought back.

After losing a day in this search, we went ahead, both preceded and followed on the road by Turks and Greeks.[20] In that place were the mountains, still stained with the blood of the Germans, and there appeared the very enemies who had killed them.[21] Wherefore, the king, who had been forewarned in vain, upon seeing the enemies' lines and the German corpses, drew his men into battle array. Here Geoffrey of Rancon,[22] the man whom he had sent ahead with his uncle, the count of Maurienne, earned our everlasting hatred. Around noon of the second day an accursed mountain which the king had planned to use an entire day in crossing (and hence had ordered us to pitch camp at its foot)

association with Louis VII and Eleanor by entertaining them at his castle during their wedding journey. For references to his life see A. Richard, *op. cit.*, Vol. II.

rex die integro transire disposuerat et[a] ideo[t] ibidem tentoria figi
praeceperat. Quo venientes primi (satis cito quia non erant ab
aliquo impediti), regis immemores, qui tunc ultimos conservabat,
montem ascendunt et sequentibus aliis tentoria circa nonam in
partem alteram figunt. Mons erat arduus et saxosus, et nobis erat
per clivum eius ascensus cuius cacumen nobis videbatur tangere
caelum, et torrens in valle concava descendere in infernum. Crescit
hic superveniens multitudo, urget, invicem constipatur, ponit pedem,[u] equo non praevidet, haerens potius quam procedens. La-
buntur de rupibus praeruptis[v] summarii obvios quosque sternentes
usque in profundum abyssi. Saxa quoque de locis suis mota[w] stragem suam faciebant. Sic cum[x] vias quaerentes latissime se sparsis-
sent, omnes lapsum proprium vel aliorum fulminationem timebant.
Turci vero et Graeci labentium erectionem prohibentes sagittis, in
partem alteram congregantur et de tali spectaculo spe vespertini
commodi gratulantur. Inclinatur dies, et semper crescit in antro
supellectilis nostrae congeries. Hostibus autem illud non sufficit,
sed amplius audent. In nostram partem transeunt, quia primos iam
non timent et postremos adhuc non vident. Feriunt et sternunt, et
vulgus inerme pecudum more cadit aut fugit. Inde clamor oritur
quo caelum et aures regiae penetrantur. Rex autem de hoc fecit
quod potuit, sed de caelo nullum tunc adiutorium nisi nox[y] venit.
Nocte autem veniente pestis cessavit.

Ego interim, qui sicut monachus hoc solum poteram,[z] vel Dominum invocare vel ad pugnam alios incitare, mittor ad castra. Rem
refero. Turbati currunt ad arma; festinarent regredi sed vix ire
poterant, asperitate loci et occursu venientium praepediti. Rex
vero relictus in periculo cum quibusdam nobilibus, non habens
secum gregarios [36v] milites nec servientes cum arcubus (non enim
se praemunierat ad districtum quem erat ex condictu communi

---

[a] om. CM.
[t] non CM.
[u] sedem CM.
[v] praeruptis *over erasure* D2.

[w] mora D.
[x] dum CM.
[y] vox DC.
[z] potam > poteram Dx.

---

[23] See Matthew Paris, *Historia Anglorum*, ed. by F. Madden (London, 1866), I, 281 f.;
William of Tyre, ed. and trans. by Babcock and Krey, Vol. II, pp. 175–78. Kugler, *Studien*,
p. 170, n. 76, refutes the story that it was Eleanor of Aquitaine who urged Geoffrey to make
this move.

offered a fairly easy passage. When the vanguard arrived there
(swiftly, because they were not hampered in any way), unmindful
of the king, who at that time was protecting the rear guard, they
climbed the mountain and, while the rest were following, pitched
their tents on the other side at about the ninth hour.[23] The mountain was steep and rocky, and we had to climb along a ridge so
lofty that its summit seemed to touch heaven and the stream in
the hollow valley below to descend into hell. Here the throng
became congested while ascending, pushed forward, then crowded
closely together, stopped, and, taking no thought for the cavalry,
clung there instead of going ahead. Sumpter horses slipped from
the steep cliffs, hurling those whom they struck into the depths
of the chasm. Dislodged rocks also caused destruction. Thus,
when the men had scattered far and wide in order to seek out
paths, all feared that they would misstep or that others [in falling]
would strike them violently. Moreover, the Turks and the Greeks,
their arrows preventing the fallen from rising again, thronged
against the other part of our army and rejoiced at this spectacle,
in the hope that evening would bring them further advantage.
The day drew to a close, and the mass of our abandoned goods kept
increasing in the valley below. However, that did not suffice our
enemies; on the contrary, they became even bolder. They crossed
against us, since they no longer feared the vanguard and did not
yet see the rear guard. They thrust and slashed, and the defenseless
crowd fled or fell like sheep. Thence arose a cry that pierced even
to heaven and to our king's ears. Now the king did what he could
about the disaster, but at that time no aid came from heaven,
except that night fell. As night came on, however, the destruction
stopped.

Meanwhile I, who as monk could only call upon the Lord and
summon others to battle, was sent to the camp. I reported the
situation. In agitation they rushed to arms; they would have returned speedily, but since they were impeded by the rough terrain
and the swift onrush of advancing men they could hardly move.
However, the king, who had been left behind in peril with certain
of his nobles, since he was not accompanied by common soldiers
or serjeants with bows (for he had not fortified himself for crossing
the pass, which by common agreement he was to cross the next

transiturus in crastinum), contemnens vitam propriam, ut morientem liberet turbam, ultimos penetrat et mactantibus paenultimos viriliter obviat. Aggreditur praesumptuose gentem incredulam, quae numero centies superat et quam locus maxime adiuvat; ibi enim equus non poterat, non dicam, currere, sed vix stare, et tardior impetus debilitabat ictum in vulnere. Vibrabant nostri hastas in lubrico suis[a] viribus non equorum, et illi sagittabant de tuto innitentes scopulis arborum vel saxorum. Turba liberata fugit, suas deferens sarcinas vel ducendo ferentes, loco suo morti obiciens regem et comites.

Sed mori dominos ut servi viverent esset lugendum commercium nisi tale dedisset exemplum Dominus omnium. Marcescunt flores Franciae antequam fructum faciant in Damasco. Quo relatu suffundor lacrimis, et de visceribus intimis ingemisco. De hoc tamen potest mens sobria tali remedio consolari, quod haec eorum probitas et anterior mundo convivet et finis, correptis erratibus fide fervida, martyrio meruit coronari. Pugnant, et, ne quisque[b] circa se[c] moriatur impune, stragem cadaverum facit; sed numerus impugnantium, reparatus a multitudine, non decrescit. Occidunt equos qui, licet currere non possent, valebant tamen armorum pondera sustinendo, et loricati pedites inter densos hostes submerguntur velut in pelago; fundentes[d] nudorum viscera, divisi[e] sunt alter[f] ab altero. In hoc rex parvulum sed gloriosum perdidit comitatum regalem; vero retinens animum, agilis et virilis, per radices cuiusdam arboris quam[g] saluti eius Deus providerat ascendit scopulum. Post quem populus hostium ut eum caperet ascendebant, et[h] turba remotior eum ibidem sagittabat. Sed Deo volente sub lorica tutatus est a sagittis, cruentatoque gladio ne capi posset defendit scopulum,

---

[a] in . . . su- D2.
[b] quisquis CM.
[c] ne *inserted* CM.
[d] que *inserted* CM.
[e] nudorum viscera di- D2.
[f] ab > alter D1.
[g] quem D.
[h] *om.* CM.

---

[24] The importance of this passage for dating Odo's work has been pointed out above, p. xxiii.

day), careless of his own life and with the desire of freeing the
dying mob, pushed through the rear-guard and courageously
checked the butchery of his middle division. He boldly assaulted
the infidel, who outnumbered him a hundred times and whom the
position aided a great deal; for there no horse could, I shall not
say gallop, but barely stand, and the slower attack which resulted
weakened the knights' thrust when wounding the enemy. On the
slippery slope our men brandished their spears with all of their
own might, but without the added force of their horses, and from
the safe shelter of rocks and trees the Turks shot arrows. Freed by
the knights' efforts, the mob fled, carrying their own packs or
leading the sumpter animals, and exposed the king and his comrades to death in their stead.

For lords to die so that their servants might live would have
been an incident calling for lamentation, had not the Lord of all
given an example thereof. The flowers of France withered before
they could bear fruit in Damascus.[24] In saying this I am overcome
by tears, and I groan from the bottom of my heart. Concerning
this tragedy, however, the sober mind can comfort itself with the
solace that this and earlier examples of their valor will live on in
the world and that their death, whereby their errors were swept
away through fervent faith, has won the martyr's crown. They
fought, and, that no one of them should die without retaliating,
each made a pile of corpses around himself; but, even so, the number of assailants did not diminish, for it was recruited from the
horde. The Turks killed the horses, which, though not able to
gallop, were nevertheless of value in carrying the heavy armor,
and the mail-clad Franks, now on foot, were overwhelmed among
the thick-pressing enemy as if they were drowned in the sea; they
were separated one from another, spilling the vitals from their
defenseless bodies. During this engagement the king lost his small
but renowned royal guard; keeping a stout heart, however, he
nimbly and bravely scaled a rock by making use of some tree roots
which God had provided for his safety. The enemy climbed after,
in order to capture him, and the more distant rabble shot arrows
at him. But by the will of God his cuirass protected him from the
arrows, and to keep from being captured he defended the crag with
his bloody sword, cutting off the heads and hands of many oppo-

multorum manibus et capitibus amputatis. Illi ergo non cognos-
centes eum et sentientes capi difficilem, metuentes [37r] superven-
tum, revertuntur colligere spolia ante noctem.

Explicit Sextus

nents in the process. Since they did not recognize him and felt that he would be difficult to capture and feared a surprise attack, the enemy thereupon turned back to collect the spoils before night fell.[25]

End of Book Six

[25] Louis, when writing to Suger from Antioch, also tells of his troubles in Asia Minor (RHGF, XV, 496). He attributes some of them to the treachery of the emperor of Greece and some to the fault of the Franks, mentioning as special hardships the constant plundering on the part of the natives, the difficult routes, daily struggles with the Turks (whom, he says, the emperor permitted to enter Greek territory in order to pursue the crusaders), and the lack of provisions in some places. Then he mentions the death of many of his barons during the ascent of a mountain in Laodicea, saying that the crusaders' sins seemed to demand this divine judgment. Also, Louis indicates that he has been in peril of death many times but has been preserved by the grace of God. Chalandon, *Jean II Comnène*, pp. 311-12, has criticized Louis' accusations against Manuel much as we have criticized similar statements made by Odo. Cf. above, p. xxii.

Incipit Septimus

Adhuc prope turba sarcinaria pertransibat, quia quo densius eo segnius per praecipitia fugiebat. Ad quam rex veniens efficitur eques ex pedite et ibat cum eis obscurato iam vespere. Tunc occurrunt ei de tentoriis anhelae cohortes militum, quem videntes solum cruentum et fessum, quod factum est gementes sine interrogatione sciebantur, et absentes regios comites, fere quadraginta sine consolatione plangebant (videlicet Warenensem comitem et fratrem eius Evrardum de Britolio, Manassem de Bulis et Guacherium de Montegaio et alios; sed non refero nomina omnium ne iudicetur sine utilitate prolixum). Ardebant animo et abundabant numero; sed nox erat, et hostes abyssi profundae contrariam partem tenebant, et ideo locum vel horam persequendi[a] ulterius non habebant. Venerunt itaque cum rege ad tentoria nimis[b] tarde, et qui timebant ibi iam lugent certo dolore, sed domino sospite consolantur ex parte. Nox illa fuit insomnis, dum quisque suorum aliquem vel expectat numquam venturum vel laetus, damno postposito, venientem suscipit nudum. Inter haec populus omnis Gaufredum iudicabat dignum suspendio, qui de dieta non oboedierat praecepto regio; et forsitan eius avunculum quem habebat in culpa socium habuit etiam de vindicta patronum, quia, cum essent ambo rei et esset parcendum regis avunculo, non debebat alter sine altero condemnari.

Illuxit dies crastina maerosis tenebras non depellens,[c] et apparet exercitus hostium laeta et diviti multitudine montes tegens. Nostri vero ab heri pauperes, suos plangentes et sua, tarde providi, ad

---

[a] post > per D1.   [b] nimis *over erasure* D1.   [c] non depellens D2.

---

[1] Either Odo was mistaken in this relationship, or he used the phrase in the sense of "brother-in-arms."

[2] Louis wrote Suger, to preserve the property of Manasses of Bulles for his brother Reginald of Bulles, who was still in the East (RHGF, XV, 500).

[3] I have found no further information about him.

[4] In his letter to Suger (RHGF, XV, 496), Louis mentions in addition Renald of Tours. William of Tyre, ed. and trans. by Babcock and Krey, II, 177, records the name of Itiers de Meingnac.

[5] Geoffrey returned to Europe from Antioch in 1148. Far from sending him in disgrace, however, Louis entrusted to him the duty of partially repaying the Templars for funds which they had loaned the king in Syria. See RHGF, XV, 499–500, 501–2.

Beginning of Book Seven

Nearby the baggage train was still crossing the pass, because the closer packed it was, the slower it fled over the crags. When he came upon it, the king, who was on foot, secured a horse and accompanied the men through the evening, which had already fallen. At that time breathless cohorts of knights from the camp met him and groaned when they saw him alone, bloody, and tired, for, without asking, they knew what had happened and mourned inconsolably for the missing royal escort, which numbered about forty (to wit, the count of Warenne and his brother, Evrard of Breteuil,[1] Manasses of Bulles[2] and Gautier of Montjay[3] and others;[4] but I shall not record the names of all, lest I be considered unnecessarily wordy). The Franks were very numerous and glowed with courage; but it was night, and the enemy held the other side of the deep valley; and thus neither the hour nor the place was suitable for further pursuit on the part of the Franks. With the king, accordingly, they arrived at the camp late at night, and the people there who had been fearful before now mourned because their grief was actual, but they were somewhat comforted by the king's safety. There was no sleep that night, during which each man either waited for some one of his friends who never came or joyously, and with no regard for material loss, welcomed one who had been despoiled. Meanwhile the entire people judged that Geoffrey should be hanged because he had not obeyed the king's command about the day's march; and perhaps the king's uncle, who shared the guilt, protected Geoffrey from punishment, because, since they were both defendants and the king's uncle had to be spared, the one man ought not be condemned unless the other was.[5]

Without dispelling the shadows of grief from the sorrowing people, the next day dawned brightly, and the enemy army became visible, spread over the mountains in a rich and happy throng. Now, while bewailing their lost comrades and possessions, our men, who were paupers since the day before and cautious now that

residua servanda ordinati, procedunt securitate depulsa. Rex vero nobilium paupertatem non ferens et mediocribus pio animo condescendens, tam largiter egestatem expulit utrorumque quasi esset immemor se cum eis aliquid perdidisse. Iam fames vexabat equos, qui diebus pluribus herbarum[d] parum et annonae nihil comederant; iam cibus deficiebat hominibus, qui duodecim dierum adhuc iter habebant; hostesque [37v] nos, sicut fera quae sanguine gustato fit trucior, hoc cognito securius et post lucrum avidius infestabant.

Quos contra magister Templi domnus Evrardus de Barris, religione venerandus et ad militiam exemplar probitatis, cum fratribus suis vigilanter et prudenter conservabat res proprias et tuebatur pro posse viriliter alienas. Rex quoque illorum diligebat et libenter imitabatur exemplum, et ad hoc voluit conformari exercitum, sciens quod si eius robur fames valida infirmaret, et debiles unitas animi confirmaret. Inducitur itaque communi consilio ut omnes mutuam et cum illis in hoc periculo fraternitatem statuerent, firmantes fide dives et pauper quod de campo non fugerent et magistris ab illis sibi traditis per omnia oboedirent. Accipiunt itaque magistrum[e] nomine Gislibertum, et ille[f] socios quibus assignaret milites quinquagenos. Iubentur pati usque ad praeceptum [eos] qui nos vexant, quia cito refugiunt inimicos, et, cum iussi restituerint,[g] ilico regredi praemonent revocatos. Cognita lege docentur et gradum, ne qui de primo est vadat ad ultimum vel ne se confundant custodes[h] laterum. Illi vero quos natura fecerat pedites vel fortuna (multi enim nobiles rebus perditis vel expensis more insolito ibant in turba) ordinati sunt extremi omnium ut habentes arcus resisterent sagittis hostium. Rex quoque legum dominus volebat oboe-

---

[d] habarum D.
[e] magister > magistrum D1.
[f] illi > ille Dx.

[g] restiterint M.
[h] se . . . custo- *over erasure* D2.

---

[6] The elementary nature of these commands makes the former disorder of the army very apparent.

[7] In the sense of the king as "the fountain of justice."

it was too late, banished their carelessness and advanced in an order designed to save what they still had. But because our king could not endure the fact that his nobles were impoverished and because his pious heart made him have regard for those below them, he dispelled the wants of both classes as generously as if he had forgotten that he had shared their loss at all. Already hunger was assailing the horses, which for many days had eaten little grass and no grain; already there was no food for the men, who still had to march for twelve days; and, like a beast which becomes more savage after tasting blood, the enemy harassed us the more boldly after learning of our weakness and the more greedily after profiting thereby.

Against them the Templars and the Master of the Temple, Lord Evrard of Barres, who should be revered for his piety and who furnished the army an honorable example, saved their own possessions wisely and alertly and protected those of other people as courageously as possible. Now the king liked the example which they set and was glad to imitate it, and he wanted the army to be influenced in that direction, for he knew that, even if extreme hunger should weaken them, unity of spirit would also strengthen them in their weakness. By common consent, therefore, it was decided that during this dangerous period all should establish fraternity with the Templars, rich and poor taking oath that they would not flee the field and that they would obey in every respect the officers assigned them by the Templars. Thus they were given a commander named Gilbert, and he was given associates, to each of whom he should assign fifty knights. Because the Turks were quick to flee, our men were commanded to endure, until they received an order, the attacks of the enemies; and to withdraw forthwith when recalled, even though they should be making a stand as originally commanded. When they had learned this, they were also taught the order of march, so that a person in front would not rush to the rear and the guards on the flanks would not fall into disorder.[6] Moreover those whom nature or fortune had made foot soldiers (for, because they had lost or sold their equipment, many nobles were marching among the crowd in a manner unusual for them) were drawn up at the very rear in order to oppose with their bows the enemies' arrows. Although the king is the lord of laws,[7]

dientiae legibus subiacere; sed nullus ausus est ei quicquam ex praecepto iniungere, hoc excepto quod aciem copiosam haberet et, sicut dominus omnium et provisor, imbecilles quosque missis de illa sociis roboraret.

Fiebat iuxta praeceptum processio, et de plano descensis montibus gaudebamus, et protervos assultus hostium sine damno vallati tutoribus[i] ferebamus. Erant autem in via duo rivi uno miliario distantes ab invicem lutosa profunditate transitum habentes difficilem. Primum transivimus in partem alteram, ultimos expectantes et de luto summarios debiles manibus sublevantes. Ultimi quoque milites et pedites hostibus fere mixti[j] transierunt sine damno mutua probitate defensi. Tendebamus ad secundum, inter duos scopulos transituri de quorum verticibus poterat turba [38r] gradiens sagittari. Ad hos Turci ab utraque parte festinant, sed unum eorum milites nostri praeoccupant. Illi vero alium ascendunt, et capillos[k] de capitibus ad pedes proiciunt, quo signo dictum nobis est praemonstrari illos de tali loco nulli timore moveri. Sed illa significatio tunc falsum vel nihil significavit, quia turba nostrorum peditum illos ilico propulsavit. Sed dum illi de montis vertice contendebant, milites posse fugam illorum inter duos amnes intercipi cogitabant. Unde, data licentia a magistro, omnes unanimiter illos invadunt, et quos possunt consequi mortes suorum et damna propria vindicantes[l] occidunt. Quorum multi venientes ad lutum, in loco idoneo mortem sortiti sunt et sepulcrum. Dum perimit fugitivos irae impetus et fuga longior, erat omnibus fames levis[m] et dies laetior.

Sed Turci[n] et Graeci modis pluribus de nostro interitu cogitabant. Ad hoc enim, cum prius essent inimici, foedus inierant. Illi ergo congregatis undique pecoribus et armentis,[o] depascentes foedabant ante nos quicquid non poterat urere ignis. Ob hoc fessi vel

---

[i] vallati tutoribus sine damno CM.
[j] fere mixti *over erasure* D2.
[k] capellos M.
[l] vidicantes D.

[m] levior CM.
[n] curci > turci D1.
[o] et armentis D2.

he, too, wished to be subject to these laws; but no one dared to
impose any command on him except that he should maintain a
full battle line and, as befits the lord and protector of all, strengthen
the weak by sending them reinforcements from his group.

We advanced according to this arrangement, and, after descend-
ing the mountains, rejoiced at reaching level ground, and, since
we were surrounded by protectors, we endured the enemies' bold
attacks without any loss. On this route, however, were two rivers
a mile apart, and the deep mud on their banks made crossing difficult. After crossing the first we awaited the rear guard and pulled
the feeble sumpter horses from the mud with our hands. Almost
mingling with the enemy, the knights and foot soldiers in the rear
guard crossed, too, but they suffered no loss, for they were protected by the pact of mutual aid. We went toward the second river
with the intent of passing between two crags from whose summit
it was possible to shoot at the crowd as it approached. From both
sides the Turks hastened to the crags, but our knights seized one
of them first. The Turks climbed the other, however, and threw
on the ground hair plucked from their heads, and by this sign, we
were told, they indicated that they could not be dislodged from
that spot by any kind of fear. But that sign was either false in
this instance or did not mean anything, because the throng of our
foot soldiers routed them immediately. But, while they were
struggling for the top of the crag, the knights thought that the
Turks' retreat could be cut off between the two rivers. Therefore,
when permission had been granted by the commander, all attacked
the Turks at once, and they killed those whom they could overtake, thus avenging the death of their comrades and their own
losses. Upon reaching the mud flats many Turks found death and
a grave in a place suited to their filthy natures. While our wrathful
attack and lengthy pursuit destroyed those fugitives, everybody's
hunger was slight and his day was brighter.

But the Turks and the Greeks were planning our destruction in
many different ways. For, although they were formerly enemies,
they entered into an agreement for this very purpose. And so, by
gathering the flocks and the cattle from everywhere and by allow-
ing them to graze ahead of us, they destroyed the produce which
they could not burn. For this reason horses were left on the road

mortui equi remanebant in via et eorum onera, tentoria, vestes, et
arma et alia multa quae nostri, ne remanerent hostibus, combure-
bant, exceptis his quae pauperes asportabant. Comedebat igitur
exercitus, et has abundanter habebat, carnes equorum, et qui non
erant habiles ad portandum contra famem dabant remedium, quibus
dapibus contenti erant etiam divites quando habebant de farina
subcinericium. Tali providentia temperata est fames, et fraterni-
tate praescripta quater fugavimus, et semper vicimus hostes, et
usque Satelliam sine damno viribus illato labore provido tutati
sumus, excepto illo die quo Gaufredum de Rancone mortis et damni
praevium fecimus.

In hac urbe nuntius imperatoris Landulfus, qui cum Turcis, sicut
ipse fatebatur, partem[p] viae[q] venerat, ex voto praestolabatur nostrum interitum vel venientibus, si de imperatore quaereremus,
excusationis praeparabat responsum. Sed quia nemo veniret in ius
cessavere querelae, erat enim victualibus opus famelicis, fessis
quiete. Ille ergo, conscius sceleris, causa fori cogit iterum nobiles
pacem firmare imperatori. Tunc [38v] quae nobis in via pepercerant
inundantissimae venere pluviae, quas sentientes subtus et desuper
in parvis tentoriis (quia maiores remanserant) celebravimus purifi-
cationem beatae Mariae. Nam certe rex in tota via nulla die
missam vel horas perdidit nec inundatione imbrium nec oppressione
hostium.

Habebamus, licet solito carius, ciborum abundantia, sed equis
qui remanserant nullo pretio inveniebamus annonam, Graecis hoc
dolose agentibus, sicut nostrorum multi dicebant; illi autem sui
loci monstrantes asperitatem, se non habere dicebant. Erat extra
urbem usque ad quemdam fluvium saxosa planities, et hostes ultra

<p partim CM.   <q illic CM.

---

[8] They arrived there *ca.* January 20, 1148.

[9] William of Tyre (Babcock and Krey, II, 178) gives the following information about
Adalia: "Attalia lies on the seacoast and is subject to the emperor of Constantinople. It
possesses very rich fields, which are, nevertheless, of no advantage to the townspeople, for
they are surrounded by enemies on all sides who hinder their cultivation. Therefore the
fertile soil lies fallow, since there is no one to work it. Yet the place has many other advantages which it offers freely to visitors. It is most delightfully situated, it abounds in
clear and healthful waters and it is planted with fruit-bearing trees. The grain supply is
brought from overseas in ample quantities, so that those resorting there are well supplied
with the necessaries of life" . . . "It borders very closely, however, on the land of the
enemy, and since it was found impossible to endure their continual attacks, it became tribu-
tary to them. Through this connection, Attalia maintains trade in necessaries with the
enemy."

exhausted or dead, and also left behind were their packs, tents, clothing, arms, and many other things which, with the exception of those that the poor carried away, our men burned in order to prevent their falling into the enemies' hands. Therefore the army ate and kept on hand plenty of horse flesh, and the horses which were not fit for the pack train alleviated our hunger; with this food and bread baked in the ashes of the campfires even the wealthy were satisfied. By such provision our hunger was relieved, and as a result of the aforesaid fraternity we routed the enemy four times and were victorious each time, and by careful endeavor, until we reached Adalia,[8] we kept ourselves safe, without suffering any loss to our forces except on the day when we made Geoffrey of Rancon our leader to death and destruction.

In Adalia[9] the emperor's messenger Landulph, who had made part of his journey with the Turks, as he admitted, was hopefully anticipating the news of our death and, in the event that we should come and complain about the emperor, was preparing an excuse in reply. But because no one approached him for justice, for the starving had to have food and the weary rest, the complaints stopped. He therefore, as an accomplice of the crime, forced the nobles to reconfirm the pact made with the emperor for the sake of market privileges. Then came the deluging rains, which had spared us during the journey, and, while feeling them above and beneath us in the small tents (for the larger ones had been left behind), we celebrated the feast of the Purification of the Virgin;[10] for it is true that during the entire journey the king never forgot mass or the hours because of floods of rain or the enemy's violence.

We obtained an abundance of food, though at a higher price than usual, but for the horses which had survived we could not obtain grain at any price, because, as many of our men said, the Greeks betrayed us in this respect; pointing out the barrenness of the soil, they said that they had no grain.[11] Outside the city lay a rocky plain which extended to the brink of a certain river, and

---

[10] February 2.

[11] William of Tyre, *op. cit.*, Vol. II, confirms this: "At Attalia the king of the Franks and his people suffered from a serious shortage of food brought on by the great number of people who had come thither; in fact the survivors of the army, and above all the poor, nearly perished of famine."

forum venientes[r] a foris et pabula prohibentes, unde nec etiam
herbas habebant equi nisi eos ducerent et reducerent armati milites.
Videns ergo rex paucos equos qui remanserant non quiete refici sed
fame mori nec in urbe venales aliquos inveniri, loquitur de processu
baronibus convocatis, dicens, "Ubi fame moriuntur equi non habere milites locum quietis. Insuper poenitentis esse pro quiete
votum tardare et devoti fessum et aegrotum[s] ad metam propositi
festinare, et coronari ut martyres quorum Deus animas de tali sumit
labore."

Illi vero, servantes oboedientiam domino et possibilem solventes
perseverantiam[t] voto, dixerunt, "Sicut regis est iubere fortia, sic
prudentis est militis audere possibilia. Omnes vestri exercitus gre-
garii milites his diebus armis proiectis pedites sunt effecti, et cum
eis de nobilioribus multi. Alius horum non potest equos emere
quia sua omnia perdidit vel expendit; alius cui superest venales non
invenit. Illi didicerunt ab istis civibus esse per mare usque Antiochiam tres dietas de portu in portum[u] parvas, opulentas et tutas,
et per terram quadraginta torrentibus invias, hostibus obsitas, et
egestate continuas. Ob hoc volunt se mari committere, et cum eis
copia peditum quibus iam deest virtus ad laborem, census ad vic-
tum. Et Graeci omnibus de vicinis villis et insulis superabundans
promittunt navigium. Nos autem vobiscum mori et vivere volumus, et libenter secundum hoc quod[v] vobis placuerit audiemus."

Rex igitur illis regio more suoque respondit, "Me divite nullus
vir probatus egebit[w] qui[x] mecum paupertatem in necessitate patien-
ter pertulerit. His [39r] ergo electis et de nostro reparatis, inermem
turbam navigio committamus[y] quae semper nocuit nobis,[z] pro qua
victus carior et gressus tardior extitit; et nos nostrorum parentum
gradiamur iter, quibus mundi famam et caeli gloriam probitas
incomparabilis dedit."

---

[r] veniens CM.
[s] egrorum CM.
[t] persoverantiam > perseverantiam D1; perseverentiam CM.
[u] portu in D2.
[v] et libenter . . . quod D2.

[w] Me . . . ege- *over erasure* D2.
[x] non *deleted* Dx.
[y] committimus CM.
[z] nobis nocuit CM.

---

[12] See above, p. 125.
[13] Cf. Conrad's desire to separate his army into two groups in Asia Minor, as discussed
above, p. 51, n. 29.
[14] The precedent of the first crusaders, already noted on p. 59, was strong with Louis.

since the enemy outside prevented the horses from coming beyond the gates and to the pastures the animals did not even get grass to eat unless armed knights led them to and fro. Seeing that the few horses which had survived were not being refreshed by rest, but were dying of hunger, and that no horses were to be bought in the city, the king, calling his barons together, therefore spoke about departing, saying: "Knights do not have the privilege of resting in a place where their horses die of hunger. A penitent should, moreover, suppress his desire to rest; and a devout man, even though weary and ailing, should hasten to the goal of the undertaking, and it befits both to be crowned as martyrs whose souls God takes from such toil to Himself."

But, although preserving obedience to their lord and adhering to his wish as fully as possible, the barons said: "Just as a king should command what is brave, so, too, should a wise knight attempt only what is possible. Since they have cast their arms aside, all of the common knights in your army have been reduced to foot soldiers in these days, and the same fate has befallen many of the more noble ones.[12] Of these, one knight cannot buy horses because he has lost or sold his property; another, who still has property, cannot find horses for sale. From the natives they have learned that the journey to Antioch by sea takes three short, well-provisioned, safe days from one port to another and that by land the journey takes forty days in territory blocked by torrents, beset by enemies, and consistent in barrenness. Therefore they wish to put to sea, as does the throng of foot soldiers who now lack courage for toil and money for food. And the Greeks promise to collect a very large fleet from all the neighboring villages and islands. However, we wish to live and die with you, and we will gladly agree to the course which pleases you."

Therefore the king replied to them in his own regal fashion: "While I shall be rich, no man of tried valor who has patiently endured poverty with me in a time of great need shall want. Thus, when such men have been selected and equipped from my means, let us entrust to the fleet the defenseless mob, which has always harmed us and on whose account food is more expensive and progress slower;[13] and let us follow the route of our fathers, whose incomparable valor endowed them with renown on earth and glory in heaven."[14]

Ad haec illi, "Non," inquiunt, "Volumus deprimere, nec possumus, laudem parentum, sed levius cum eis hucusque actum est[a] quam nobiscum. Cum enim illi Constantinopolim et Brachium pertransissent, voti compotes Turcos et eorum terras ilico reppererunt, et, de exercitio militiae alacres, et de captione urbium et castrorum sese divites servaverunt. Nos autem Graecos fraudulentos in locis illorum[b] invenimus, quibus (malo nostro) velut Christianis pepercimus; otioque torpentes taedio et molestiis aegrotantes, fere omnia nostra expendimus. Alii, stulta securitate vel aspera paupertate, arma etiam vendiderunt vel equis morientibus reliquerunt. Tamen hoc quod iubetis honestum est, sed supradictis de causis tutum non est. Sed nos illud, labore et timore postposito, faciemus si equos ad reparandos milites invenire poterimus."

Qui requisiti cum paucitate non sufficerent et debilitate nihil valerent, coegerunt regem vellet nollet marina naufragia experiri, ut "periculis in mari, periculis in solitudine, periculis ex gentibus, periculis ex falsis fratribus," sicut et Pauli, permitteret Deus eius patientiam exerceri. Denique dux urbis et nuntius imperatoris super hoc negotio consuluntur, qui respondent ad placitum navesque cito venturas toto exercitui[c] pollicentur. Hiems interim exercet quod distulerat; pluit, ningit, tonat, et fulgurat; et differtur ventus usque ad quinque hebdomadas quem cito sperabamus a Domino, navesque amplius quas expectabamus de Graecorum promisso. Graeci autem scientes quoniam modicum tempus habent, omnem quam possunt malitiam exerunt,[d] rebus in foro nos spoliantes et quantum possunt suis consiliis vita privantes. Inveniebant sanus et aeger quicquid requirebat eorum qualitas, sed gravabat eos pretii quantitas. Habebant gallinam pro decem solidis et ovum unum pro sex vel quinque denariis. Unum caepe vel allium pro septem vel octo (secundum grossitudinem pretio temperato) nuces-

---

       [a] eis . . . est D2.   [c] exercitu C.
       [b] illo > illorum D2.   [d] exierunt > exerunt Dx; exercent CM.

---

[15] This series of speeches has a very authentic ring. It is significant that the knights recognized that they had become enfeebled because of lack of combats; that the anti-Greek feeling was strong. Almost staggering is the importance of horses.

[16] Louis reports this series of conferences to Suger by saying that after they had deliberated for a long time about continuing the journey the council of nobles and churchmen advised him to go to Antioch by water, because the supply of horses had been exhausted and the more difficult part of the road still lay ahead. Thus, following their advice, Louis and most of his nobles arrived at Antioch on March 19. See RHGF, XV, 496.

To these remarks they answered: "We do not want to and cannot depreciate our fathers' renown, but events went more easily for them than they have thus far for us. For when they had passed through Constantinople and crossed the Arm, they encountered the Turks immediately and entered their lands, just as they had wished, and while they maintained their alacrity by practicing warfare, they kept themselves rich by capturing cities and fortresses. Instead of the Turks, however, we met with the wily Greeks, whom we spared, to our bad luck, as if they were Christians; and, sluggish with idleness and ailing from weariness and annoyances, we have spent nearly all our wealth. Out of a foolish sense of security or from bitter poverty, some have even sold their arms or abandoned them after their horses died. For the aforesaid reasons the course which you command, though honorable, is not safe. But, disregarding fear and hardship, we will follow it if we can find horses with which to re-equip the knights."[15]

Horses were sought for; but since they did not suffice, because they were few and of no account by reason of their weakness, the barons forced the king to risk shipwreck willy-nilly,[16] so that God might permit his patience, like Paul's, to be tried "in perils in the sea, in perils in the wilderness, in perils by the Heathen, and in perils among false brethren."[17] Then the commandant of the city and the emperor's messenger were consulted about this undertaking, and they answered the plea favorably and promised that ships for the entire army would arrive soon. Meanwhile the winter loosed the bad weather that it had delayed; it rained, snowed, thundered, and lightened, and the wind with which we were hoping that the Lord would soon favor us did not come until the fifth week; and the same was true, too, about the ships which we were awaiting on the promise of the Greeks. Now, since the Greeks knew that the time at their disposal was short, they performed all the evil deeds which they could, robbing us of goods in the market and, insofar as they could by their plots, depriving us of life. The well and the sick found whatever their condition demanded, but the high price grieved them. They got a hen for ten solidi and a single egg for five or six denarii. We got an onion or a bulb of garlic for seven or eight denarii, the price adjusted to the size, and

[17] Cf. II Corinthians 11:26.

que duas habebamus pro uno. Quibus equus vel mula remanserant eos [39v] pro panibus cambiebant vel more boum in macello vendebant. Haec enim nostra fuit cum Graecis conditio, vendere sine pretio et care emere sine modo.

Itaque Turci militibus equos deesse Graecis referentibus didicerunt, et hac usi securitate ad invadendum exercitum se unanimiter paraverunt. Quod notum factum est regi et contra illos abscondit secum viros ditiores qui dextrarios suos, quamvis famelicos, adhuc servaverant[e] et fratres Templi. Venientibusque apparens subito coegit eos occidendo sine ponte fluvium retransire et credere deinceps in exercitu equos optimos abundare. Parant interim Graeci naves, sicut res alias, pretio inaudito. Dabat unus homo quattuor marcas usque Antiochiam, quo venturi[f] eramus, sicut ipsi praedixerant, in die tertio. Haec paucae et parvae regi quasi donum gratuitum a duce et imperatoris nuntio praesentantur, et ab eo episcopis et baronibus dividuntur. Voluit eas habere, tamen pretium aegre tulit et, querelas inutiles tegens silentio reliquo exercitui, sicut promiserant, naves quaerit. Illi vero dum divites expectant pauperes, illud diu procrastinant, et rebus utrosque tali latrocinio spoliabant. Credo autem quod quietem carius emimus huius urbis quam labores totius itineris.

Dicturi vero sunt ignari talium hanc urbem debuisse capi et vindictam sumi de dolis civium. Recogitent illi dextra laevaque privatis et extraneis hostibus sine victualibus nos obsessos et esse impossibile turres arduas sine machinis ruere[g] vel cito posse suffodi duplices muros. Poterant quidem dux et imperatoris nuntius capi quando veniebant ad regem, sed cives pro illorum suspendio non redderent civitatem. Eratque regi abominabile, contra morem suum hanc[h] proditione capi et commune periculum sine captione

[e] servan- > servav- Dx.	[g] ruire > ruere D1.
[f] v/venturi > venturi Dx.	[h] hac M.

[18] It is difficult to say whether the "they" and the "we" refer to the sick and the well or whether they are the result of a grammatical slip.

[19] The account of the business transaction concerning the ships is rather confusing. Probably some ship space was sold directly to private people by the Greeks and some ships were sold to Louis, who divided them among the prelates and the barons. It is hard to reconcile the expression "free gift" with Louis' dissatisfaction with the high price.

two nuts for one denarius.[18] Those who still had a horse or mule exchanged them for bread or sold them in the meat market as if they were cattle. For, when among the Greeks our plight was to sell without profit and to buy at an extremely dear price.

From the Greeks, then, the Turks learned that our knights had no horses, and, taking advantage of this security, prepared to attack the army in full force. This was made known to the king, and for a move against the Turks he concealed with him the Templars and the wealthy knights, who still had kept their chargers even though they were starving. Appearing suddenly before the advancing Turks, he killed some, thus forcing the rest to recross the river without using a bridge and to believe from that time forth that the army had plenty of excellent horses. Meanwhile the Greeks furnished ships at an outrageous price, as was true of their other wares. One man paid four marks for passage to Antioch, where we were to arrive on the third day, as the Greeks had said. These few poor vessels were presented to the king as if they were a free gift from the commandant and the emperor's messenger and were divided among the bishops and the barons by him. Although he resented the high price, he wanted ships, and, burying useless complaints in silence, sought the vessels promised for the rest of the army.[19] But while the wealthy waited for the poor the Greeks delayed for a long time and, by such villainy, robbed both classes of their possessions.[20] I really believe that we paid more dearly for our respite in this town than we did for all the hardships on the journey.

Those who are ignorant of such things will say that this city should have been captured and that revenge should have been exacted for the citizens' frauds. Let such people reflect that we had no food and were besieged on the right and on the left by enemies within and without and that it was impossible to destroy the lofty towers or to undermine the double walls quickly without siege machinery. The commandant and the emperor's messenger could have been seized when they were coming to see the king, but the citizens would not have given up the city in order to save these two from being hanged. And the king found it abhorrent and contrary to his custom to have the city seized by treachery and to

---

[20] That is, because of the high cost of food and other commodities.

temptari. Parcat[i] Deus Alemanno imperatori, cuius fortunam vitantes et indocto consilio acquiescentes[j] in haec mala devenimus; sed Graeco quomodo parcet iustus iudex, Deus vel homo, qui dolosa crudelitate[k] tot Christianos occidit utriusque exercitus?

Populus ergo novorum pauperum affectus taedio, spoliatus argento, corruptus[l] morbo, cognitoque de navibus Graecorum mendacio, ad regem veniunt cui suam voluntatem et paupertatem[m] his et [40r] similibus verbis exponunt, "Domine rex, in vestrae maiestatis praesentia merito astamus confusi,[n] tamen illud audemus, de vestra bonitate confisi; quando enim Graecis credentes vobiscum per terram ire noluimus,[o] in hoc inertes in alio decepti sumus. Modo vero paupertate cogente, illud volumus facere sine duce. Vadimus in mortem, sed Deo volente valere[p] poterit vitare praesentem.[q] Tolerabilior[r] erit forsitan Turcorum[s] gladius quam, post discessum[t] vestrum, istorum civium dolus."

Quibus rex solita miseratione condoluit, et eorum egestate tam larga effusione consuluit ut crederes eum nihil antea expendisse vel de cetero curam domus propriae contempsisse. Deinde, volens eos in itinere tutos fore, pactum facit cum nuntio imperatoris et duce ut ab eo quingentas[u] marcas[v] acciperent et suos ultra duos fluvios qui erant prope cum magna manu conducerent et postea darent eis competentem[w] comitatum qui posset eos securos ducere Tarsum. In urbe vero debiles et infirmi susciperentur quousque convalescentes invento navigio alios sequerentur. Illi ergo, de argento cupidi et contra Turcos timidi, prius cum illis locuti sunt et, sicut tunc putavimus, cum eis pretium diviserunt; et reversi, sumptis secum divitibus civitatis, pactum simul sicut praedictum est iuraverunt. Redditur argentum, et illi iubent debiles civitatem intrare et alios

---

[i] paccat > parcat D1.	[q] praesentem *over erasure* D1.
[j] et . . . acquies D2.	[r] tolelabilior > tolerabilior D1.
[k] crudelita- *over erasure* D1.	[s] turcorum *over erasure* D1.
[l] corrruptus D.	[t] dicessum D.
[m] pauptatem D.	[u] quingentes M.
[n] consusi D.	[v] in arcas D.
[o] voluimus D.	[w] competens D.
[p] volere > valere D1.	

---

[21] Probably a less scrupulous leader would have been more advantageous for the success of the expedition. Although Louis hesitated to endanger his army in the matter of seizing the city, he allowed it to incur disastrous losses because he took no decided action during his campaign in Asia Minor.

[22] Because he suggested the shore route rather than the direct road through Philadelphia. See above, p. 105.

hazard the danger of all without seizing it.[21] May God spare the German emperor, even though it was by avoiding his ill fortune and following his inexpert advice that we came into these evil straits;[22] but how will a just judge, either God or man, spare the Greek emperor, who by cunning cruelty killed so many Christians in both the German and the Frankish armies?[23]

Thus, when the host of new paupers, succumbing to tedium, robbed of their money, and wasted with disease, learned that the Greeks had lied about the ships, they came to the king and set forth their will and their poverty to him in these words and others like them: "O Lord King, in the presence of your majesty we stand confused, as is right, but we dare to come because we put our trust in your goodness; for when we did not wish to march with you by land, because we believed in the Greeks, we were both lazy and deluded. But, because we now feel the compulsion of poverty, we wish to make the march without our leader. We are rushing to meet death, but, if God wills us to prevail, we can avoid the death which threatens us. Perhaps it will be easier to endure the Turk's sword than the treachery of these natives after your departure."

With his usual compassion the king sympathized with them, and he provided for their needs with such generous largesse that you would have thought that he had spent nothing heretofore or else that he disdained to take further care for his own household. Since he wanted his subjects to be safe during their journey, he then made an agreement with the commandant and the emperor's messenger to the effect that they should receive five hundred marks from him and that, with a large troop, they should lead his men beyond the two rivers nearby and afterwards give them an escort able to lead them safely to Tarsus. The weak and the invalids were to be admitted to the city until, having recovered and obtained passage, they might follow. Then the Greek officers, who were greedy for money and afraid of the Turks, conferred with the Turks first and, as we thought at that time, divided the money with them; and upon returning, they and some wealthy citizens whom they brought along, swore to the aforesaid agreement. The money was paid; and the Greeks ordered the invalids to enter the city and the rest of the men to prepare themselves for the journey

[23] For a discussion of this point, see above, p. xxii.

ad iter se in crastinum praeparare. Adhuc suis[x] rex providet equos
quos invenire potuit congregans et probatis militibus eos donans;
fraudemque timens ubi saepius illam invenerat, comitem Flandren-
sem et Archembaldum[y] Burbonensem usque ad processum illorum
dimisit, et ipse cum benedictione remanentium naves ascendit.

In crastinum pedestris exercitus duces itineris expectabat, et ecce
Turcorum populus regem discessisse[z] per Graecos edoctus quasi ad
certam praedam contra illos veniebat. Quos contra comes Flandrensis et Archembaldus Burbonensis acies suas ordinant, animosas
sed pigras quia paucos et debiles equos habebant. Hostibus occurrunt, confligunt, dant terga qui veniebant ad spolia; sed quoniam
non fuit qui posset illos velociter insequi, pauci sunt illorum occisi.
Post haec ducem nuntiumque imperatoris et cives[a] de pacto requi-
runt quod regi iuraverant, et illi tunc primum de [40v] impossibili-
tate, Turcos monstrantes et hiemem, se excusant. In hoc dies aliquos et verba plurima perdiderunt, nec illos iure, ratione, vel hone-
state vicerunt. Tandem querela deposita de conductu, vix conce-
dunt nostro infra murum propugnaculi[b] hospitari[c] et eis ibidem
usque ad navigium forum praeberi. Quo facto viri regii vadunt ad
naves, eo quod suas iniurias non possunt vindicare dolentes.

Deinde Turci urbi appropriant,[d] intrant, et exeunt et aperte
Graecis communicant. Vident inter duo genera hostium et murorum suos hostes densos includi, sicut pecudes in ovili, et eos, qui
non audent exire vel ingredi, posse ibidem sagittari. Erat murus
humilis et inflexus, et ei non poterat inhaerere tam densus populus;
unde remotiores patebant vulneribus. Turci ergo de locis congruis
sagittas immittunt et vulnerant aliquos vel occidunt. Tunc probati

---

[x] *om*. M.
[y] archebaldum > archembaldum Dx.
[z] decessisse D.
[a] et cives *om*. W.

[b] propugnali D.
[c] hospitari *over version of itself* D2.
[d] approximant CM.

---

[24] That Louis feared the agreement would not be carried out seems obvious. His departure
under such circumstances appears to have been a sort of desertion; and yet it is hard to say
how he could have salvaged his army at that time, when it was so demoralized and badly
equipped.

[25] Although Odo had evidently left Adalia when Louis did, he could have learned of these
happenings from the count of Flanders and Archibald of Bourbon. After their departure the
source of his information is not apparent.

on the morrow. In addition the king provided for his men by collecting all the horses which he could find and giving them to knights of proven valor; and, since he feared the presence of deception where he had often experienced it, he had the count of Flanders and Archibald of Bourbon stay behind until the people should depart, and he himself embarked, accompanied by the blessing of those who remained behind.[24]

On the morrow, when the army of foot soldiers was awaiting its guides, suddenly the Turks, who had been informed by the Greeks of the king's departure, marched upon our men as if to certain prey. Against these the count of Flanders and Archibald of Bourbon arranged battle lines, in which the men were courageous, but slow, because they had only a few feeble horses. They rushed against their enemies and engaged with them, and those who had come for plunder fled; but since there was no one who could follow them quickly, few of the enemy were killed. After this incident the Franks demanded that the commandant and the emperor's messenger and the natives fulfill the agreement which they had sworn to the king that they would observe; and then for the first time the Greeks absolved themselves on the ground that the agreement was impossible, indicating the Turks and the winter as reasons. In this discussion the Franks lost several days and a great many words, and they did not win the Greeks over even by appealing to their sense of justice, reason, or honor. Finally, when the dispute about the escort had been abandoned, the Greeks hardly allowed our men to be lodged within the fortress wall and to have a market furnished them there until they sailed. When the fleet arrived the king's deputies hastened on board, grieving at their inability to avenge the wrongs done them.[25]

Then the Turks drew near the city, went in and out, and openly communicated with the Greeks. They saw their enemies confined close-packed between two kinds of enemies and walls, just like sheep in a fold, and they realized that since they dared to go neither in nor out they could be mowed down with arrows there. The wall was low and curving, and such a large crowd of people could not gain protection by clinging to it; and thus the ones farther away were likely to be wounded. Therefore the Turks shot arrows in from advantageous points and wounded or killed some of the

iuvenes coeperunt de muro,[e] sumptis arcubus, prosilire, suam suo-
rumque vitam tueri vel mortem vendere; quaerentesque[f] pacem
viribus hostes longius cogunt refugere. Haberent pacem, sed eos
Graeci sine vulnere perimebant, qui sanos cum aegris in arto et
immundo loco recluserant. Et dum hos fames occidit nummis
deficientibus luesque corrumpit alios, vicinis cadaveribus corruunt
multi, Graecis non inferentibus mortem sed expectantibus. Ob hoc
virorum fortium duae turmae trium et quattuor milium, ne more-
rentur, sunt mortuae, iudicantes idem foras mori et intus vivere.
Qui sumptis armis, exeunt duos fluvios transituri, loco vicinos sed
magnitudine dispari. Primum facile transierunt, sed ad secundum
duplici obstaculo restiterunt. Amnis enim non nisi natando, nec
hostis ibi congregatus nisi pugnando poterat pertransiri, sed utrumque simul non poterat exerceri; et ideo revertentes, fugati sunt
capti vel mortui.

Sanguine istorum sitis Turcorum extincta est et dolus Graecorum
in violentiam conversus est. Illi enim reversi sunt eos videre qui
remanserant, et deinceps aegris et pauperibus largas eleemosynas
faciebant; Graeci vero, cogentes fortiores ad sua servitia, loco mer-
cedis verberabant. Quidam Turcorum a suis sociis nostras monetas
emebant et inter pauperes plena manu dividebant; Graeci[g] vero illis
quibus aliquid remanserat auferebant. Vitantes igitur sibi [41r]
crudeles socios fidei inter infideles sibi compatientes ibant securi;
et, sicut audivimus, plusquam tria milia iuvenum sunt illis rece-
dentibus sociati. O pietas omni proditione crudelior, dantes panem
fidem tollebant, quamvis certum sit, quia contenti servitio, nemi-
nem negare cogebant. Deus autem, execrans civitatem, tam districte
cives eius subita morte percussit, ut multae domus in ea vacuae
remanerent, et vivi stupentes et timentes eam omnino relinquere

---

[e] muris W.
[f] q *erased, rewritten to make space between* vendere *and* quaerentesque D1.
[g] Graecis DCM.

people. Then, taking their bows in hand, the seasoned youths began to leap down from the wall, so that they might either protect their own lives and those of their comrades or sell their lives dearly; and by seeking peace thus forcibly they compelled the enemy to withdraw farther. They would have had peace; but the Greeks, by confining well and ailing people in one narrow and unclean place, killed them without inflicting a single wound. And while some starved because they had no money and disease wasted others, many died from the effect of the corpses left near at hand, with the Greeks not inflicting death but awaiting it for the Franks. For this reason two troops of three or four thousand strong men died in order to avoid dying, judging that living within the city was tantamount to dying without. After taking up their arms they went forth with the intention of crossing the two rivers, which were similarly situated, but unlike in size. The first they crossed easily, but at the second they halted before a double obstacle. For they could cross the stream only if they swam across, and they could penetrate the enemy drawn up there only if they fought through, but both they could not accomplish at the same time; and, turning back for this reason, they were routed and either captured or killed.

By the blood of these soldiers the Turks' thirst was quenched and the Greeks' treachery was transformed into violence; for the Turks returned to see the survivors and then gave generous alms to the sick and the poor, but the Greeks forced the stronger Franks into their service and beat them by way of payment. Some Turks bought our coins from their allies and distributed them among the poor with a liberal hand; but the Greeks robbed those who had anything left. Therefore, avoiding the fellow-believers who were so cruel to them, the Franks went safely among the unbelievers, who had compassion on them; and, we have heard, more than three thousand young men went with the Turks when they departed. O, pity more cruel than any betrayal, since in giving bread they took away faith (although it is certain that the Turks, content with the service they gained, did not force anyone to deny his faith)! Now God, cursing the town of Adalia, smote its people so severely with sudden death that many houses there remained empty, and the living, stunned and fearful, planned to leave it

cogitarent. Imperator quoque Deo contrarius in iudicio eo, quod illa regi forum paraverat et navigium, illam[h] penitus auro et argento spoliavit. Sic Deus et ille contraria sentiebant, tamen hanc uterque punivit.

Rex autem cum in hac quinque complesset hebdomadas, quibusdam suorum navibus confractis vel cassatis, non tamen Deo volente submersis, usque Antiochiam naufragando consummavit tres alias. Gravia sunt quae pertulit damna et pericula, pater Sugeri, sed ipso debetis sospite consolari. Illi etiam proderit laborasse, qui scitur in periculis tutus et post[i] damna[j] laetus constanter et prudenter omnia pertulisse. Sola illi gravis erat adversitas subditorum,[k] quibus semper pro posse consuluit, putans esse regis non sibi nasci sed utilitatibus aliorum, et sicut regis est habere pietatem, sic eiusdem esse numquam timere paupertatem. Ad probitatem cautelam regiam postponebat, et tutelam primam vel ultimam, et excubias noctium vicibus alternis faciens, algorem noctium dierumque fervorem sub lorica tolerabat. In tot laboribus servatus est incolumis sine medicina pro exercitio sanctitatis quia semper a divinis sacramentis obviabat viribus hostium et revertens ab hostibus requirebat vesperas et completorium, Deum[l] semper faciens alpha et omega suorum operum. Sic liberalis ut rex, animosus ut princeps, acer ut miles, ut iuvenis alacris, maturus ut senior, locis et temporibus et virtutibus singulis se aptabat; et de probitate favorem hominum, de religione divinam gratiam conquirebat.

[h] illa > illam Dx.   [k] subitorum D.
[i] per W.   [l] dominicum W.
[j] dampno > dampna D1.

altogether.[26] The emperor, although opposed to God in judgment, also completely despoiled the city of silver and gold, because it had prepared a fleet and a market for the king. Thus, God and he held opposite opinions, but both punished the city.

Now after the king had spent five weeks in this city he spent three more weeks suffering shipwreck on the way to Antioch, for some of his vessels were battered and damaged, but yet, by the will of God, not sunk.[27] Serious were the losses and hazards which he endured, Father Suger, but you ought to be comforted by the fact that he is safe. For it will even be to his advantage to have toiled thus, since he is recognized as one who is prudent in time of danger and serenely happy after suffering losses, and he has borne all kinds of fortune wisely and steadfastly. His only grief was for the misfortune of his subjects, of whom he always took as much care as possible, on the theory that a king is born, not for his own benefit, but for the advantage of others and that a king should be not only pious but also without any fear of poverty. In order to live up to his ideal of honor he disregarded the caution usual for a king and, clad in mail, endured the nights' cold and the days' heat while protecting alternately the van and the rear guard. Amid so many hardships his safe preservation was owed to no other remedy than his religion, for he always took communion before he went to attack the enemy forces and on his return requested vespers and compline, in such wise always making God the alpha and the omega of his deeds.[28] Thus, as a generous prince, a brave knight, a lively youth, a mature older man, he adapted himself to various situations, circumstances, and capacities; and by his integrity he procured the favor of men, by his piety the favor of God.[29]

---

[26] The citizens evidently succumbed to the illness which had been among the crusaders. This fact seems to belie Odo's accusation that they left the corpses around so that the Franks would die of disease. Had the Greeks been subtle enough to plan such a death, they surely would have foreseen the damage which would ensue for themselves.

[27] Louis describes this journey as pleasant sailing (*felici navigatione*). See RHGF, XV, 496. On p. 135 above Odo says that he arrived in Antioch on the third day after leaving Adalia. Evidently he was not in Louis' vessel.

[28] Revelation 21:6, 13.

[29] For other eulogies of Louis see *Fragmentum historicum de Ludovico VII*, RHGF, XII, 89–91; *Liber III historiae regum Francorum, ibid.*, pp. 220–21; *Anonymi chronicon, ibid.*, p. 120.

BIBLIOGRAPHICAL ABBREVIATIONS

CSHB   *Corpus scriptorum historiae Byzantinae;* ed. by J. Reiske, Vol. VIII, Bonn, Weber, 1829; ed. by I. Bekker, Vol. XXII, Bonn, Weber, 1835; ed. by A. Meineke, Vol. XXV, Bonn, Weber, 1836.

GC   *Gallia Christiania in provincias ecclesiasticas distributa;* ed. by Denis de Sainte-Marthe and others, Vol. III, Paris, 1725; Vol. IV, Paris, 1728; Vol. XI, Paris, 1759; Vol. XIII, Paris, 1785.

MGSS   *Monumenta Germaniae historica: Scriptores;* ed. by O. Holderegger and others, Vol. XIII, Hanover, Hahn, 1881; ed. by H. Simonsfeld and others, Vol. XIV, Hanover, Hahn, 1883; ed. by G. H. Pertz and others, Vol. XVI, Hanover, Hahn, 1859; ed. by W. Arndt, R. Wilmans, and others, Vol. XX, Hanover, Hahn, 1868; ed. by M. Lappenberg and others, Vol. XXI, Hanover, Hahn, 1869; ed. by G. Waitz and others, Vol. XXVI, Hanover, Hahn, 1882.

PL   *Patrologia Latina;* ed. by J.-P. Migne, Vols. CLXXXII, CLXXXV, Paris, Garnier, 1879.

RHCHO   *Recueil des historiens des croisades: Historiens occiden-taux;* ed. by [Ch. Hase and others], Vol. I, Paris, Imprimérie royale, 1844; Vol. III, ed. by [H. Wallon and Ad. Régnier], Paris, Imprimérie impériale, 1866.

RHGF   *Recueil des historiens des Gaules et de la France;* ed. by M. Bouquet and others, Vols. XII and XIV, Paris, Palmé, 1877; Vol. XIII, Paris, Palmé, 1869; Vol. XV, Paris, Palmé, 1878.

Select Bibliography

SOURCES

Annales Herbipolenses; edited by G. H. Pertz, in MGSS, Vol. XVI. Hanover, Hahn, 1859.

Annales Magdeburgenses; edited by G. H. Pertz, in MGSS, Vol. XVI. Hanover, Hahn, 1859.

Annales Palidenses; edited by G. H. Pertz, in MGSS, Vol. XVI. Hanover, Hahn, 1859.

Breve chronicon ecclesiae sancti Dionysii, in M. Bouquet and others (eds.), RHGF, Vol. XII. Paris, Palmé, 1877.

Chronicon Mauriniacense, in M. Bouquet and others (eds.), RHGF, Vol. XII. Paris, Palmé, 1877.

Chronicon Senonense sanctae Columbae, in M. Bouquet and others (eds.), RHGF, Vol. XII. Paris, Palmé, 1877.

Cinnamus. Epitome rerum ab Ioanne et Alexio Comnenis gestarum; edited by A. Meineke, in CSHB, Vol. XXV. Bonn, Weber, 1836.

Constantinus Porphyrogenitus. De ceremoniis aulae Byzantinae; edited by J. Reiske, in CSHB, Vol. VIII. Bonn, Weber, 1829.

Continuatio Sanblasiana; edited by R. Wilmans in MGSS, Vol. XX. Hanover, Hahn, 1868.

De expugnatione Lyxbonensi; edited and translated by C. W. David. New York, Columbia University Press, 1936. Columbia University Records of Civilization, XXIV.

De tributo Floriacensibus imposito, in Bouquet and others (eds.), RHGF, Vol. XII. Paris, Palmé, 1877.

Epistolae Bernardi, in Migne (ed.), PL, Vol. CLXXXII. Paris, Garnier, 1879.

Epistolae Conradi, in M. Bouquet and others (eds.), RHGF, Vol. XV. Paris, Palmé, 1878.

Epistolae Eugenii III papae, in M. Bouquet and others (eds.), RHGF, Vol. XV. Paris, Palmé, 1878.

Epistolae Ludovici VII, in M. Bouquet and others (eds.), RHGF, Vol. XV. Paris, Palmé, 1878.

Gaufridus. Vita et res gestae sancti Bernardi, III, in M. Bouquet and others (eds.), RHGF, Vol. XIV. Paris, Palmé, 1877.

Gesta abbatum sancti Bertini: Continuatio; edited by O. Holder-Egger, in MGSS, Vol. XIII. Hanover, Hahn, 1881.

Gesta Eugenii III papae, in M. Bouquet and others (eds.), RHGF, Vol. XV. Paris, Palmé, 1878.

Gesta Ludovici [printed at the bottom of pages as reference for Grandes chroniques], in M. Bouquet and others (eds.), RHGF, Vol. XII. Paris, Palmé, 1877.

Guillelmus. Vita Sugerii abbatis; edited by A. Lecoy de la Marche, in Suger, Œuvres complètes, Paris, Renouard, 1867.

Helmold. Chronica Slavorum; edited by I. M. Lappenberg, in MGSS, Vol. XXI. Hanover, Hahn, 1869.

—— The Chronicle of the Slavs; translated by F. J. Tschan. New York, Columbia University Press, 1935. Columbia University Records of Civilization, XXI.

Historia ducum Veneticorum; edited by H. Simonsfeld, in MGSS, Vol. XIV. Hanover, Hahn, 1883.

Historia pontificalis; edited by W. Arndt, in MGSS, Vol. XX. Hanover, Hahn, 1868.

Historia Vizeliacensis monasterii, in Bouquet and others (eds.), RHGF, Vol. XII. Paris, Palmé, 1877.

John of Ypres. Chronicon sithiense sancti Bertini, in M. Bouquet and others (eds.), RHGF, Vol. XIII. Paris, Palmé, 1869.

Nicetas. Historia; edited by I. Bekker, in CSHB, Vol. XXII. Bonn, Weber, 1835.

Odo of Deuil. De profectione Ludovici VII in orientem, in M. Bouquet and others (eds.), RHGF, Vol. XII. Paris, Palmé, 1877.

—— De profectione Ludovici VII in orientem; edited by F. Chifflet, in Sancti Bernardi genus illustre assertum. Dijon, Chavance, 1660.

—— De profectione Ludovici VII in orientem; translated by M. Guizot, in Collection des mémoires relatifs à l'histoire de France, Vol. XXIV. Paris, Dépot central de la librairie, 1825.

—— De profectione Ludovici VII in orientem, in Migne (ed.), PL, Vol. CLXXXV. Paris, Garnier, 1879.

—— De profectione Ludovici VII in orientem; edited by G. Waitz, in MGSS, Vol. XXVI. Hanover, Hahn, 1882.

Origo et historia brevis Nivernensium Comitum, in M. Bouquet and others (eds.), RHGF, Vol. XII. Paris, Palmé, 1877.

Otto of Freising. Gesta Friderici; edited by G. Waitz. Hanover, Hahn, 1912.

—— Chronicon; translated, under the title "The Two Cities," by C. C. Mierow. New York, Columbia University Press, 1928. Columbia University Records of Civilization, IX.

Richard of Poitou. Chronicon; in M. Bouquet and others (eds.), RHGF, Vol. XII. Paris, Palmé, 1877.

Robert de Monte. Appendix ad Sigebertum, in M. Bouquet and others (eds.), RHGF, Vol. XIII. Paris, Palmé, 1869.

Suger. Vita Ludovici Grossi; edited and translated by H. Waquet. Paris, Champion, 1929.

William of Tyre. Historia, in RHCHO, Vol. I. Paris, Imprimerie royale, 1844.

—— A History of Deeds Done beyond the Sea; translated and annotated by E. A. Babcock and A. C. Krey. New York, Columbia University Press, 1944. Columbia University Records of Civilization, XXXV.

SECONDARY AUTHORITIES

Analecta Bollandiana, XXXIV (1915), 228–49.

Bédier, Joseph. Les Légendes épiques. 4 vols. Paris, 1908–13.

Bernhardi, Wilhelm. Konrad III. Leipzig, Duncker & Humblot, 1883. Jahrbücher der deutschen Geschichte.

Cahen, Claude. La Syrie du Nord à l'époque des croisades. Paris, 1940.

Cartellieri, Otto. Abt Suger von Saint-Denis. Berlin, Eberling, 1898.

Chalandon, Ferdinand. Jean II Comnène (1118–1143) et Manuel I Comnène (1143–1180). Paris, Picard, 1912.

Delisle, Léopold. Le Cabinet des manuscrits. 3 vols. Paris, Imprimerie impériale, 1868–81.

Ebersolt, Jean. Le Grand Palais de Constantinople et le livre des cérémonies. Paris, Leroux, 1910.

Erdmann, Carl. Die Entstehung des Kreuzzugsgedankens. Stuttgart, Kohlhammer, 1935.

Giesebrecht, Wilhelm von. Geschichte der deutschen Kaiserzeit. Vol. IV. Leipzig, Duncker & Humblot, 1877.

Hirsch, Richard. Studien zur Geschichte König Ludwigs VII. Leipzig, Fock, 1892.

Hüffer, Georg. "Die Anfänge des zweiten Kreuzzugs," in Historisches Jahrbuch, VIII (1887), 391–429.

Jaffé, Philipp. Geschichte des deutschen Reiches unter Conrad dem Dritten. Hanover, Hahn, 1845.

Kugler, Bernhard. Analekten zur Geschichte des zweiten Kreuzzugs. Tübingen, Fues, 1878.

—— Neue Analekten zur Geschichte des zweiten Kreuzzugs. Tübingen, Fues, 1883.

Kugler, Bernhard. Studien zur Geschichte des zweiten Kreuzzugs. Stuttgart, Ebner & Soubert, 1866.

Luchaire, Achille. Études sur les actes de Louis VII. Paris, Picard, 1885.

Michaud, J. F. Bibliothèque des croisades. Paris, Ducollet, 1829.

Millingen, Alexander van. Byzantine Constantinople; the Walls of the City and Adjoining Historical Sites. London, Murray, 1899.

Neumann, Carl. Bernhard von Clairvaux und die Anfänge des zweiten Kreuzzugs. Heidelberg, Winter, 1882.

Sybel, F. von. "Über den zweiten Kreuzzug," Zeitschrift für Geschichtswissenschaften, IV (1845), 197–228.

Vacandard, E. Vie de Saint Bernard. 2 vols. Paris, Gabalda, 1910.

Wilken, F. Geschichte der Kreuzzüge. Vol. III. Leipzig, Crusius, 1817.

Index